Love, Sex, and Disability

Disability in Society

Ronald J. Berger, series editor

Love, Sex, and Disability

The Pleasures of Care

Sarah Smith Rainey

LYNNE
RIENNER
PUBLISHERS

BOULDER
LONDON

Published in the United States of America in 2011 by
Lynne Rienner Publishers, Inc.
1800 30th Street, Boulder, Colorado 80301
www.rienner.com

and in the United Kingdom by
Lynne Rienner Publishers, Inc.
3 Henrietta Street, Covent Garden, London WC2E 8LU

Library of Congress Cataloging-in-Publication Data
Rainey, Sarah Smith.
    Love, sex, and disability : the pleasures of care / Sarah Smith Rainey.
        p. cm. — (Disability in society)
    Includes bibliographical references and index.
    ISBN 978-1-58826-777-1 (hardcover : alk. paper)
    1. People with disabilities—Sexual behavior.   2. Intimacy (Psychology)
3. Interpersonal relations.   4. Man-woman relationships.   I. Title.
    HQ30.5.R35 2011
    306.7087—dc22

                                                        2010041200

British Cataloguing in Publication Data
A Cataloguing in Publication record for this book
is available from the British Library.

Printed and bound in the United States of America

The paper used in this publication meets the requirements
of the American National Standard for Permanence of
Paper for Printed Library Materials Z39.48-1992.

    5   4   3   2   1

For Max

Contents

Acknowledgments

I am deeply indebted to my advisers and mentors at Ohio State University, including Cynthia Burack, Brenda Brueggemann, Mary Thomas, and Christine Keating, who guided me at the beginning of this project. I would also like to acknowledge the Department of Women's Studies at Ohio State and the Coca-Cola Critical Difference for Women grant that helped fund my focus group research.

This book was a very difficult endeavor because I lost my partner, Max, in the middle of writing it. My relationship with Max was the inspiration for this research. I know that I could not have returned to the project after his death without the help of my family and friends, especially Inez and Victor Smith, Emily and Brian Corbin, Zachary Rice, Janice McCabe, Alina Bennett, Susan Burch, Allison Ricket, and Chickie Rice. They did not read drafts, but instead provided the emotional support that I needed to complete the work.

Others were both friends and helpful readers. I especially thank Anne Mitchell, Stephanie Young, Emily Lutenski, Bruce Jeffers, and Jessica Rainey for providing invaluable copyediting and suggestions. I also thank Andrew Berzanskis, acquisitions editor at Lynne Rienner Publishers, and Ron Berger, editor of the Disability in Society series of which this book is a part, for guiding me through my first book project. Two anonymous reviewers also provided insightful comments and suggestions.

Many thanks go to all the disabled/nondisabled couples who participated in the focus groups. Your candor made the book possible. I thoroughly enjoyed the time I spent with all of you.

Finally, I thank my new love, Jessica Teaman Rainey, for helping me see this to completion. I am looking forward to our new chapter.

1

Introduction:
Love, Sex, and Disability

My late partner, Max, had secondary progressive multiple sclerosis (MS). We met in an online dating forum during the summer of 2003. When he contacted me, I read his profile and was struck by the many things that we had in common personally, socially, and politically. We obviously were a good match and he was very handsome. I definitely was interested in chatting, but he had been upfront about his disability and I felt that I had to consider what that meant for a relationship before pursuing it any further. I did not want to begin chatting online, then on the phone, and maybe meeting in person only to back out because the disability was too much for me to handle. For several days, I read everything I could get my hands on about multiple sclerosis. I learned that Max's form of MS was not the worst (e.g., primary progressive), but not the best either (relapsing remitting). Max had gone downhill quickly, remitted, and was now in a slow, but supposedly continual decline. There were medications that could help slow the progress of the disease, but there was no cure. The medications usually worked so well that it was no longer common to die from MS. Before these medications became widely available, people with MS died when the disease began attacking their respiratory system. Nevertheless, a number of physical symptoms could come and go: poor vision, cognitive problems, inability to walk or stand or move any part of the body, depression, erectile dysfunction, low sex drive, pain, numbness, and poor coordination. Did I want to start dating such a person? What if we fell in love? Would caring for Max on a daily basis make me resentful, tired, or depressed? Could I handle it when he got worse? How would my friends and family react?

Obviously, I decided to jump in. I spent five wonderful years with Max before his death in April 2008. I am recounting this story because the questions that I initially asked myself reflect popular culture's assumptions about care, disability, and the nature of relationships. I think it is telling that my first questions were not: How will Max love me and take care of me? What kind of fun

1

will we experience? How could taking physical care of Max be part of our intimacy? I did not ask such questions because they were not available to me. The cultural script for relationships in which one person is physically disabled and the other is nondisabled is one of despair and pity.

This script is enforced by portrayals of care burden on television, in film, and by the questions and comments of friends, family members, health care professionals, and strangers. For example, it was common for strangers at the grocery store to assume that I was Max's personal care assistant. Checkout clerks would ask if I "enjoy my job." It was inconceivable to them that Max and I could be a couple. Once while flying to Chicago for a family vacation, the airline bumped Max up to first class without asking if he was traveling with anyone else. When confronted, the airline attendants said they assumed he was traveling alone. Both of these examples illustrate that people with disabilities are imagined as single, sexless, and pitiable—definitely not intimate partners, fathers, or mothers. Conversely, the partners of people with disabilities are either viewed suspiciously or as martyrs. When I was filing travel grant paperwork after presenting a portion of the research that I describe in this book, the student assistant who was helping me asked if I was "in such a relationship." When I responded affirmatively, he said, "Wow, you must be a really great person. That has to be really hard on you." I said that I was just as much work for Max as he was for me, but I could tell that my correction was not heard—the image of burden was too strong. In writing about women with disabilities, Adrienne Asch and Michelle Fine relay a similar story:

> Disabled women who have partners, especially if they are non-disabled men, are likely to discover that they and their partners are subjected to curiosity, scrutiny, and public misunderstanding. Ubiquitously perceived as a social burden, the disabled woman evokes pity that spreads to her partner. "Whenever my husband and I are shopping and he is pushing my wheelchair, people stop us and say [to him], 'You must be a saint.' What about me? Do you think it's easy to live with him?" The public assumption is that this woman is a burden and her husband is either saintly or a loser himself.[1]

Even if the disabled/nondisabled couple does not experience physical care as a burden, it is impossible to escape the prevailing beliefs about care burden and dependency. Strangers usually exhibit an amazing level of audacity when confronted publicly with disability, revealing their beliefs about disability, care, and relationships.

Family members and friends also may freely express doubt and concern over disabled/nondisabled intimate relationships. In Rose Galvin's qualitative study on disabled identity, disabled people described numerous examples of discriminatory attitudes about their sexuality and ability to be in a relationship. For example, one of Galvin's research participants, Craig, says that friends and family members "advised his wife against marrying him, saying 'He's a nice man, but he's disabled.'"[2] Similarly, in Dikaios Sakellariou's study of men with spinal cord injury, family members' disapproval of intimate relationships between disabled and nondisabled people is a frequent theme. "Alexandros shared a story, where the brother-in-law of a man with spinal cord injury suggested that his sister should find a lover, since she wouldn't be possibly getting any sexual satisfaction from her spinal cord injured husband."[3] Another participant in Sakellariou's study, John, says that his girlfriend left him because she could not present him to her family.[4]

Some disability theorists argue that the cultural taboo against disabled/nondisabled intimate relationships is a form of "erotic segregation," similar to the social taboos placed on interracial relationships.[5] Writing about the discriminatory treatment and sexual shame that people with disabilities receive on a daily basis, Barbara Faye Waxman notes, "I believe this is done tacitly to keep us from doing the thing that poses an overwhelming threat to our disability-phobic society: taking their sons and daughters as sexual and life partners, bearing their grandchildren."[6] Fearful that a disabled person will partner with a nondisabled person, burdening nondisabled family members and potentially creating more disability, people with disabilities are erotically segregated—socially through taboo and institutionally by way of separate education for people with disabilities, institutionalization in nursing homes, and isolation due to inaccessible physical environments and economic strain. I find the concept of erotic segregation helpful in thinking through the construction of disabled/nondisabled intimate relationships, but it does not explain all the forms of discrimination that such couples experience. In particular, it does not approach the particular constructions of care and dependence/independence that seem to root many of the biased statements outlined above.

As a feminist scholar, I turned to feminist research for further understand ings of the causes and consequences of stereotyped constructions of care disabled/nondisabled intimate relationships. I found that feminist scholars more likely to critique the meaning of independence woven into many di ity stereotypes; however, caring between intimate partners is largely ab the formidable body of work that examines the gendered nature Instead, feminists more commonly address issues of caregiving ir caring for dependent children or elderly parents.[7] Ellen K. Fed Feder Kittay describe care as "interactions of unequals . . . betw giver and the dependent to be cared for."[8] In *Love's Labor: Ess Equality, and Dependency*, Eva Feder Kittay goes even furth cared-for a "charge" to indicate that self-direction and car ability or entitlement of the charge."[9] Within this sche charges are rarely also intimate partners and producers of Furthermore, the vast majority of contemporary femir nondisabled partners as victims of a system that ref who are statistically female.[10] For example, the

Women conducts campaigns for both disability rights and mothers' and caregivers' economic rights; however, these platforms are not linked. In fact, disabled people are not addressed in the mothers' and caregivers' economic rights statement of policy and program goals.[11] Suggested solutions involve respite care, paying informal caregivers, and job protection for caregivers. These reforms are all aimed at helping the (nondisabled) caregiver. Reforms aimed at disabled people—including direct funds to the disabled so that they can hire and manage their own personal care assistants—are not listed. It is true that family caregivers need help, but it is symptomatic of the beliefs about disability in intimate relationships that the disabled partners are erased in much feminist care research and policy.

Thus, much of the feminist research on care and disability supports the predominate image of the burdened and asexual disabled/nondisabled couple. I find this ideological hegemony remarkable. Of course, the hegemony is never complete—there are individuals who approve of disabled/nondisabled intimate relationships, and there certainly are plenty of couples who resist attempts to construct their relationship as burdensome and asexual. In this book, I begin the necessary process of understanding and countering the dominant representations of disabled/nondisabled intimate relationships. I examine two key discursive sites that contribute to the ideological hegemony—popular culture (e.g., mainstream film, television, and magazines) and the applied fields (e.g., rehabilitation sciences, medicine, and psychology). To provide alternative understandings of care and sexuality in disabled/nondisabled relationships, I turn to the words and images of people involved in such relationships. Their experiences help construct new scripts about care, love, and sexuality.

Such a holistic approach to the topic is a radical departure from most studies on the relationship between disabled/nondisabled partners. As Chapter 2 details, this topic is common in the applied fields; however, such relationships are typically viewed as burdensome for the nondisabled partner and the couple's sexuality is consistently absent in the research. Importantly, the couple's "problems" are rarely framed within the social world. In other words, how films, media, social movements, and the people around them shape (and are shaped by) the couple is seldom part of the framework in scientific studies on disabled/nondisabled relationships. To date, there have been only a handful of studies that adopt a social view, incorporating questions about the couple's treatment and how stereotypes about sexual and care relationships involving disability affect people with disabilities and their partners.[12] Most notably is Gillian Parker's book-length study of couples in England during the late 1980s and early 1990s, which is called *With This Body: Caring and Disability in Marriage*. Parker interviewed twenty-one couples (using both couple and individual interviews) in which one partner had become physically disabled since marriage. She was particularly interested in how the couple negotiated independence and dependence, and how the preexisting relationship shaped the roles adopted in the presence of disability. However, Parker weaves in information about the influence of public policy on the relationship, and positive and negative effects of prejudice and support from friends, neighbors, and extended family members. Thus, Parker understands that the couple exists in a social and political matrix that influences the experience of disability and care in marriage. Similarly, Celia Shultz's more recent study of collaboration within intimate relationships situates the people with disabilities and their partners within a social world.[13] Shultz examined four physically impaired people, three of whom were married to other people with disabilities. Shultz's participants were all physically impaired at the time of their marriage. Like Parker, Shultz found high levels of collaboration, problem solving, and reciprocity between partners. Caregiving and receiving were blended into the couples' daily interactions.

Parker, Shultz, and other researchers are beginning to simultaneously investigate the social, political, and experiential dimensions of care in intimate relationships involving disability.[14] However, the sexual aspects of these relationships are typically left out or downplayed in the little research that does exist. Thus, this study is unique in that I look at care and sexuality/intimacy in disabled/nondisabled intimate relationships. Additionally, the study includes both pre- and postdisability couples. In other words, some of the examples involve couples in which the disabled partner was impaired after they became a couple and some before they became a couple.

This project is also unique because I was interested in both (1) understanding how dominant narratives of care and intimacy are circulated and enforced in contemporary society; and (2) how disabled/nondisabled couples work with and against dominant narratives of care and intimacy. To adequately carry out such an extensive, holistic study, I had to draw on a wide range of disciplines and employ several different kinds of research methods. With respect to the circulation of norms, I focused on popular culture and the applied fields because these two arenas are particularly powerful for people with disabilities. I used feminist, textual analysis to analyze popular culture representations, and content analysis to examine research from the applied fields. While I acknowledge that these sites help shape the experiences of disabled/nondisabled couples, they do not determine their lives. In other words, popular culture and the applied fields research influence, but do not dictate realities. Couples adopt, alter, and resist dominant narratives about their lives. Thus, I also systematically examined alternative renderings of disabled/nondisabled relationships by turning to a variety of self-representations. I used three sources of self-representations in this study: autobiographies written by people in disabled/nondisabled relationships, filmic self-representations, and both oral and written statements of participants in the four focus groups that I conducted as part of this research project.

Key Voices and Concepts

The voices of the focus group participants, along with the authors of the written and filmic self-representations, ground the analysis in this book. In other words, I used their understandings of care, intimacy, and love to analyze the dominant representations of disabled/nondisabled relationships and to help make sense of their complicated self-representations. Thus, before outlining the chapters of this book, I will introduce my "coauthors" and explain how their specific deployment of key concepts helped guide the subsequent analysis.

I start by introducing the authors of the autobiographies because use of autobiographies as a data source is atypical. And at least from the perspective of disability rights activism, it is a somewhat controversial move because disability autobiography often features individuals overcoming impairment and downplays interdependence (the way each of us is dependent on others for survival) and disability pride.[15] However, the six autobiographies that I reference throughout this book do not reify popular understandings of the self as separate and independent of others, nor do they tell tales celebrating the return to disability-free bodies.[16] The autobiographies that I selected put forth new paradigms about interdependency, the relationship between self and others, by highlighting the relationality of the body. Four of the authors—Nancy Mairs, Bonnie Sherr Klein, Robert Francis Murphy, and John Hockenberry—write from the perspective of the disabled partner.[17] The other two—Marion Deutsche Cohen and Morton Kondracke—write from the perspective of the nondisabled partner.[18] All of these authors narrate what Paul John Eakin calls the "relational life," stories that describe a "relational model of identity, developed collaboratively with others, often family members."[19] The relational life makes connection very obvious. The lives of others figure prominently in the autobiographies of relational selves, so much so that the text becomes partially a biography of the proximate other.[20] Physical impairment can facilitate the saliency of relationality because the disabled person needs the other in atypical ways. Indeed, the disability rights movement puts forth the concept of interdependency[21] to emphasize how the disabled and nondisabled alike are dependent on others for daily survival. The authors of the autobiographies that I analyzed are aware of the way in which caregiving and receiving can help them see their connection to others, and they mark this connection using a variety of strategies.

One way that interdependency is marked in the texts is through what Susanna Egan calls "mirror talk": the dialogue between two characters, the dialogue between reader and author, and the internal dialogue of the narrator in autobiographical texts.[22] Mirror talk includes all of the dialogic moments that create the relational self. Egan argues that this mirror talk exemplifies intersubjectivity because it stresses the need for a subject to be recognized by another subject. The dialogic moments in the autobiographical texts enact intersubjectivity, producing a self in relation to another, producing a narrator always in the process of subject formation. In other words, through dialogue with the writer, with the reader, and between characters, the narrator emerges into subjectivity.

I selected these six authors because they speak to—and speak back to—the dominant representations of care and sexuality in disabled/nondisabled. In different ways, each author shows that care is not necessarily a binary relationship and that their disabled body can be a site of pleasure. The autobiographies are case studies of self-representations that bring alternative constructions of care and sexuality into relief.

In addition to written autobiographies, I used three autobiographical documentary films made by or with people with disabilities—*Shameless: The ART of Disability* (2006), *Want* (2007), and *Sick: The Life and Death of Bob Flanagan Supermasochist* (1997).[23] These filmic self-representations also offer new understandings of disability and intimacy, and all three films engage in filmic practices that blur the boundaries between self and other, highlighting interdependence. Each film also features intimate, sexual relationships between people with disabilities and those that help care for them. In doing so, these films emphasize reciprocity between partners, suggesting that care can increase (not hinder) intimacy.

As self-representations, the autobiographies and films offer viewers a rich portrait of life with physical impairment, but they also were typically produced by people with certain levels of social and economic privilege.[24] Disabled authors and performers/filmmakers have the means and experience to create and produce their representations. The relative privilege of disabled authors and performers/filmmakers may impact their experience of care and sexuality, limiting the applicability of the research findings. In order to diversify the self-representations that I analyzed in this study, I also conducted focus groups with couples in disabled/nondisabled relationships (for a more detailed discussion of my focus group methodology, including recruitment and data analysis, please see Appendix A). I recruited twelve couples into four focus groups in four different areas of Ohio. The demographics of all the participants who framed this study are displayed in Table 1.1, but I will now introduce each couple.

The makeup of each of the focus groups was somewhat determined by the organizations that helped me recruit participants. For example, I recruited three of the four couples in Focus Group 1 through a multiple sclerosis group. Although they did not know each other, these three white couples share the experience of dealing with MS, an unpredictable and progressive disease. Tracy and Jeff are a thirty-something couple who married about a year after Tracy's diagnosis with MS. She works part-time and cares for their toddler daughter while he works full-time. Sabrina and Adam are also a thirty-something couple who married after Sabrina's diagnosis with MS. However, they are a blended family with four children between them. These two couples are newlyweds

Table 1.1 Participants

Demographics	Sex	Age	Race/Ethnicity	Marital Status	Disabled/Nondisabled	When Disabled	Time Lived Together (years)	Length of Relationship (years)
Focus Group 1								
Tracy	F	31	White	Married	Disabled (MS)	Before	4	4.5
Jeff	M	31	White	Married	Nondisabled	Before	4	4.5
Sabrina	F	34	White	Married	Disabled (MS)	Before	1	1.5
Adam	M	33	White	Married	Nondisabled[a]	Before	1	1.5
Kevin	M	44	White	Married	Nondisabled	After	16	25.0
Ellen	F	43	White	Married	Disabled (MS)	After	16	25.0
Rachel	F	32	White	Not married	Disabled (spinal muscular atrophy type 2)	Before	2	5.0
Jack	M	33	White	Not married	Nondisabled	Before	2	5.0
Focus Group 2								
Richard	M	64	White	Married	Nondisabled	Before	7	7.0
Emma	F	48	White	Married	Disabled (CP)	Before	7	7.0
Olivia	F	30	White	Married	Nondisabled	Before	7	7.0
Randall	M	36	Black	Married	Disabled (CP)	Before	7	7.0

continues

Table 1.1 Continued

Demographics	Sex	Age	Race/ Ethnicity	Marital Status	Disabled/ Nondisabled	When Disabled	Time Lived Together (years)	Length of Relationship (years)
Focus Group 3								
Victoria	F	37	White	Not married	Disabled (muscular dystrophy)	Before	11	12.0
Gene	M	52	White	Not married	Nondisabled	Before	11	12.0
Ted	M	35	White	Not married	Nondisabled	Before	5	7.0
Sofia	F	37	White	Not married	Disabled (SCI)	Before	5	7.0
Kay	F	40	White	Married	Nondisabled	Before	14	19.0
Dan	M	46	White	Married	Disabled (SCI)	Before	14	19.0
Focus Group 4								
Allison	F	23	White	Not married	Disabled (vision impairment)	Before	3	6.0
Jason	M	23	White	Not married	Nondisabled	Before	3	6.0
Bob	M	55	White	Married	Nondisabled	After	14	15.0
Connie	F	55	White	Married	Disabled (MS)	After	14	15.0
Frank	M	Not disclosed	White	Not married	Nondisabled	Before	1	1.5
Jennifer	F	44	White	Not married	Disabled (SCI)	Before	1	1.5

Notes: All couples self-identified as heterosexual. Abbreviations: CP, cerebral palsy; MS, multiple sclerosis; SCI, spinal cord injury.
a. Adam also has MS but was considered the nondisabled partner in my study because he was largely not symptomatic.

compared to Kevin and Ellen, who have been married sixteen years. Now in their forties, Kevin and Ellen were married well before Ellen's diagnosis of MS. Although Ellen can no longer work outside the home, both remain active in their church and keep busy with their two teenaged daughters. The fourth couple in Focus Group 1 is Rachel and Jack. Rachel was born with spinal muscular atrophy type 2. She and Jack met online and dated three years before moving in together. Both Rachel and Jack work full-time and they are the only pair in the first group without children.

I recruited both of the couples in Focus Group 2 through a disability rights organization and they knew each other quite well. Richard and Emma are a middle-aged white couple and have been married for seven years. Although they do not have children together, they are close to Richard's adult daughters from a previous marriage. Emma was born with cerebral palsy and does not work full-time and Richard is now retired (he is about fifteen years older than Emma). Olivia and Randall are an interracial couple and, like their friends Richard and Emma, have been married for seven years. Randall is a black man who was born with cerebral palsy and Olivia is a nondisabled white woman. Together they raise Randall's teenaged son from a previous marriage and they have recently adopted a daughter together. Ironically, both couples met through online dating websites.

I also recruited the three couples in Focus Group 3 through a disability rights organization and they too knew each other well from working closely on activist and educational projects. Kay and Dan are the only couple in this group with children. They have been married fourteen years and have two small children. Dan is disabled from a spinal cord injury and they both work full-time. Gene and Victoria are a middle-aged white couple. Victoria was born with muscular dystrophy and requires the care of a paid nurse. Both Gene and Victoria work full-time. Ted and Sofia have been married five years. Sofia is disabled from a spinal cord injury and uses a wheelchair. Ted works full-time.

Focus Group 4 was diverse in the sense that I recruited all three couples from different sources, they had different disabilities, and they did not know each other prior to the group. Connie and Bob are a middle-aged couple with adult children. They have been married fourteen years. Although they both used to work full-time, Connie had to leave her job after her diagnosis of MS. Jennifer and Frank are both in their forties and have lived together for only about one year. Jennifer is disabled from a spinal cord injury. Jennifer and Frank do not have any children, and neither do Allison and Jason, the youngest couple (both twenty-three years old). Allison was diagnosed with macular degeneration as a child and is blind.

Although all of the recruitment announcements indicated that I was interested in talking with both same-sex and opposite-sex couples, only opposite-sex couples contacted me. In addition, only one participant was African American. All other participants, including his wife, identified as white or Caucasian.

The sample was more diverse with respect to age. The mean age was thirty-nine years old, ranging from age twenty-three to sixty-four. Based on representations in popular culture and research from the applied fields that indicate it is more likely for disabled women to be divorced or abandoned by male partners than disabled men by female partners,[25] I expected the sample to be heavy with disabled men. However, the woman was the disabled partner in ten of the twelve couples in the focus groups. As expected, only two couples experienced the onset of the disability after the start of their relationship: for the vast majority of the sample, the disability was present when the pair met.

The self-representations included in this book—autobiographies, films, and focus groups—are obviously not a representative sample, nor were they intended to be. My intention was to focus on couples outside of a clinical, therapeutic setting. As Chapter 3 shows, so much of what we know about disabled/nondisabled couples has come from scientific studies on couples in distress. Although "relationship satisfaction" was not a qualification for the focus groups, it is likely that the couples whom I recruited into the focus groups are not distressed because they were willing to talk in a group setting about their experiences. The couples had experienced some problems, but they were not on the brink of divorce or caregiver burnout. Likewise, the autobiographies and films I selected feature couples that are still in love. My goal was to make visible disabled/nondisabled couples that "make it work"; therefore, the fact that the data I drew on were all from couples that are happy and in love is important. Nevertheless, these couples do not erase the hardships. Instead, these self-representations paint a complex picture of life with disability.

Almost all of the focus group participants and authors of the written and filmic self-representations included in this book are connected to the disability rights movement, in which disability is figured as a normal aspect of life. Following the lead of Nancy Mairs, one of the key autobiographical voices, and Simi Linton, a disability studies theorist and activist, my use of the term "nondisabled," instead of "ability" or "able-bodied," signals a centering of disability.[26] Mairs says that she calls people who lack disabilities "the nondisabled" because "in relation to me, they are the deficient ones."[27] By using the terms "disabled" and "nondisabled" to describe group membership and identity, disability becomes the privileged perspective and the typically unexamined position of the nondisabled is moved to the margins. Naming the nondisabled, like naming and analyzing whiteness, also reveals the way in which the able body is set as the standard in society, the way it is positioned as supposedly natural or neutral, and the starting point on which impairment is layered. Reversing this and centering disability suggest that the impaired body may be the natural state, the neutral perspective. In this book, then, nondisabled is situated as the negative position, as not having disability.

With disability firmly at the center of this analysis, I am critical of any force that impedes or discourages the disability point of view and life. I use the term "ableism" to describe the many ways in which the participants and authors whom I discuss in this book experienced explicit and implicit acts of discrimination, marginalization, and violence because they deviated from the nondisabled norm. For many of the participants, ableist attitudes surround them, punctuating their daily lives. The pervasiveness of ableism should not be too surprising considering society's long history of eugenic policies that actively sought the elimination of people with disabilities as well as a dominant medical model of disability that seeks to fix, cure, or otherwise "normalize" the impaired body. As I show in detail in Part 1 of this book, the medical model informs almost all of the medical and social science research on disability, and curing or overcoming disability is a common narrative in popular culture. The medical model is ableist in the sense that it views the disabled person as a problem that needs to be solved.

For the focus group participants and self-representation authors and performers/filmmakers in this study, their love relationship is a vital component to combating the negative effects of ableism. All of them understand that in our culture, care is typically associated with physical and emotional stress, even burnout. They know that outsiders see the physical caregiving required in their love relationship as a problem, an indicator that their love is bound to fail. However, their concept of care deviates from dominant representations. For them, care is sometimes physical (dressing, bathing, and so on), but it is also emotional, mental, and instrumental. Randall, who has cerebral palsy and requires the help of his wife Olivia for bathing and dressing, says that "caring is more than just the physical. Caring is mental, caring is—I define caring as something that you do or say to help that other spouse." Because physical needs are so immediate and pressing, the couples in this study place care at the foundation of a love relationship. Care is not something performed intermittently, as needed; for disabled/nondisabled couples care is a regular, integral part of their lives, and it is how they learn about each other, express love and devotion, and become intimate.

This perspective on care is actually quite radical. As I mentioned at the beginning of this chapter, when I began to investigate care, I first came across what I call "feminist care research," feminist studies from the social science fields that position women as victims of informal care. From this standpoint, care is a burden and drain on women. Bound to feminine gender roles, women disproportionately serve as caregivers to children, parents, partners, relatives, and friends. Thus, according to this research, caregiving isolates women, prevents them from engaging in wage work or other activities outside the home, and exposes them to harmful physical and emotional toil.[28]

Although aspects of this research rang true for me—physical care was sometimes physically and emotionally draining, and there were times when my activities outside of the home were foiled because of Max's needs—I felt that, overall, the research failed to capture the complexity of our care relationship and the way care was defined and experienced by the focus group participants. Most significantly, this research erased the disabled partner's subjectivity and caregiving. Max's subjectivity and the ways that Max cared for me were ignored. Disabled feminists, like Jenny Morris, have also critiqued the way in which feminist research on care has erased disabled people. Morris argues that the feminist critique of community care, which grew from the socialist analysis of women's role in the family, creates an us-and-them dichotomy between female caregivers and "dependents."[29] Concerned with women's roles as caregivers, most feminist care research has failed to recognize that most recipients of care are also women. Thus, as Margaret Lloyd argues, "polarized constructions of the disabled person as a burden and the informal carer as an oppressed woman do an injustice to the real issues for many women."[30] Furthermore, treating the disabled as "passive recipients of that care" fails to adequately capture the experience of caregivers.[31] And it ignores the "reciprocity involved in caring relationships."[32]

Jan Walmsley and other disabled feminists have pointed out that many women, including disabled women themselves, want to care for others and that this desire should be supported by feminist activism. Walmsley finds that "for some women who are denied the opportunity to be carers [because they are themselves disabled] caring becomes a valued activity to be sought, rather than an oppressive burden to be shifted. For others, caring is burdensome and exploitative."[33] Thus, Walmsley argues that "it is not that caring in itself is valuable, but that the dignity of choice is important to all adults."[34] Obscuring the subjectivity of the disabled person therefore produces a biased and problematic picture of family care. In addition, I *enjoyed* caring for Max. I refused to believe that my pleasure was some kind of false consciousness because, as a feminist, I was highly aware that the government benefited from my unpaid labor in the home, that Max and I deserved formal assistance, and that I had been socialized to assume caregiving responsibilities as a woman. Despite this knowledge, I gained concrete physical and emotional pleasure from caregiving. Feminist care research, however, portrays care as physically, socially, and emotionally harmful to women.

Eventually, I picked up the work of Nel Noddings and other feminist philosophers who focus on the moral and interpersonal dimensions of care.[35] It is through their work that I began to see Max's and my experiences reflected, and found a language from which to frame the voices of the focus group participants. Noddings focuses on "the caring relation" because, as she puts it, "relations, not individuals, are ontologically basic."[36] She is concerned with the role of both the caregiver and the cared-for, how both contribute to the care relation. According to Noddings, when caring is working, the pair is locked into a mutually reinforcing connection: "Clearly, the cared-for depends upon the one caring. But the one caring is also oddly dependent upon the cared-for."[37] The cared-for reciprocates in a variety of ways, including direct response ("thank you"), personal delight ("Oh, that feels so much better"), and growth (care allows the cared-for's pursuit of happiness).[38]

This reciprocity sustains the caregiver, provides purpose, and helps define his or her sense of self. Reciprocity, then, blurs the roles of caregiving and care receiving. As Noddings puts it, "I could as easily say 'I am giving' as 'I am receiving.'"[39] This was so true for me. Max was a brilliant man and I bounced all of my ideas off him. Many nights we discussed feminist theory until the morning's first rays of light peeked through our bedroom window. Even while I performed various care activities, we talked. While I helped with toileting, we talked about the boundaries of the body, privacy, and body image. Dressing could generate a conversation about the role of touch in moral agency; shaving could lead to a discussion of gender performativity. Such constant discourse was immensely useful to me as an academic. But Max did other things for me as well, including editing all of my papers, giving me neck and foot rubs, holding me when I was sad, and making fantastic, healthy meals for us. Max also qualified for Social Security Disability Insurance and received money from disability insurance paid by his former employer. So, even though Max could not work, he had a reliable source of income that was his and that he could use to contribute to the overall financial health of our household. I may have helped with activities of daily living that he could not complete alone, but I certainly never felt that our relationship was one-way. We both gave and we both received.

Noddings's formulation of the care relation made both of our contributions visible. In an effort to focus on reciprocity and to honor the care work that both the disabled and nondisabled partners perform in the relationship, I therefore avoid making the distinction between caregiver and care receiver unless I am talking about a specific example of someone giving and someone receiving care. Instead, I conceptualize the couple as disabled/nondisabled. Using the terms "disabled partner" and "nondisabled partner" allows for the possibility that both partners give and receive care, that the roles of caregiver and cared-for are not fixed or defined by the presence or absence of physical impairment. In this book, I assume that the disabled and nondisabled both provide and receive care. I suggest that this dynamic is fundamental to the spark of the intimate relationship. In other words, the care relation contributes to the sustainability of the couple and the individuals.

To help theorize care's role in the subjectivity of both partners, I also draw on the work of Jessica Benjamin, a feminist psychoanalyst who is most famous for her work on "intersubjectivity" in *The Bonds of Love: Psychoanalysis, Feminism, and the Problem of Domination*. Benjamin suggests that the provider/dependent or caregiver/cared-for dynamic is essential to selfhood. As an alternative to ego psychology in which the self is formed through differentiation, "the intersubjective view maintains that the individual grows in and through the relationship to other subjects."[40] Paramount to intersubjectivity is the recognition that, although connected and in fact dependent on each other, the self and the other are separate entities. Significantly, these entities do not need to be social equals to enact intersubjectivity. To emphasize the freestanding nature of the other, Benjamin draws on D. W. Winnicott's work on the use of objects. According to Winnicott, a child can only "'use' the object when he perceives it 'as an external phenomenon, not as a projective entity,' when he recognizes it *as an entity in its own right*.'"[41] The other's separate, but connected, subjectivity is affirmed by the other's survival: "When I act upon the other it is vital that he be affected, so that I know that I exist— but not completely destroyed, so that I know he also exists."[42] Later, in *Like Subjects, Love Objects: Essays on Recognition and Sexual Difference*, Benjamin elaborates and suggests that "'like subjects' refers to the possibility of both recognition and identification."[43] In other words, intersubjectivity allows us to see both the other's difference and sameness from the self. Like subjects are both like and dislike our selves; like enough to see an equivalent subjectivity in the other, and dislike enough to not see the other simply as an extension of one's self.[44]

This is a particularly relevant point for sustainable care relationships because care is primarily viewed as a burdensome activity that often leads to burnout and dissolution of the care relationship. To keep the care relation viable, the disabled and nondisabled partners must recognize each other's separateness. More than this, the other must recognize the subjectivity of the other, and how his or her own subjectivity is dependent on that subjectivity. As Benjamin eloquently puts it, "the need for recognition entails this fundamental paradox: at the very moment of realizing our own independence, we are dependent upon another to recognize it."[45] Further, Benjamin suggests the term "mutual recognition" to describe this fundamental need, "the necessity of recognizing as well as being recognized by the other."[46] Reaching mutual recognition is a psychologically ideal state in which the self and the other attain emotional attunement and distinction; "in the ideal balance, a person is able to be fully self-absorbed or fully receptive to the other, he is able to be alone or together."[47] Maintaining this "constant tension" between the self and the other is the ideal resolution to the paradoxes of recognition and is precisely how intersubjectivity can facilitate an appreciation for difference while confirming one's sense of self.[48] Benjamin later adds that "mutual recognition is meaningful as an ideal only when it is understood as the basis for struggle and negotiation of conflict . . . , when its impossibility and the striving to attain it are adequately included in the concept."[49] Thus, mutual recognition describes the process in which the relationship between the self and the other is maintained.

It is particularly important for this study that physical bodies remain visible when thinking about mutual recognition and intersubjectivity. Ironically, bodies have occupied a precarious position in disability activism. For decades, disability scholars and activists have offered the social model of disability as an alternative to the historically predominant medical model as mentioned above. The social model, however, views the physical and social environment as the problem. Inaccessible buildings and transportation, prejudice, and fear of people with disabilities cause poverty, isolation, and depression—not the impairment itself. The solution, then, is to change the built environment and to shift attitudes. The social model has led to many significant improvements for people with disabilities, including passage of the historic Americans with Disabilities Act in 1990. However, it has also obscured the realities of the disabled body. In fact, some scholars and activists purposively discourage attention on the disabled body[50] because, they believe, such attention individualizes and sentimentalizes the problem, distracts from the real problem of disabling social conditions, and is a poor political organizing platform.[51] In other words, the disabled body is strategically ignored for the political good.

Disabled women and people whose disabilities are not fixed with physical and social accommodations are increasingly critiquing the social model for its inability to account for the body and its refusal to think critically and openly about impairment.[52] Cheryl Marie Wade argues that the social model of disability creates people who are the "able-disabled" by focusing on those people with disabilities who live "normal" lives once physical accommodations are in place.[53] This marginalizes the vast majority of people with disabilities whose bodies continue to impede and shape their existence, even when their environments are barrier free. To rectify this situation, Wade advocates airing the realities of the disabled body, especially those aspects that "ain't exactly sexy": "To put it bluntly—because this need is as blunt as it gets—we must have our asses cleaned after we shit and pee. Or we have others' fingers inserted in our rectums to assist shitting. Or we have tubes of plastic inserted inside us to assist peeing or we have re-routed anuses and pissers so we do it all into bags attached to our bodies."[54] Disabled bodies break the boundaries of privacy and politeness around bodily functions associated with adult control. Wade argues: "If we are ever to be really at home in the world and in ourselves, then we must say these things out loud. And we must say them with real language. So they are understood as the everyday necessity and struggle they are. How can we assert a right (for personal care) if we are too ashamed of the need to state it openly?"[55] The right to care depends on drawing attention to the body. Likewise, Julia Twigg argues that making visible the body in care work is important for disabled people and the people that provide their care.[56] Attention on the body and "personal care" (e.g., shitting and peeing) can improve social policy.[57] "Enabling policy to look at bodily issues" does imply different political strategies than the equal rights and inclusion model offered with the social model of disability, but it will likely lead to better policy.[58] In addition, bringing the body back into the discourse allows disability scholars to acknowledge physical pain (and pleasure).[59] And it allows them to consider the medical response to impairment, including issues of prevention, quality of life, and "cure."[60]

Attention to the body does not, however, have to be reductionist, focusing only on the physical/biological. On the contrary, the new scholarship views "the materiality of the body [as a] dynamic interrelationship with the social and cultural context in which it is lived."[61] The new body scholars eschew the nature/nurture, social/biological, and impairment/disability binaries. The social can influence the body and vice versa. As Kelly Oliver puts it:

> All human relationships are the result of the flow and circulation of energy, thermal energy, chemical energy, electrical energy, and social energy. Social energy includes affective energy, which can move between people. . . . Just as thermal energy from our bodies can warm the bodies of others, affective energy from our psyches can affect the psyches of others. In important ways, the psyche is a material biological phenomenon, a biosocial phenomenon.[62]

Thus, there is no easy distinction between impairment (biological) and disability (social) because they are mutually influential. Tobin Siebers calls this the "new realism of the body." He states that "the body is alive, which means that it is capable of influencing and transforming social languages as they are capable of influencing and transforming it."[63] Similarly, Janet Price and Margrit Shildrick put forth a model of "embodied subjectivity" that accounts for the ways in which we are "actively and continuously produced through social interactions with other body-subjects."[64] Both new realism and embodied subjectivity privilege the dialectic between physical body and social experience and thus seek to expose how "impairment is social and disability embodied."[65]

I am invested in this new disability politics that embraces corporeality and acknowledges interdependency; therefore, I pay special attention to the role of the physicality in care activities. The physical care in disabled/nondisabled relationships requires touching and contact between bodies. As Margrit Shildrick notes, "to touch another . . . is in some sense always to compromise control, to feel my sense of wholeness and self-sufficiency dissolve, for even where the intent is outward and aggressive, I am also touched in return. An undecidable moment of exchange occurs, a crossing of corporeal boundaries, which unsettles the dimensions of the embodied self."[66] Touch emphasizes the connection between bodies, and I argue touch is also a necessary component to the fundamental paradox of dependence. In other words, witnessing and recognition are not enough. Subjectivity is also dependent on touch, specifically a caring touch, thus bodies are central to my analysis of care in disabled/nondisabled relationships. Gail Weiss's concept of intercorporeality is particularly useful because it emphasizes the role of the physical body and subjectivity. As Weiss notes, "the experience of being embodied is never a private affair";[67] it is an unconscious, "ongoing exchange between bodies and body images."[68] By "body image," Weiss is referring to proprioception or the sense of one's body in space, how it looks, feels, and is bounded. Individuals have many different body images (although relative stability is needed for reliable movement and response) and these body images adjust in response to physical changes within the body, the physical environment, and other bodies one encounters. Intercorporeality "implies that body images are in continual interaction with one another, participating in a mutually constitutive corporeal dialogue that defies solipsistic analysis."[69]

Sometimes the caring touch is also clearly an erotic touch. Yet in contemporary Western societies, care touching is explicitly associated with mothering. And although from a psychoanalytic perspective, this touching initiates sexuality in the infant, care and erotics are unambiguously disconnected for mature adults. To be turned on by someone helping you dress, bathe, or toilet is certainly not normative and maybe even taboo. Nevertheless, as the self-representations in this research show, the line between care touch and erotic touch is frequently blurred for disabled/nondisabled couples. In those parts of the book, I draw from the theoretical tradition of queer theory, which challenges the dominance of heteronormativity. As Diane Richardson notes, queer "displace[s] the categories of 'lesbian' and 'gay' *and* heterosexual."[70] Furthermore, Richardson explains:

> Ideas about what is "normal" and "acceptable" sexual behaviour, indeed what is regarded as sexual practice, also reflect dominant constructions of sexuality as heterosexual (vaginal) intercourse. . . . Not only does this affect how forms of sexual activity are evaluated as sexually satisfying or arousing or even as counting as "sex" at all, it also serves to "discipline" the body . . . , marking out the boundaries which represent our private and public zones, and distinguishing the potentially sexual from the non-sexual bodily surfaces action.[71]

Even though most of the people represented in this book self-identify as heterosexual, almost all of them had expansive, nonheteronormative definitions of what counted as sexually intimate. Thus, I read the sexuality that they describe as "queer." Describing the many ways he has gotten to know his wife's body while dealing with her MS, Kevin says, "as far as intimacy goes, intercourse isn't [the] only intimacy." For Kevin and many other people involved in disabled/nondisabled relationships, intimacy can include not only sexual acts, but also acts that exemplify a high level of connection between two bodies, including massage, touching, dressing, and even toileting and feeding. Intimacy is used, purposely, as an umbrella term and includes feelings of love and devotion as well as sexual desire and attraction.

Another useful concept related to queer and queer theory is Tobin Siebers's "sexual culture."[72] Siebers uses sexual culture to define the way in which intimacy is figured differently for people with disabilities, including people in disabled/nondisabled relationships. It refers to the expansive, nongenital focus that an erotics based on care expresses. The need for care opens up a diffuse sexuality in which touch and connection are ongoing intimate expressions. In addition, it exposes the ways in which disabled/nondisabled sexual intimacy violates the notion that there are proper erotic zones, and that sexuality (and personal care) are private matters. For people with disabilities, a sex life is not a discreet, personal matter. Sex is not limited to the bedroom behind closed doors; it happens in the shower while being bathed, in the bathroom while being dressed, and in the kitchen while being fed. It may also involve additional assistance beyond the normative dyad. Thus, sexual culture refers to the way of being sexual that the care opens up.

Limitations and Overview of the Book

The analysis in this book is limited to couples experiencing physical disability; however, I do not focus on any one particular disability. Paralleling the move away from sexual identity to sexual behavior in sex research, I am more interested in care needs and activities than in the medical identity of people with disabilities. In other words, this book examines people who need help with one or more activities of daily living (bathing, dressing, toileting, eating) regardless of what caused or continues to cause that impairment. Of course, I also recognize that diseases have social histories that influence how the disabled person and his or her partner experience life,[73] and there are places in which I mention the person's specific disability because it is contextually significant. However, my decision to include all physical impairments that created a need for daily care reflects the disability rights movement's goal to foster a common group identity among people with disabilities.[74] Although the exact type of care may vary with each disability or illness, all of the people with disabilities highlighted in the book need help with at least one activity of daily living and their partners provide most or all of this care. That is their commonality. I limited this study to physical impairment, however, because cognitive and emotional disabilities raise additional questions and concerns around consent (both sexual consent in their relationships and consent to research) and self-direction, and highlight completely different kinds of care.

Although the project did not start this way, it has become, for a variety of reasons, a project about heterosexual disabled/nondisabled relationships. There are few representations of same-sex disabled/nondisabled relationships. In fact at the time of this writing, I could find no mainstream, popular culture examples. I found a few studies on disabled/nondisabled same-sex intimate relationships, as well as a few self-representations (documentary film examples), but the rest of the studies, autobiographies, and documentaries analyzed are straight. In addition, despite attempts to recruit same-sex couples, the focus group research that I conducted is composed entirely of couples that identify as heterosexual. Regardless of the straightness of the couples, what I discovered was sexual expression that did not fit normative understandings of sex and intimacy. Thus, while future work should investigate the specificities of same-sex disabled/nondisabled relationships, the data that I present in this book also should not be read as fully straight.

The book is divided into two parts. In Part 1 I focus on dominant representations and beliefs about disabled/nondisabled intimate relationships. Chapter 2 examines popular culture representations—films, television shows, and magazine and newspaper articles—featuring disabled/nondisabled intimate relationships. Popular culture typically represents disability as a tragedy that dooms sexual relationships and strains love. In addition, love—as an institution and expression—is something available only to those who can perform in certain nondisabled physical and emotional ways. Love itself is apparently able-bodied. Significantly, the message is highly gendered. Disabled women are more frequently represented as "doomed" than disabled men. I argue that this disparity stems from heteronormative beliefs about gender roles in intimate relationships. Disability impedes a woman's ability to care for her husband and is therefore more disruptive than disability in men.

In Chapter 3, I conduct a content analysis of literature from the applied fields, including rehabilitation, medicine, and nursing. Much of this literature focuses on caregiver burden and barriers to sexuality for people with disabilities. I argue that the dissemination of these study results—on the evening news, on the Internet, and in the newspapers—contributes to the negative perception of disabled/nondisabled relationships. The self-representations that I analyze in Part 2 of the book are full of stories of discrimination. Parents, friends, family members, health care professionals, and even strangers make biased and damaging comments about disabled/nondisabled relationships based on the popularization of research from the applied fields.

Part 2 of the book speaks back to dominant representations as I present the self-representations—autobiographies, documentaries, and data from focus groups with disabled/nondisabled couples. Looking at the self-representations together, it is clear that "successful" disabled/nondisabled couples were able to (1) move beyond traditional gender roles, (2) find strength and pride in disability identity and culture, (3) focus on reciprocity and mutuality in their love relationship, and (4) redefine sex and eroticize care intimacy. Thus, Part 2 is divided into these four major themes: gender, disability pride, love, and sex.

Chapter 4 suggests that one reason the disabled/nondisabled couples whom I study are so successful is their gender role flexibility. Sometimes this meant that as individuals and as a couple, they would flat out ignore gender norms. Other times it meant creatively appropriating gender norms to fit physical difference. Regardless, most of the couples viewed gender flexibly and were able to forge gendered positions that worked for them: rarely did the couples get hung up on gender stereotypes.

When their ability to be flexible with gender and to endure adversity were tested, disabled/nondisabled couples weathered this prejudice through disability pride and humor as well as the strength of their love for one another. Thus, Chapter 5 focuses on pride and humor in disabled/nondisabled intimate relationships, arguing that these tools are used as effective survival mechanisms, countering the prejudicial views reflected in the popular culture and opinion.

Chapter 6 moves more fully into a discussion of what love means in these relationships, especially how disabled/nondisabled couples stay in love in spite of the outside forces that discourage their love and the internal stress of physical impairment. The expression of love in the self-representations emphasizes the role of care, reciprocity, and commitment.

Finally, Chapter 7 focuses on intimacy and sexuality in disabled/nondisabled relationships. Because disabled/nondisabled couples are dealing with bodies that deviate from the norm, their sexual expression often also is non-normative. The chapter explores how these relationships are different from other love relationships, especially how disability may queer sexuality for people in disabled/nondisabled relationships. Thus, Chapters 4–7 focus on four different ways in which people in disabled/nondisabled relationships manage, even flourish, through gender role flexibility, the ability to find humor and pride in the face of prejudice, paying careful attention to reciprocity and creating new forms of sexual intimacy.

What emerges from this comparison of dominant representations and self-representations is a complicated, nuanced picture of care and intimacy in disabled/nondisabled relationships. Self-representations contradict the binary and asexual relationship between disabled and nondisabled partners popularized in academic research and the mainstream media. Disabled/nondisabled couples emphasize reciprocity, mutuality, and eroticized daily care in their relationships. These findings help correct popular stereotypes and suggest that reciprocal relationships and alternative forms of sexuality should be considered in future research on care and disability. Thus, on a practical level, understanding the ways in which disabled/nondisabled relationships are characterized by reciprocity, and the ways that couples are intimate and sexual, may improve the treatment of people in disabled/nondisabled relationships. Instead of assuming burden and asexuality, professionals, friends, and family may be able to see love and mutuality.

These findings are also significant on a theoretical level. As Robert McRuer argues in his groundbreaking book *Crip Theory: Cultural Signs of Queerness and Disability*, queer theory and disability studies have much to learn from each other. Both are dedicated to the intellectual project of "working the weakness in the norm" by exposing compulsory heterosexuality and compulsory able-bodiedness, respectively.[75] McRuer puts forth "crip theory" as a way to understand how the "severely disabled/critically queer body . . . remaps the public sphere and reimagines and reshapes the limited forms of embodiment and desire proffered by the systems that would contain us."[76] Disabled/nondisabled couples expose how limited the dominant understandings of care really are—how care has become synonymous with burden, and how care can be otherwise. By expanding care to include sexual intimacy, and by focusing on the ways in which disabled partners reciprocate in the care relationship, disabled/nondisabled couples crip or queer the meaning and nature of care, disability, and intimacy.

Notes

1. Asch and Fine, "Nurturance, Sexuality, and Women," p. 245.
2. Galvin, "Researching the Disabled Identity," p. 407.
3. Sakellariou, "If Not Disability," pp. 104–105.
4. Ibid., p. 104.
5. Wilkerson, "Disability, Sex Radicalism," p. 42.
6. Waxman, "It's Time," p. 86.
7. For example, Meyer, *Care Work.*
8. Feder and Kittay, "Introduction," p. 2.
9. Kittay, *Love's Labor*, p. 31.
10. See, for example, Bubeck, "Justice"; Folbre, "Reforming Care"; Schutte, "Dependency Work"; and Suthers, "Women Still Shouldering."
11. National Organization for Women, "NOW and Disability Rights"; NOW, "Mothers and Caregivers Economic Rights"; NOW, "A Feminist Future."
12. See Crawford and Ostrove, "Representations of Disability"; Parker, *With This Body*; Schulz, "Collaboration in the Marriage"; and Shuttleworth, "The Search for Sexual Intimacy."
13. Schultz, "Collaboration in the Marriage Relationship."
14. For example, see Asch and Fine, "Nurturance"; Fine and Glendinning, "Dependence"; and Walmsley, "Contradictions in Caring."
15. Disability scholars and activists, however, have mixed reactions to this boon in disability autobiography. David Mitchell, for example, is suspicious of the current celebration of disability autobiography because "even the most renowned disability autobiographers often fall prey to an ethos of rugged individualism that can further reify the longstanding association of disability with social isolation" ("Body Solitaire," p. 312). Because disabled people's "lives are so inextricably tethered to the lives of others," Mitchell believes that disability autobiography could promote a new model of interdependency, undermining notions of independence and autonomy that are so valued in contemporary society (p. 314). However, Mitchell argues that disability autobiography is just as likely—perhaps even more likely—to express a singular self (p. 312). In an effort to convince the nondisabled that "we are just like you," people with disabilities may downplay the interdependence that characterizes their lives.

In addition, the most popular disability autobiographies are "overcoming stories" or what Arthur Frank calls "restitution narratives." Such a narrative "affirms that breakdowns can be fixed," easing the anxiety that the nondisabled may have about illness and disability (*The Wounded Storyteller*, p. 90). Because restitution narratives are about the body overcoming the illness or disability, characteristic of the medical model of disability, they are not politically viable tools. Following the social model of disability, in which attention is drawn to the social and physical barriers in the environment that disable the impaired, it would be best to have narratives that critique ableism and celebrate the disabled body instead of healing it. These narratives are out there; indeed, the autobiographies that I analyzed in this chapter are prime examples, but they do not yet outnumber the more popular story of overcoming.

16. See Appendix B.

17. Hockenberry, *Moving Violations*; Klein, *Slow Dance*; Mairs, *Waist-High*; Murphy, *The Body Silent*.

18. Cohen, *Dirty Details*; Kondracke, *Saving Milly*.

19. Eakin, *How Our Lives*, p. 57.

20. Ibid., p. 86.

21. Although I will use both interdependence and intersubjective to signify this fundamental connectivity, I prefer intersubjective because it foregrounds subjectivity.

22. Egan, *Mirror Talk*.

23. *Want*, directed by Loree Erickson, 2007 (Toronto, Ontario: Femmegimp Productions), DVD; *Shameless: The ART of Disability*, directed by Bonnie Sherr Klein, 2006 (Montreal, Quebec: National Film Board of Canada), DVD; *Sick*, directed by Kirby Dick, 1997 (Santa Monica, CA: Lions Gate Home Entertainment), DVD.

24. Couser, *Recovering Bodies*, p. 4.

25. Singh and Sharma, "Sexuality and Women," p. 29.

26. See Linton, *Claiming Disability*, especially chapter 2, for a thorough discussion of the term *nondisabled*.

27. Mairs, *Waist-High*, p. 14.

28. See, for example, Bubeck, "Justice"; Feder and Kittay, "Introduction"; Folbre, "Reforming Care"; Meyer, "Care Work"; Schutte, "Dependency Work"; Suthers, "Women Still Shouldering."

29. Morris, "'Us' and 'Them'?" pp. 28–29.

30. Lloyd, "The Politics of Disability," p. 721.

31. Morris, "'Us' and 'Them'?" p. 34.

32. Ibid., p. 35.

33. Walmsley, "Contradictions in Caring," p. 131.

34. Ibid., p. 139.

35. I make a distinction between feminist care research and feminist care philosophy. Feminist care research focuses on the negative health outcomes of a system that makes informal care the sole responsibility of women. Feminist care philosophy focuses on the moral, ethical, and social dimensions of giving and receiving care. However, I believe that it is time for the care research to incorporate the disabled point of view and to more carefully consider how feminist care research portrays care. In other words, research on care activities and care policy should begin with the insights about care relations formulated in feminist care philosophy. Recognizing care as a valued activity for disabled and nondisabled women alike does not abandon the feminist project of removing care burdens.

36. Noddings, *Caring*, p. xiii.

37. Ibid., p. 48.

38. Ibid., p. 74.

39. Ibid., p. 52.

40. Benjamin, *The Bonds*, pp. 19–20.

41. Ibid., p. 37, emphasis added.

42. Ibid., p. 38.

43. Benjamin, *Like Subjects*, p. 7.

44. Ibid., p. 7.

45. Benjamin, *The Bonds*, p. 33.

46. Ibid., p. 23.

47. Ibid., p. 28.

48. Ibid., p. 36.

49. Benjamin, *Like Subjects*, p. 23.

50. See, for example, Finkelstein, "The Social Model"; and Michael Oliver, *Understanding Disability*.

51. Thomas, *Sociologies*, p. 122.

52. See, for example, Hughes, "Disability and the Body"; Morris, "'Us' and 'Them'?"; Wade, "It Ain't"; and Wendell, *The Rejected Body*.

53. Wade, "It Ain't," p. 89.

54. Ibid., p. 88.

55. Ibid., p. 89.

56. Twigg, "The Body," pp. 428–430.

57. Ibid., p. 430.

58. Ibid., p. 431.

59. Ibid.

60. Shakespeare, *Disability Rights and Wrongs*, p. 40.

61. Thomas, *Sociologies*, p. 137.

62. Kelly Oliver, "Subjectivity as Responsivity," p. 329.

63. Siebers, "Disability in Theory," p. 749.

64. Price and Shildrick, "Bodies Together," p. 63.

65. Hughes, "Disability and the Body," p. 66.

66. Shildrick, "Unreformed Bodies," p. 329.

67. Gail Weiss, *Body Images*, p. 5.

68. Ibid., p. 3.

69. Ibid., p. 33.

70. Richardson, "Heterosexuality," p. 5.

71. Ibid., p. 6.

72. Siebers, *Disability Theory*, pp. 137–139.

73. For examples of cultural histories of disease, see Finger, *Elegy for a Disease* (on polio); Sontag, *Illness as Metaphor* (on cancer); Sontag, *AIDS and Its Metaphors*; and Irvine, "Regulated Passions" (on sexual addiction).

74. See, for example, Shapiro, *No Pity*.

75. Judith Butler, quoted in McRuer, *Crip Theory*, p. 30.

76. Ibid., p. 31.

PART 1
Mainstream Representations

2

Images in Popular Culture

In a recent Mothers Against Drunk Driving commercial, a young man is reading on a park bench and the screen reads "your best friend."[1] An attractive woman walks up and kisses him as the screen reads "your girlfriend." The camera moves to the inside of an institutional-looking room with a man in a wheelchair gazing upon the pair and the screen reads "you." The screen fades to black and reads, "You have a lot to lose." The intent of the commercial is to deter drunk driving, but the message hinges on understanding disabled people as sexless and isolated. Within this discourse, disabled people are not adequate friends or lovers because they need constant care to maintain their disabled bodies. They are burdens, not active participants in relationships, particularly in a sexual sense.

Representations reflect social attitudes, but they also set limits of possibility—they help define what is socially imaginable. As Hilde Zitzelsberger notes, "relationships between cultural representations of bodies and people's experiences are fundamental to understanding the conditions that shape the lives of people with physical disabilities and differences in western societies."[2] In popular culture, people with disabilities are rarely represented as caregivers or sexual partners. Such images can negatively affect disabled people and their partners at the psychological level by lowering self-esteem.[3] In addition, the stereotype of the dependent, needy disabled person—prolific in popular culture—influences social service providers and likely factors into public policy. For example, in the United States, disabled adults often lose most or all of their Social Security and Medicare benefits if they marry or cohabitate. Such "marriage penalties" leave people with disabilities who want to live with their partners with three unappealing choices: (1) live alone and keep their health care and income; (2) cohabitate and lose their financial autonomy; or (3) cohabitate and hide their living arrangement from the government.[4] Although it is difficult to know conclusively which factors policymakers considered when making such

27

policies, it is clear that the nondisabled spouse, constructed as the caregiver, is expected to provide fully for the disabled partner.[5] In addition, Medicare calls in-home assistance with activities of daily living (bathing, dressing, toileting, eating) "custodial care." Such terminology clearly marks the disabled person as a ward whose rights and autonomy are withdrawn for his or her own good. Assumptions about disability, sexuality, and care, reflected in representations, factor into the allocation and delivery of services.

In this chapter, I closely examine how love, sex, and disability are represented in popular culture, focusing on Hollywood cinema, theater, and the news media. Although there are a few notable exceptions, some of which I will review later in this chapter, love between disabled and nondisabled people is rarely represented. I argue that this is the result of our able-bodied ideals of love. In other words, the scripts that surround love are possibilities only for those that can perform in certain physical and emotional ways. Considering this, it is not too surprising that disabled lovers are extraordinary finds in popular culture. When disabled/nondisabled love is represented, it is almost always a tragic affair. The physical care required is represented as a burden that makes sexual intimacy impossible, dooming disabled/nondisabled relationships to eventually fail. This is especially true for a disabled woman in love with a nondisabled man. Disabled men are much more likely to be shown in intimate relationships than disabled women because it is more acceptable for men to be cared for by their female partners.[6] In the heteronormative environment of popular culture, it is simply unthinkable, and thus unrepresentable, for male partners to care for disabled women.

Love Is Nondisabled

In her groundbreaking study of middle-class couples, Ann Swidler argues that, although we never fully participate in the love myths that are perpetuated in popular culture, we do use them as threads to sew together our own meaning of love.[7] These threads form "tool kits" or repertoires that each of us use, alter, and sometimes reject entirely. Regardless, these repertoires are constantly with us, shaping the contours of our identities, the limits of our actions. Feminist theorist bell hooks makes a similar argument in *All About Love: New Visions*.[8] The love myths that circulate in popular culture may not determine our actions, but they certainly shape our choices by providing the raw materials to construct our realities. This is why studying what popular culture has to say about love, sex, and disability is so important. Images in popular culture are particularly powerful. As Rosemarie Garland-Thompson states, "in our ocularcentric era, images mediate our desires and the ways we imagine ourselves."[9] Since people with disabilities are still isolated from the nondisabled world, film is one of the primary ways in which the nondisabled learn about disability and people with disabilities learn about themselves as a social group. Indeed, Madeleine A. Cahill and Martin F. Norden argue that "it is not simply a matter of movies reflecting reality; for some people, movies are the reality on which to draw for ideas about disability."[10] Popular culture portrayals create the repertoires that disabled and nondisabled people alike use to make sense of love, disability, and sexuality.

Unfortunately, the images and narratives available about love typically leave out people with disabilities. Although it is easy to find people with disabilities in popular culture,[11] it is not easy to find these characters in love relationships, especially with nondisabled people. I argue that this omission is not entirely surprising if we consider the way in which love—as an institution and a mythology—is able-bodied. Most (although not all) of the popular ideals of love are possibilities only for people with nondisabled bodies and minds. For example, "love at first sight," "falling in love," and being "swept off one's feet" are clichés that idealize an instant connection that would be difficult if not impossible when there is a significant impairment. Disabled/nondisabled couples often have to learn how to interact and how to communicate using a letter board, voice box, or just patiently learning the unique cadence and pronunciation of a disabled tongue. Intrigue and curiosity may be instant, but love certainly is not.

Indeed, the entire concept of learning and work in love relationships contradicts popular love scripts. As hooks notes, "the message received from the mass media is that knowledge makes love less compelling; that it is ignorance that gives love its erotic and transgressive edge."[12] Thus, to have to learn to communicate, to find accessible restaurants for that first date, and any other number of trials a disabled/nondisabled couple may face would all be indications of incompatibility according to the popular notion of true love. Since real love is effortless—it's how you know it is "right"—love that requires work must not be true. The notion of natural ease is especially pronounced when it comes to sex. We are inundated with sexual imagery in magazines and film, on television and the Internet, and it all sends a clear, consistent message: sex is a natural, graceful, polished coordination of motions. Sex that does not go smoothly, that takes work, is taken as a sign of incompatibility.

This work is what ultimately drives Joel (Eric Stoltz) and Anna (Helen Hunt) apart in the film *Waterdance* (1992).[13] Joel becomes paraplegic after a hiking accident and the film chronicles his recovery and acceptance of his new body. He and his girlfriend, Anna, try to continue their relationship, even having sex in the hospital bed at the rehabilitation center. However, the injury has made them so different that the amount of work it would take to bridge their divide becomes insurmountable for the couple and they break up at the end of the film.

Key to Joel and Anna's decision to separate is the notion of compatibility, a belief that has become the hallmark of what Swidler calls "prosaic" love myths since the end of the Victorian era. From this perspective, real love depends on "compatibility and on practical traits that make persons good life partners."[14] Companionate lovers have the same hobbies, like to watch the same television shows, and have different, but necessarily equitable, careers and life aspirations. Their relationship makes sense because they are such natural companions. They can take long walks together on the moonlit beach, go see a concert, or ride bikes in the mountains. Most of all, they both work, help raise the family, and take care of the house. She may do the cooking, but he mows the lawn. Physical disability is viewed as a wrench in that compatibility, a hurdle that could make enjoying companionate activities impossible. Although the Romeo and Juliet myth of lovers who are drawn together in defiance of social forces continues to be romanticized in our culture, disability creates too wide of a gulf between starstruck lovers. Physical similarity is a prerequisite for companionate love.

This need for physical sameness can be found in numerous animated Disney and Dreamworks love stories. The potentially compatible lovers are barred from consummating their love until physical otherness is overcome. In the classic tale of *Beauty and the Beast* (1991), Belle (nondisabled) falls for the ugly, hairy Beast (disabled); however, their love cannot be secured until the Beast turns into a nondisabled human.[15] We can see a similar version of this tale in *The Little Mermaid* (1989) and *Shrek* (2001).[16] Ariel can be with her true love only after her mermaid tail has been exchanged for a pair of usable legs. Putting a slight spin on the theme, Fiona and Shrek can realize their love only after Fiona has been transformed back into an ugly ogre. Shrek falls in love with Fiona when she is a beautiful princess, but they can be lovers only once they look the same. Then, there is *The Hunchback of Notre Dame* (1996).[17] Quasimodo is not transformed into a nondisabled character or made physically similar to his love Esmeralda; therefore, their love is doomed.

Perhaps the most recent Hollywood film that enforces this theme of physical sameness as a prerequisite for compatibility is the blockbuster *Avatar* (2009).[18] Paraplegic Marine Jake Scully (Sam Worthington) falls in love with a Na'vi woman, Neytiri (Zoe Saldana) while he is inside a Na'vi avatar that can walk, talk, and move just like a real Na'vi. They are soul mates, but their love cannot be real until Jake is permanently inside his Na'vi avatar. In a magical ceremony at the end of the film, Jake's soul is removed from his disabled human body and transferred into the nondisabled Na'vi body, and Jake and Neytiri live happily ever after on Pandora as similarly, compatibly, matched Na'vi.

Although tied up in feminist notions of equality, the ideal of companionate marriage based on similarity is bound up with capitalist notions of productivity and exchange. To be equal partners means that both are providing meaningfully to the relationship, usually in economic or material ways. This ideal assumes, and is sometimes correct to assume, that disabled bodies cannot function as productively as able bodies in contemporary neoliberal context. As Robert McRuer argues, disabled bodies (usually) fail at the neoliberal economic imperative for flexibility.[19] Bodies and minds that can adapt quickly and easily to changing contexts and circumstances, that can be readily molded to perform new tasks and have new desires, are what work in economies marked by flexible accumulation. Few disabled (and nondisabled) bodies are ever so flexible; thus, they cannot compete in this ever-expanding, ever-changing marketplace. Disabled bodies become deadweight in a relationship. However, if they are able to manage and overcome their disability, they can join the ranks of couples in love.

According to McRuer, this is exactly what happens to Jack Nicholson's character, Melvin, in the popular film *As Good As It Gets* (1997).[20] After falling in love with Carol (Helen Hunt), Melvin decides to treat his disabling obsessive compulsive disorder. For Melvin, "able-bodied status is achieved in direct proportion to his increasing awareness of, and need for, (heterosexual) romance."[21] Carol and Melvin can be a happy couple in love only once Melvin's disability is overcome. McRuer uses this example to show the connection between compulsory heterosexuality and compulsory able-bodiedness, but I believe it points to the able-bodiedness of love more generally. Melvin must participate as Carol does in the relationship in order for the mutual exchange of companions to be realized. Key here is that the exchange has to be similar. In other words what Carol gives, Melvin also has to give. This is what makes physical disability such a hurdle. The nondisabled partner can provide physical care; however, this physical care may not be reciprocated in the case of severe disability. The exchange is not equal; thus, the couple fails the ideals of companionate love.

The Stuff of Dramas

Of course, even though love is an able-bodied institution, love between disabled/nondisabled people nevertheless makes the popular culture radar screen. When it does, however, it is almost always the stuff of drama. Over and over, love between a disabled person and a nondisabled person is represented as a tragedy. Thus, there are a number of dramas that feature disabled/ nondisabled love, but never does such love appear in romantic comedies. In fact, the only romantic comedy that I could find that featured disabled/ nondisabled love was *The Ex* (2006).[22] In this film, Sophia (Amanda Peet) has a brief affair with Chip (Jason Bateman), who uses a wheelchair; however, Sophia ends up with her nondisabled husband (Zach Braff) in the end. In addition, it turns out that Chip was faking his disability at the time of their affair. All the other films, plays, and television shows that I found presented the disabled/nondisabled love affair as tragic.

The Men (1950) is a classic example of the emotional drama that disabled/nondisabled love can bring.[23] The film is about Lt. Kenneth "Bud" Wilcheck's (Marlon Brando) struggle to come to terms with his paraplegia, including his reconciliation with fiancée Ellen Wilosek (Teresa Wright). We meet Lt. Wilcheck during the opening credits when he is shot in the back by enemy fire. He falls to the ground and Wilcheck's voice-over begins as the image dissolves to the hero lying in a hospital bed. Wilcheck is clearly depressed and has given up hope, breaking up with Ellen and refusing to see her because he believes himself to be a worthless cripple. It is the task of Dr. Brock (Everett Sloane) and the men in the rehabilitation hospital (most of whom are members of the Paralyzed Veterans of America and oversee hospital governance) to help Wilcheck accept his impairment and move on with his life. Ellen contacts Dr. Brock and convinces him to set up a meeting with Bud against his will. She insists that she wants to marry him, not out of pity, but out of true love. Although resistant at first, Bud begins to accept Ellen's love and his disability. However, after they marry, Ellen suddenly expresses doubt about their relationship. Shaken by Ellen's moment of uncertainty, Bud returns to the rehabilitation hospital, taking up the role of a drunken, bitter cripple. Eventually, his peers kick him out so that he will attempt to reconcile with Ellen. The ending shows Bud driving to the home of Ellen's parents and asking her on a date, implying (but not confirming) that Bud has finally accepted his disability and the two will reconcile.

The film is particularly dramatic when it comes to the subject of care. Rehabilitation makes Bud less dependent and more mobile, but he will always need help. Early in the film, there is a scene in which Dr. Brock addresses a room of women—presumably the mothers and lovers of the hospitalized men—to explain the nature of spinal cord injury, what to expect in terms of recovery, and so on. The scene functions primarily to inform members of the audience and to introduce Ellen, but it also speaks volumes about the expectations of women and care. Dr. Brock is shot from a low angle and the women are shot from high angles, indicating the unequal power relations. He instructs the women that there "will be problems," but that it is their duty to help their men accept their limitations and move on with their lives. Because there are no men in the audience, it is clearly the expected job of these women to help, care for, and assist the men. Nevertheless, the film also makes it clear that this level of personal care is horrifying. As Dr. Brock explains that the word "walk" should be forgotten, that some men will never regain bladder and bowel function, and that some men will not be able to father children, the camera cuts to reaction shots of the women. Each close-up reveals the women's complete shock and horror, instructing the audience too on how to react. As the women anxiously ask about surviving as a married couple, Dr. Brock says that it takes "a special kind of woman," but that they should try. Later, when Ellen is telling her parents that she plans to marry Bud, her father says that he fears she will get married and then realize that she has "signed a contract to be his nurse." These moments highlight the film's anxiety over care of disabled men. In one sense, it is clearly the proper role of women, natural and unproblematic. In another sense, the film seems to suggest that no women or only a few could handle such a relationship.

During Ellen and Bud's wedding, Bud decides to stand at the altar with his bride but, when he tries to hold her hand, he begins to fall. Foreboding music floods in and there is a cut to Ellen's disturbed reaction. After the wedding, the two enter their new home. Ellen appears shaken by the fall at the wedding, but proceeds to feign excitement as she shows Bud the house and gets the champagne. As Bud wheels around the family room his chair begins to squeak loudly, further troubling Ellen. He spills the champagne and, as she frantically cleans up "her carpet," he begins to have a leg spasm. The camera zooms in on his leg and the dark music returns. Ellen's look has turned to horror. Her groom is a helpless, grotesque body dependent on her care. She breaks down and he leaves.

Although the ending of *The Men* suggests that Bud and Ellen will reconcile, the audience is never awarded the typical happy ending. The specter of disability remains so we are not sure that Bud and Ellen will survive as a couple. The drama of *The Men* is not exceptional. Other films that portray disabled/nondisabled love as serious and potentially tragic include *An Affair to Remember* (1957), *My Left Foot* (1989), *Theory of Flight* (1998), and *Passion Fish* (1992).[24] Even when the love itself is not overcast with doubt, the vehicle is dramatic; for example, *The Bone Collector* (1999).[25]

Gender and Dependency

Significantly, not all disabled/nondisabled love affairs are as doom and gloom as others. In contemporary popular culture, it is much more tragic when the disabled partner is female. Part of this gender difference is the result of a representational inequity: there are many more portrayals of disabled men than of disabled women. Cahill and Norden argue that Hollywood portrayals of disabled women are constrained by women's role as object of the male gaze. Thus, there are fewer portrayals of disabled women because physical disabilities disrupt women's sexual attractiveness.[26] As Susan Wendell points out, "physical 'imperfection' is more likely to be thought to 'spoil' a woman than a man by rendering her unattractive in a culture where her physical appearance is a large component of a woman's value."[27] When women with disabilities are represented, they are usually blind, deaf, mute—disabilities that do not adversely affect their attractiveness.[28] Cahill and Norden note that "the tradition of Hollywood movie heroines whose disabilities always affect their fates but never their looks is long indeed," citing *Orphans of the Storm* (1921), *City*

Lights (1931), *The Spiral Staircase* (1946), *Johnny Belinda* (1948), *Magnificent Obsession* (1954), *Wait Until Dark* (1967), *Ice Castles* (1979), *Children of a Lesser God* (1986), *Jennifer 8* (1992), and *Blink* (1994).[29] In many of these films, the women are cured (often by men) and are in a heterosexual relationship by the end of the film.

I agree with Cahill and Norden's analysis of the gendered nature of disability representation in Hollywood films; however, I add that the differences between disabled male and female characters are also influenced by gendered understandings of dependency.[30] In our culture, it is socially acceptable for a nondisabled man to be intimately cared for by his wife; thus, it is not a large imaginative leap to see a disabled man taken care of by a loving woman. The disabled man does not necessarily violate the expectations of heteronormative companionship, and he may be able to continue to fulfill his social role as economic provider and decisionmaker, despite his physical impairment. A disabled woman, however, is perceived to be incompetent because her value is determined by her ability to provide care, especially to her husband and children.[31] Adrienne Asch and Michelle Fine argue that, "if men can accept emotional sustenance only from women who can provide the maximum in physical caretaking, the woman with limitations may be viewed as inadequate to give the warmth, companionship, and shelter men traditionally expect from their mates."[32] Physical dependence is not acceptable for women because nurturance is associated with the ability to "make house" and provide physical care to the family. As a participant in William Hanna and Betsy Rogovsky's 1991 study on women and disability aptly puts it, "there is a big difference between a disabled husband and a disabled wife. A disabled husband needs a wife to nurture him, but a disabled wife is not seen by society as capable of nurturing a husband who is not disabled."[33] Thus, I add to Cahill and Norden's understanding of the gendered nature of disability representations by noting that a woman's value in patriarchy remains connected to her ability to care for her husband and children.

For both men and women, disability signifies dependency in popular culture and, in the West, dependency is a state to be feared.[34] This fear is also gendered. It is much more common to find examples of men with physical disabilities in popular culture. Disabled men's "failure"—their dependency—is often recuperated in film and popular culture through demonstrations of how closely they embody what R. W. Connell has called "hegemonic masculinity" in other aspects of their lives. According to Connell, "hegemonic masculinity can be defined as the configuration of gender practice which embodies the currently accepted answer to the problem of the legitimacy of patriarchy, which guarantees (or is taken to guarantee) the dominant position of men and the subordination of women."[35] In other words, hegemonic masculinity is culture's normative ideal of masculinity. It is not necessarily the most prevalent form of masculinity; rather, it is the most socially endorsed. Men are supposed to be cunning, strong, aggressive, potent (connote their phallic authority), and decisive. Making these qualities salient in representations of disabled men can work to shore up their need for physical care. For example, in *The Bone Collector*, Detective Lincoln Rhyme (Denzel Washington) is quadriplegic and dependent on the help of his assistant (Queen Latifah) for all of his personal care. However, he is also a potent and cunning detective who not only solves the crimes and finds the serial killer, but wins the love of Amelia Donaghy (Angelina Jolie). Rhyme's masculinity is thus shored up by his superior skills as a detective and his ability to "get the girl." Parallel stories for women simply do not exist because, I argue, a woman's femininity—her ability to meet societal expectations about womanhood—is entirely dependent on her ability to care for others and her sexual attractiveness. Unable to care for others or satisfy men, women with disabilities are rendered socially useless. Thus, women with physical disabilities who require care from others are killed off or rendered invisible in popular culture.

On stage, disdain for women's physical dependency can be found in *Wicked: A New Musical* (2005). Based on the novel *Wicked: The Life and Times of the Wicked Witch of the West* by Gregory Maguire, the musical, billed as the "untold story of the witches of Oz," focuses on the unlikely friendship between Elphaba and Galinda that blossoms at Shiz University, explaining how Elphaba becomes the Wicked Witch of the West and Galinda becomes Glinda the Good Witch.[36] Early, we learn that Elphaba has green skin because her mother drank a potion called Green Elixir when she was conceived. Marginalized by her unusual appearance, she is sent to Shiz primarily to watch over her much favored younger sister Nessarose, who is beautiful, but "wheelchair-bound."[37] At Shiz, Elphaba's natural talent is discovered and she is given a sorcerer position. But she eventually turns on the Wizard and others in charge when she learns they are part of the anti-Animal force in Oz that is taking the voices away from Animals, including her beloved Professor Dillimaud. Her disavowal is labeled subversive and dangerous by those in charge and she is named the Wicked Witch of the West. Thus, the moral of the story is that Elphaba was really just misunderstood, and that it is discrimination that is truly wicked.

Green skin and species status serve as metaphors for people oppressed based on race and gender; however, the progressive message of *Wicked: A New Musical* is not extended to disability. While at school Nessarose falls in love with Boq, a munchkin who is more interested in Galinda. Bitter over her unrequited love, Nessarose becomes governor of Munchkinland (after her father dies) and enslaves Boq. Seeking refuge from her sister, Elphaba attempts to gain her favor by casting a spell on Nessarose's silver shoes, turning them ruby red and giving them the power to let her walk. Nessarose, however, only becomes more tyrannical, refusing Elphaba, turning Boq into the Tin Man, and becoming the Wicked Witch of the East, who dies when

Dorothy's house falls on her. Nessarose is the embodiment of the bitter cripple—isolated, angry, and viewed as an unsuitable sexual partner in the play's narrative. Nessarose is dependent on the help of others. Her difference exceeds the play's embrace of diversity; therefore, she is quite literally stamped out when Dorothy's house falls on her.

In the popular culture, falling in love and caring for someone with a disability (especially a disabled woman) is almost unimaginable, maybe even heroic. In June 2007, *Glamour* published a spread, "Real Women, Real Courage," in which Maria Corona is featured alongside Jessica Gaulke, a beauty queen fighting in Iraq; Melissa Hawkinson, a woman who saved a young boy from drowning; and Kendra Kern, who started an organization called Safe Passage that has helped more than 600 kids in Guatemala City attend school. What was Maria's heroism? She reunited with her life partner, Krystina Jackson, when Krystina became paralyzed in a snowboarding accident. "After the accident, Maria moved in. She feeds me, showers me, takes me to the bathroom and goes to class with me and writes my notes; someday I'll get my business degree. We're a couple again, and our love is stronger than ever."[38] By juxtaposing Maria and Krystina with women who have saved lives and helped hundreds of needy people across the globe, *Glamour* sends a clear message that being in a relationship with a disabled woman is exceptional.

The representation in *Glamour*[39] is drawn from a well-established tradition in Hollywood film, television, and theater of isolating disabled women (e.g., *What Ever Happened to Baby Jane?* [1962] and *Passion Fish*), or even ending their lives when they cease to fulfill expected gender roles (e.g., *Million Dollar Baby* [2004] and *Wicked: The Musical*).[40] Audiences are also frequently warned that such displaced women may become dangerous and manipulative. In a 2006 *Law & Order: Special Victims Unit* episode titled "Manipulated," we meet Tessa, a paraplegic woman, and her husband, Linus, who explains that he stays with his wife out of guilt because he caused the accident that left her paralyzed. Linus says he is having an affair because "I haven't been able to have sex with my wife since her accident." The twist is that Tessa has framed her husband for murder as punishment for the affair because "I need him, I couldn't survive without him." The psychologists evaluating Tessa tell her that "you crave attention so much that you made your husband into a servant," and you are "too invested in assuming the sick role." Tessa's queer position as cared-for becomes connected, then, to her depraved and criminal behavior. In an ironic turn, we learn at the end of the episode that Tessa's paralysis has been cured and she has been playing paralyzed to gain attention, to keep being cared for. Thus, it is questionable whether Tessa counts as a disabled character; however, I argue that it is the show's portrayal of pathological female dependence that is important in this case. Tessa plays the manipulative cripple who saps those around her for attention and care. Once again, the message is clear: beware of women with disabilities. They can only be cared for, and this drain is eventually, inevitably dangerous.

Disabled women in mainstream popular culture are represented as threatening to heteronormative expectations embedded in intimate relationships and family affairs. These women are supposedly unable to fulfill their roles as caregivers; their dependency is social excess that must be eliminated (by killing them off) or controlled—lest they become too draining or too manipulative of the system. Psychological research suggests that attitudes toward people with disabilities are gendered, and that ideas about disabled women are generally much more negative. Reporting on Hanna and Rogovsky's 1986 study with college students, Asch and Fine write:

> When asked how women and men using wheelchairs became disabled, nondisabled students attributed male disability to external situations such as war, work injury, or accident. They attributed female disability to internal causes, such as disease. The authors suggest that attributing disability to disease may foster more negative attitudes because disease stimulates primitive fears of contagion or the person's inherent moral badness. Thus, the disabled woman may be viewed as more dangerous than a similarly disabled male, more morally suspect, or more deserving of her fate.[41]

Thus, attitudes toward women with disability and popular culture representations appear to reinforce each other. Even when disabled through injury (e.g., *Million Dollar Baby* and *What Ever Happened to Baby Jane?*), the disabled woman is depicted as pitiable and fully dependent.[42] She is not shown caring for others or being in a sexual relationship. These fictional portrayals are reinforced by a steady flow of news stories and human interest stories in the popular press that discuss the problems that disability creates for intimate relationships. The many newspaper articles about the frequency of divorce when one partner becomes disabled,[43] and the difficulty that people with disabilities have finding partners (especially nondisabled partners),[44] help maintain the norm.

There are two films that suggest the *possibility* of a romantic relationship for the disabled main character but, tellingly, the films end with this prospect (e.g., *Passion Fish* and *An Affair to Remember*).[45] And the films in which the women are allowed romance on screen end with their death (e.g., *Frida* [2002] and *Theory of Flight*).[46] The only exception to these rules that I could find was for supporting characters. For example, in *Notting Hill* (1999), Gina McKee plays Bella, one of William's (Hugh Grant) friends.[47] Bella is in a wheelchair and she is married; she is presented as a successful, loving, and funny woman. Such representations, however, are usually marginalized (quite literally, as in the case of supporting characters), when not entirely absent, in mainstream popular culture. Women with disabilities are usually portrayed as socially useless, if not threatening, an excess that must be contained and even eliminated.

Sexual Perversion

As the previous section makes clear, it is rare to see people with disabilities, especially women, in romantic relationships in popular culture. It is even more extraordinary to see disabled/nondisabled sex scenes, which is remarkable considering how sex-saturated popular culture has become. I believe that the possibility for sexuality and intimacy in disabled/nondisabled relationships is often obscured because it is antithetical to care in the popular imagination. As Michael Davidson notes, "for many able-bodied persons, disability *is synonymous* with dependency, the former framed as a condition of tragic limit and loss requiring regimes of care and rehabilitation."[48] I would add to this astute observation that dependency is synonymous with childlike asexuality. Children are bathed, dressed, and helped with the bathroom, and sexualizing children is extremely taboo. Physical care is desexualized so that helping with potty, putting on underwear, and the countless other intimate ways in which physically able adults help children are never confused with sex or sexuality.

The same desexualization of intimate care happens in the personal care assistant world. When I worked for several years as a professional personal care assistant, disabled clients were consistently desexualized in my training. The sexual desires of the clients or the aid's sexual desires were never explicitly addressed. To do so would admit that what we do involves sex organs that may respond in desirous ways. Thus, sex functioned as the elephant in the room, constantly present, but never acknowledged. I argue that this consistent bifurcation of care from sex makes it difficult to even think of a disabled/nondisabled sexual relationship. Thus, it is not too surprising that representations of disability rarely include a sexual component.

In films that feature disabled/nondisabled relationships, sex consistently occurs offscreen or is visually hidden in some way. The exception is *Coming Home* (1978), which I will discuss in the final section of this chapter. For example, in *The Bone Collector* and *Passion Fish* sex between disabled and nondisabled lovers is mentioned—we are told that it happens or will happen—but it is never shown. In *Theory of Flight* and *Waterdance*, there are the beginnings of "proper" sex scenes, but each is foiled for the viewer. Joel and Anna begin to have sex while he is at the rehabilitation hospital and both of their naked upper bodies are visible, but the rest of their bodies are under the sheet and the scene quickly ends when Joel's catheter slips and he wets the bed. In *Theory of Flight*, the sex scene fades quickly into the next scene so that the audience sees it beginning, but little visual time is spent on sexual intimacy.

Part of this refusal to show disabled/nondisabled sexual relationships may also stem from the long history of nonconsensual sterilization of people with disabilities. Between 1907 and 1974, thirty-two states had sterilization laws on the books and about 64,000 Americans were forcibly sterilized.[49] Anna Stubblefield points out that "sixty percent of those sterilized were women, and a large majority of those sterilized were white and poor."[50] Pamela Block's historical analysis of the management of women with cognitive impairments notes that, in the 1920s, "sterilization and parole came to be seen as a more economically viable solution" than forced institutionalization.[51] The model law, drafted by Harry H. Laughlin of the Eugenics Record Office, listed ten "socially inadequate" groups that were targeted for nonconsensual sterilization:

> 1) feeble-minded; 2) insane (including psychopathic); 3) criminalistic (including the delinquent and wayward); 4) epileptic; 5) inebriate (including drug habituees); 6) diseased (including the tuberculous, the syphilitic, the leprous, and others with chronic, infectious, and legally segregable diseases); 7) blind (including those with seriously impaired vision); 8) deaf (including those with seriously impaired hearing); 9) deformed (including the crippled); and 10) dependent (including orphans, ne'er-do-wells, the homeless, tramps and paupers).[52]

What is clear from this model law is the desire to erase bodies that fail the expectations set by white male civilization builders. The legality of sterilization laws was upheld by the famous 1927 Supreme Court case *Buck v. Bell*, in which Justice Oliver Wendell Holmes Jr. wrote that "three generations of imbeciles are enough," attesting to the belief that feeblemindedness—discursively linked to other forms of deficits including pauperism and sexual promiscuity—is inherited and a drain on society. Holmes argued that people with disabilities "sap the strength of the State"; therefore, it made sense to prevent further degeneracy and further costs.[53]

Most nonconsensual sterilization laws were removed after World War II; however, Kevin O'Reilly adds that "today, 10 states still have eugenics sterilization laws on the books, although they are not used."[54] While it is true that nonconsensual sterilization laws are not frequently used, it is not true that they are never used. For example, in 1994 Cindy Wasiek was sterilized through laws that were still on the books in Pennsylvania.[55] What is more common today is the use of so-called substitute consent laws. Such laws allow legal guardians to consent to sterilization if the disabled person is determined as unable to consent. For example, in the recent Pillow Angel case, the doctors and parents of a six-year-old girl with severe brain damage created the "Ashley treatment" in which Ashley's uterus and breast buds were removed (to reduce the risk of rape and pregnancy as well as to improve "comfort") and she was subjected to high-dose estrogen treatments to close her growth plates and stunt her growth. Although the case sparked much controversy, it is a testament to the continued presence of nonconsensual sterilization of people with disabilities.[56]

Nonconsensual sterilization and substitute consent laws seek to differentiate the fit from the unfit and to minimize the reproduction of "degeneracy" in all its many forms by controlling the disabled. In addition, desire for the disabled has also historically been (and continues to be) policed. As Stubblefield notes, anyone desiring someone considered "feebleminded" (whether by virtue of race, sexuality, class status, or other form of "degeneracy") must also be "feebleminded."[57] People with such perverse desires do not "get" that reproduction must contribute to civilization building; "thus, failing to understand the importance of white racial purity was itself evidence of moronity in white women."[58] The eugenics discourse punished desire for people with disabilities and other degenerates by labeling those who love people with disabilities as unfit and in need of social control and sterilization. Today, however, policing continues through shunning and more subtle forms of discrimination. People who enter intimate relationships with the disabled are often scrutinized and viewed suspiciously. Writing in the British context in the late 1970s, Wendy Greengross notes:

> The principal problem for a marriage between an able-bodied and someone handicapped is one of motivation. It begs the cruel and unavoidable question: "What normal person would saddle him/herself with someone who will probably need a lifetime of care?" Many "normal" people when they enter a marriage of this nature are not marrying an equal but someone they want to treat like a child.[59]

Considering how normal it has become to see explicit sex, it is revealing that disabled sex, including desire for people with disabilities, remains a fetish subgenre—connoting perversity and depravity—in the pornography industry. By many accounts, pornography is now mainstream.[60] The industry's estimated annual revenue is $10 billion to $14 billion and there are over 420 million pages of pornography online.[61] Each year 13,000 porn videos are released.[62] The porn industry now also has expanding links to more legitimate popular culture industries like music, television, and film. For example, Gregory Dark, who directs porn films, has also directed music videos for Britney Spears and Mandy Moore, and porn stars appear in popular music videos, on popular television shows, and so on.[63] Clearly, porn is no longer the seedy underbelly of popular culture. Porn involving people with disabilities, however, remains in the shadows. To come out as a porn fan is no longer stigmatizing, but to say that you specifically like porn with amputees, little people, or people in wheelchairs is definitely something to hide. It is quite easy to find pornography featuring people with disabilities on websites such as devoteedelites.com, amputee-devotee.com, and gimpsgonewild.com. In addition, mainstream adult stores like the Lion's Den carry titles like *Hump the Stump* (2009) and *Lesbian Handicap Sex* (2009).[64] Despite this apparent popularity, "disability" is not one of the dozens of categories at the annual Adult Video News (AVN) Awards. Best Squirting Release, Best Foot/Leg Fetish Release, and Best Interracial Series are award categories, but not Best Disability Release. When a fetish is excluded from the menu at AVN, it is clearly depraved.

Many disability rights activists and scholars feel conflicted about the fetishization of disability in pornography. For example, Raymond Aguilera critiques research on the devotee phenomena that characterizes desire for people with disabilities as a "disorder." Aguilera notes, pathologizing devotees and other people that are attracted to people with disabilities as sexual predators is not only based on assumption instead of research, but also "fails [to] take into account the agency of a disabled individual in choosing to form a relationship with a devotee."[65] Feminist and disability activist scholar Alison Kafer's analysis of the amputee-devotee community reveals that, contrary to the image of the unsuspecting prey, female amputees have begun to produce their own images, including pornographic ones, in which they are "icons of strength and endurance."[66] Nevertheless, Kafer also offers readers several examples of unwanted attention from devotees that she and other female amputees have received, including being stalked and harassed. Thus, on the one hand, making sexualized images of people with disabilities can help correct the image of asexual or childlike people with disabilities. On the other hand, the tone of such portrayals often remains that of a perverse fetish, something that pushes the limits of even mainstream pornography, encouraging the objectification of people with disabilities (especially women).

The Exceptional Homecoming

I will conclude this chapter with an exception to the popular culture landscape outlined above. *Coming Home* is a film about the fallout of the Vietnam War, but it is also about the love triangle of Luke Martin (Jon Voight), Sally Hyde (Jane Fonda), and Bob Hyde (Bruce Dern).[67] Like *The Men*, the film opens in a Veterans Affairs (VA) hospital, introducing the audience to Luke, a sergeant who has become paraplegic from a combat injury.[68] Luke is depressed, alcoholic, and violently resistant to rehabilitation. Next introduced is Captain Bob Hyde, who is being sent overseas to fight, and his naïve wife Sally. After seeing Bob and his friend Sgt. Dink Mobley (Robert Ginty) off, Sally befriends Dink's girlfriend Val Munson (Penelope Milford) and decides to volunteer at the VA hospital (against her husband's wishes). This experience opens Sally's eyes to the atrocities of the war and the government's treatment of veterans, and reunites her with Luke, a friend from high school. The sexual tension between Luke and Sally is palpable from the beginning, even though they encounter each other when Luke crashes his mobile hospital bed into Sally, spilling the urine from his catheter bag all over her. The film makes a point to emphasize lingering glances, tense conversation, and nervous laughter to draw out the potential intimacy between the two. This meeting seems to encourage

Luke to quit drinking and accept his paralysis. Sally, empowered by her new experiences away from her husband and by Luke's advances, quite literally blossoms—changing her hair, buying a new car (a sporty roadster), and renting an apartment on the beach (none of which she shares with her husband overseas). Confident and invigorated, Sally invites Luke over to her new apartment for dinner. From here the two begin an intense and mutually beneficial affair (both seem to grow from the experience), all the time knowing that it will end upon Bob's return. At the end of the film, Bob returns in relatively good physical health (he limps because he shot himself in the leg), but emotionally broken. He learns about the affair and, in the final scene, undresses on the beach and walks into the ocean. It is implied that Bob intends to kill himself; however, the audience does not see this or how Luke and Sally go on.

Although typical for its "portrayal of adjustment," *Coming Home* is unique because so much attention is spent on the sexual and romantic connection between Luke and Sally, and the way in which mutual care functions in their relationship. As the nondisabled partner, Sally helps Luke into bed during the sex scene, over the stairs to her apartment, and into her car. She is also an emotional helpmate, calling him out on his self-centered loathing early in the film. However, Luke also helps Sally. He holds the door open for her and helps her with beds at the VA hospital, and literally rescues her when Bob almost assaults Sally after finding out about the affair. Emotionally, he encourages Sally's independence and righteous outrage toward the military's refusal to acknowledge problems at the VA hospital. Luke even gives Sally her first orgasm. This mutuality and reciprocity are emphasized through the film's narration. Two shots[69] (as opposed to shot-reverse-shot sequences) of Sally and Luke dominate the film, adding to the sense of equality between the two. In contrast, conversations between Sally and Bob often occur in shot-reverse-shots, literally separating the couple, or the composition of the shot emphasizes Sally's subservient position to Bob and her disapproval of Bob's values and behavior. For example, when Sally goes to Hong Kong to visit Bob during his R & R, there is an interesting shot in which Bob is in the foreground, obscuring Sally. This is significant because the dialogue indicates the couple's growing distance, including Bob's inability to see Sally as a full partner. The shot emphasizes the pair's inequality and cements their disconnection. Bob wants Sally to remain naïve and in the private sphere, but Sally has already outgrown such restrictions. The film is critical of heteronormative relations and offers Luke and Sally as an alternative (which is also alternative in terms of disability). The relationship between Luke and Sally is a bond that allows both to grow, to be more themselves together. It also undercuts the binary position of caregiver and care receiver; Sally and Luke are equal partners in the film's narrative.

I believe that it is this sense of mutuality and equality as well as the film's overtly radical nature that allows for the explicit sexual representation. In other words, the potential for sex and intimacy is not forestalled in this film because the disabled partner is not equated with dependency. The sex scene occurs after Luke has been arrested for protesting the war. Sally bails him out of jail and tells him that she would like to sleep with him (he propositioned her earlier in the film when he came over for dinner). He tells her they can go back to his place. When they enter Luke's apartment, he says he needs to do a few things in the bathroom and that he will be only a few minutes. The film then cuts to the bedroom and the audience sees Sally waiting on the bed with her long coat on (she is naked underneath). Without cutting, the film then shows Luke rolling into the bedroom (toward the camera and Sally) and up to the bed. He is naked except for a hand towel he has placed across his lap. He asks Sally to position his sheepskin in the center of the bed and then he transfers. She lifts his legs into the bed and then turns off the light. The screen turns to black and then the audience hears Luke tell Sally to turn the light back on because "I want to see you." The next shot lasts almost a full minute (average shot duration in film is only ten seconds) and is a close, tight shot that pans their bodies, following their hands as they touch each other and kiss. The lighting is soft and warm tones are used, adding to the sense of closeness and heat. In the final part of this scene, Sally's face is shown in close-up as she orgasms. She then begins to sob because "that has never happened to me before," and Luke comforts her. The last shot is of Luke resting his head on Sally's breasts.

Cinematically, this scene looks and feels much like the typical sex scene in a Hollywood film; however, as the sequence above indicates, female pleasure is foregrounded. In addition, the dialogue addresses audience anxieties about "how a disabled person has sex." After Sally turns on the lights, the audience hears the following exchange while the camera pans over Sally's and Luke's bodies.

SALLY: What do I do?

LUKE: Everything. I want you to do everything.

SALLY: Where can I touch you? Where can you feel?

LUKE: That's nice. I'm real sensitive in all the areas that I feel. Real sensitive.

SALLY: Can you feel that?

LUKE: Can't feel it but I can see it.

SALLY: I wish you could feel me.

LUKE: I feel you.

The dialogue lets the audience know that people with paralysis are still sexually aroused by touch in the numb areas because they can see the touching and feel through body memory. It also suggests that the rest of the body becomes hypersensitive to touch. It is, in fact, possible for some men with paraplegia to learn how to orgasm through caresses on their chest, nape of their neck, or other areas. In other words, the dialogue combats the notion that paraplegia deadens sexual feeling and desire.

This sex scene is remarkable for Hollywood film because the audience watches for over four minutes as a disabled/nondisabled couple has physically hot and emotionally intimate sex. Their physical differences are present. The dialogue highlights Luke's paraplegia as Sally helps him into bed and there is a glimpse of the scar on his spine. However, these physical differences do not undercut the scene's sexiness; instead, they are blended seamlessly into the eroticism of the encounter. I know of no other Hollywood film that treats disabled sexuality in this way. As I outlined above, it is much more typical for sexuality to be suggested than shown.

Coming Home's treatment of sex and disability is exceptional in the cinematic landscape and it helps put the normative representations of disabled/nondisabled love into sharper focus. Since disabled bodies do not fit with popular understandings of love, it is common to portray people with disabilities as unsuitable intimate partners. They require a level of care that burdens the nondisabled partner, draining interpersonal relationships and state support. It is clear from these representations that physical dependency is a serious problem to love relationships, especially for women who are typically the caretakers in heterosexual relationships. If they are disabled, they are rendered socially worthless because they are unable to care for others (according to popular culture logic). Since it is already acceptable for men to receive care from wives and girlfriends, the care that disabled men require is not necessarily problematic. For the most part, however, disabled men and women are not favorably represented in popular culture. Disability continues to carry connotations of perversity and childlike asexuality, making it difficult to intervene with positive sexual representations of disabled/nondisabled intimate relationships. As I will demonstrate in the second part of this book, the images and beliefs outlined in this chapter influence the lives of people involved in disabled/nondisabled intimate relationships. In the following chapter, I show how such discourse frames contemporary scientific research on disabled/nondisabled intimate relationships.

Notes

1. "Girlfriend," Mothers Against Drunk Driving Canada (2005).
2. Zitzelsberger, "(In)visibility," p. 389.
3. Crawford and Ostrove, "Representations of Disability."
4. Ibid.; Waxman, "It's Time."
5. This policy can put people with disabilities at the financial mercy of their spouses because they no longer have their own income. Research on disabled women

and domestic violence suggests that such financial concerns may lead some women to stay in abusive relationships (Olkin, "Women with Physical Disabilities").

6. Asch and Fine, "Nurturance, Sexuality, and Women."

7. Swidler, *Talk of Love*.

8. hooks, *All About Love*.

9. Garland-Thomson, *Extraordinary Bodies*, p. 57.

10. Cahill and Norden, "Hollywood's Portrayals," p. 72.

11. Mitchell and Snyder, "Narrative Prosthesis," p. 205.

12. hooks, *All About Love*, p. 95.

13. *Waterdance*, directed by Neal Jimenez and Michael Steinberg, 1992 (Culver City, CA: Columbia TriStar Home Video, 2001), DVD.

14. Swidler, *Talk of Love*, p. 114.

15. *Beauty and the Beast*, directed by Gary Trousdale and Kirk Wise, 1991 (Burbank, CA: Walt Disney Home Video, 1992), VHS.

16. *The Little Mermaid*, directed by John Musker and Ron Clements, 1989 (Burbank, CA: Walt Disney Home Video, 1990), VHS; *Shrek*, directed by Andrew Adamson and Vicky Jenson, 2001 (Universal City, CA: DreamWorks Home Entertainment), DVD.

17. *The Hunchback of Notre Dame*, directed by Gary Trousdale and Kirk Wise, 1996 (Burbank, CA: Walt Disney Home Video, 1997), VHS.

18. *Avatar*, directed by James Cameron, 2009 (Beverly Hills, CA: Twentieth Century Fox, 2010), DVD.

19. McRuer, *Crip Theory*, pp. 16–17.

20. *As Good As It Gets*, directed by James L. Brooks, 1997 (Culver City, CA: Columbia TriStar Home Video, 1998), DVD.

21. McRuer, *Crip Theory*, p. 24.

22. *Notting Hill* is also a romantic comedy and there is a disabled woman in a relationship with a nondisabled man in this film; however, she is a supporting character and their relationship is not featured.

23. *The Men*, directed by Fred Zinnemann, 1950 (Santa Monica, CA: Republic Pictures, distributed by Artisan Home Entertainment, 2003), DVD.

24. *An Affair to Remember*, directed by Leo McCarey, 1957 (Beverly Hills, CA: Twentieth Century Fox Home Entertainment, 2002), DVD; *My Left Foot*, directed by Jim Sheridan, 1989 (New York: HBO Video, 1991), VHS; *The Theory of Flight*, directed by Paul Greengrass, 1998 (Fine Line Features, 1999), VHS; *Passion Fish*, directed by John Sayles, 1992 (Culver City, CA: Columbia TriStar Home Video, 1998), DVD.

25. *The Bone Collector*, directed by Phillip Noyce, 1999 (Universal City, CA: Universal Studios, 2000), DVD.

26. Cahill and Norden, "Hollywood's Portrayals," p. 57.

27. Wendell, *The Rejected Body*, p. 43.

28. Cahill and Norden, "Hollywood's Portrayals," p. 58.

29. Ibid. *Orphans of the Storm*, directed by D. W. Griffith, 1921 (Los Angeles, CA: Delta Entertainment, 2004), DVD; *City Lights*, directed by Charlie Chaplin, 1931 (Pyrmont, NSW: MK2/Warner Bros., 2004), DVD; *The Spiral Staircase*, directed by Robert Siodmak (1946; Culver City, CA: Metro-Goldwyn-Mayer Home Entertainment), DVD; *Johnny Belinda*, DVD, directed by Jean Negulesco, 1948 (Warner Home Video, 2006), DVD; *Magnificent Obsession*, directed by Douglas Sirk, 1954 (Irvington, NY: Criterion Collection, 2008), DVD; *Wait Until Dark*, directed by Terence Young, 1967 (Warner Home Video, 2003), DVD; *Ice Castles*, directed by Donald Wyre, 1978 (New York: Columbia Pictures Home Entertainment), VHS; *Children of a*

Lesser God, directed by Randa Haines, 1986 (Hollywood, CA: Paramount Pictures, 2000), DVD; *Jennifer 8*, directed by Bruce Robinson, 1992 (Hollywood, CA: Paramount Pictures, 2000), DVD; *Blink*, directed by Michael Apted, 1994 (New Line Home Video, 2003), DVD.

30. Cahill and Norden, "Hollywood's Portrayals," p. 58.

31. Asch and Fine, "Nurturance, Sexuality, and Women," pp. 244–245; Lloyd, "The Politics of Disability," pp. 722–723.

32. Asch and Fine, "Nurturance, Sexuality, and Women," p. 245.

33. Hanna and Rogovsky, "Women with Disabilities," p. 56.

34. Garland-Thomson, *Extraordinary Bodies*, p. 41.

35. Connell, *Masculinities*, p. 77.

36. Maguire, *Wicked: The Life and Times of the Wicked Witch of the West*, 1996.

37. Elphaba feels responsible for Nessarose because it is suggested that the potion their mother consumed to prevent her second child from being green-skinned caused Nessarose's physical appearance (and her mother's death during childbirth). Notice that this references "thalidomide babies"—babies born with physical deformities caused by thalidomide, a morning sickness drug prescribed to pregnant women in the 1960s.

38. "Real Women, Real Courage," *Glamour*, p. 233.

39. Ibid.

40. *What Ever Happened to Baby Jane?* directed by Robert Aldrich, 1962 (Burbank, CA: Warner Home Video, 2006), DVD; *Passion Fish*, directed by John Sayles, 1992 (Culver City, CA: Columbia TriStar Home Video, 1998), DVD; *Million Dollar Baby*, directed by Clint Eastwood, 2004 (Burbank, CA: Warner Home Video, 2005), DVD; *Wicked: A New Musical*, 2005.

41. Asch and Fine, "Nurturance, Sexuality, and Women," p. 243.

42. *Million Dollar Baby*, directed by Clint Eastwood, 2004 (Burbank, CA: Warner Home Video, 2005), DVD; *What Ever Happened to Baby Jane?* directed by Robert Aldrich, 1962 (Burbank, CA: Warner Home Video, 2006), DVD.

43. For example, Kilborn, "Divorce Rate Is Higher"; Vance, "Disability and Divorce"; Eustice and Eustice, "In Sickness and in Health"; and Kilborn, "Disabled Spouses Are Increasingly Forced to Go It Alone."

44. See, for example, Altman, "Something in the Way He Moves."

45. *An Affair to Remember*, directed by Leo McCarey, 1957 (Beverly Hills, CA: Twentieth Century Fox Home Entertainment, 2002), DVD; *Passion Fish*, directed by John Sayles, 1992 (Culver City, CA: Columbia TriStar Home Video, 1998), DVD.

46. *Frida*, directed by Julie Taymor, 2002 (Burbank, CA: Buena Vista Home Video, 2003), DVD; *The Theory of Flight*, directed by Paul Greengrass, 1998 (Fine Line Features, 1999), VHS.

47. *Notting Hill*, directed by Roger Michell, 1999 (Universal City, CA: Universal Studios), DVD.

48. Davidson, "Introduction," p. i, emphasis in original.

49. O'Reilly, "Confronting Eugenics."

50. Stubblefield, "'Beyond the Pale,'" p. 162.

51. Block, "Sexuality, Fertility, and Danger," p. 245.

52. Cited in ibid.

53. *Buck v. Bell*, 274 US 200 (1927).

54. O'Reilly, "Confronting Eugenics."

55. Block, "Sexuality, Fertility, and Danger," p. 247.

56. Gibbs, "Pillow Angel Ethics."

57. Stubblefield, "Beyond the Pale," p. 177.

58. Ibid.

59. Greengross, *Entitled to Love*, p. 29.

60. See Stein, "Porn Goes Mainstream"; and Young, *Media Education Foundation Study Guide: The Price of Pleasure*.

61. Young, *Study Guide: The Price of Pleasure*, p. 5.

62. Ibid.

63. Young, *Study Guide: The Price of Pleasure*, p. 5.

64. *Hump the Stump*, 2009 (Robert Hill Entertainment), DVD; *Lesbian Handicap Sex*, 2009 (Heatwave Entertainment), DVD.

65. Aguilera, "Disability and Delight," p. 258.

66. Kafer, "Inseparable," p. 113.

67. *Coming Home*, directed by Hal Ashby, 1978 (Santa Monica, CA: Metro-Goldwyn-Mayer), DVD.

68. *The Men*, directed by Fred Zinnemann, 1950 (Santa Monica, CA: Republic Pictures, distributed by Artisan Home Entertainment, 2003), DVD.

69. "Two shot" is a film technique in which the two people talking are filmed in the frame together. The other way of filming dialogue is called "shot-reverse-shot" in which only one person at a time is filmed and the sequence is edited together for continuity.

3

The View from Medicine, Rehabilitation, and Nursing

Popular attitudes about the meaning and nature of marriage and partnerships, care, independence, and dependence all contribute to a long-standing cultural suspicion of relationships between the able-bodied and disabled. Professionals working in rehabilitation, nursing, medicine, social work, and psychology—what I call the applied fields—are not exempt from these attitudes. Professionals in the applied fields may hold discriminatory beliefs about people with disabilities and their partners, including the faulty assumption that there are only negative aspects to caregiving.[1] For example, professionals may assume that the disabled partner is wholly dependent, unable to give care to the nondisabled partner and unable to meaningfully participate in social life. Likewise, they may assume that the care given by the nondisabled spouse is a burdensome activity that desexualizes the relationship and causes physical and mental harm to the nondisabled partner. These attitudes are characteristic of the medical model of disability aimed at curing and eliminating disability. Activists in the disability rights movement (which frames impairment as a benign social difference) have criticized the medical model approach, arguing that professionals in the applied fields need to incorporate social and political discrimination, prejudice, and isolation into their studies of disability. In this chapter, I examine whether or not the applied fields have heeded the calls for a paradigm shift by analyzing research published in peer-reviewed journals from 2003 to 2006. Although there are a few examples of ideological progress, most of the literature continues to support dominant understandings of care and sexuality between disabled/nondisabled partners. In the analysis that follows, I detail how caregiving and sexuality in disabled/nondisabled intimate relations are constructed and explore the varied ramifications of these views.

Understanding how health and rehabilitation professionals view people with disabilities and their partners is important because it is likely that couples will have repeated contact with the applied fields. Visits to doctors and nurses may be necessary to manage chronic illness or to care for acute conditions that emerge as a result of physical impairment (e.g., bed sores). Occupational therapists may be needed from time to time to help the disabled partner to improve or learn new skills for daily living (e.g., techniques for transferring from wheelchair to toilet), or to introduce the disabled person to adaptive technologies that can be used in work environments (e.g., voice recognition software). Physical therapists help people with disabilities rehabilitate from acute conditions, but also may be needed periodically to improve physical function and flexibility to prevent acute conditions. Personal care assistants and home health nurses may visit the couple in their home to provide personal (unskilled) and medical (skilled) care. Social workers and home health nurses can provide training to partners of people with disabilities. This training may involve how to dress and bathe the disabled partner, or it may involve highly skilled training such as maintenance of respirators and permanent bladder catheters. Finally, periodic assessment visits to doctors and physical therapists may be required by the government and private disability insurance companies. These visits are designed to ensure that the beneficiary remains "disabled enough." That is, they are unable to work (or work enough) and, therefore, are still in need of financial assistance. These interactions create a matrix of health professionals who are involved in the lives of people with disabilities and their partners. At each iteration, professionals subtly or explicitly relay attitudes and beliefs about disability to the couple.

Disability rights advocates argue that the attitudes of health professionals contribute to feelings of worthlessness and self-doubt as ablest beliefs are internalized.[2] Rose D. Galvin reports that, "whether being patronized or pitied, singled out for unsolicited attention or treated as invisible, being stared at or reviled, participants reported that the negative attitudes of others greatly contributed to the development of negative self-perceptions."[3] Although low self-esteem often diminishes over time (especially as the disabled person places the "problem" of disability with society), the attitudes of others continue to influence and shape conceptions of self.[4]

Candy Mung-nga Li and Matthew Kwai-sang Yau report that health professionals' attitudes are especially negative when it comes to disability and sexuality. According to Li and Yau, "when health professionals discuss sexual issues with their patients, they often do so in an overly pessimistic way. They may focus on likely difficulties without giving possible solutions, addressing fears, or reassuring patients that they are still sexual beings and can enjoy a meaningful sex life."[5] Stereotypical understandings of disabled sexuality shape the ways in which health professionals approach sexuality with clients. Li and Yau highlight research on stereotypical attitudes in the nursing profession. They state:

> Morris (32) points out that the common reactions of most nursing staff to sexual behaviors or questions from people with disabilities may include dis-

belief ("how could they be sexually active?"); revulsion or disgust ("anything but 'normal' sexual activity is a perversion"); or avoidance ("if we do not discuss it, it will not happen"; "it is not my job"). Morris (33) further highlights that nurses commonly perceive people with physical disabilities as asexual, expressing embarrassment or disgust at the thought of their sexuality, as well as being unsure of how to deal with the specific issues of the patient's sexuality.[6]

Doctors, social workers, and occupational and physical rehabilitation specialists hold similar attitudes.[7] These attitudes are also gendered so that the sexual lives of women with disabilities are more likely to be ignored in research and clinical practice.[8] Based on sexist ideas about female sexuality, researchers assume that women are passive in the sexual encounter and have lower sexual drives than men.[9] Thus, a spinal cord injury does not disrupt a woman's sexual functioning as it does a man's because "all she has to do is lie on her back and open her legs."[10] Because of these attitudes, it is more likely that disabled men, not disabled women, will receive some type of sex education in rehab.[11]

In addition, health professionals' attitudes and beliefs impinge on the lives of people with disabilities and their partners outside the immediate interaction. The research conducted in the applied fields is also disseminated in the larger culture: reformulated into thirty-second sound bites for the evening news, used as inspiration for film and television scripts, and taught in college courses. In other words, the effect of such research is far-reaching, especially in societies that highly value and trust doctors and other health professionals.

In order to better understand how disabled/nondisabled relationships are represented by the applied fields, I conducted a content analysis of peer-reviewed journal articles published from 2003 to 2006 and indexed in the Academic Search Premier[12] database (see Appendix A for more information about methods). I performed two different searches, one using "sexuality" and "disability" as keywords and the other using "caregiving" and "spouse," which yielded sixty-three articles for analysis (see Appendix B for a listing of these articles by search). Although there were a few articles that challenged normative understandings of disability, care, and sexuality, the vast majority of the research that I analyzed endorsed stereotypes either overtly in clearly ableist statements or implicitly through research choices and exclusions.

A Divided Literature

It is interesting that there was only one article in common between these two searches.[13] Clearly, sexuality and care are not conceptualized together in the literature. Instead, they are viewed as antagonistic needs. The assumption that a high need for assistance in activities of daily living results in low levels of sexual and relationship satisfaction appears to influence research design.

Indeed, it is rare for studies concerned with high levels of care to even ask participants about sexuality and romantic relationships. Such a perspective results in a bifurcated literature, which fails to conceptualize the disabled/nondisabled couple as both sexual and caring. When sexuality is the primary concern of an article, the focus is on the disabled partner. When care is the primary concern of an article, the focus is on the nondisabled partner. The needs and concerns of the nondisabled partner are considered as opposed to those of the disabled partner. In fact, only seventeen (27 percent) studies included perspectives from both partners, and three of these were literature reviews.[14] This dichotomization supports the view that the disabled partner is only the care receiver, the nondisabled partner only the caregiver, and that this dependency dynamic creates low levels of sexual satisfaction.

Thirty-three articles (82.5 percent) from the caregiving and spouse search failed to mention sex or sexual intimacy. This is a notable omission because it seems logical to assume that high marital satisfaction, including sexual satisfaction and intimacy, would buffer caregiver burden in disabled/nondisabled intimate relationships. In other words, it makes sense that marital discord would be related to increased care-related stress. However, of the seven (17.5 percent) articles from the caregiving and spouse search that do address sex or intimacy, only two[15] explore how sexual or intimate satisfaction may influence care-related stress. Significantly, both of these articles support the notion that marital satisfaction buffers caregiver burden. Heejeong Choi and Nadine F. Marks note:

> Perhaps one of the most important findings of this study is that, in comparison to noncaregiver peers, no differences in change in mental health outcomes were observed among biological parent or spouse caregivers who reported lower ratings of marital disagreement (i.e., better marital quality). This finding warrants further consideration because biological parent care and spouse care are typically two of the most demanding caregiving types. Low conflict marriage appears to protect new biological parent and spouse caregivers to the point of not only reducing but actually negating the potentially detrimental effects of caregiving on positive and negative affect.[16]

Regardless, studies that examine the relationship between marital satisfaction and caregiver burden continue to be rare. Of the remaining five articles that do address sex or intimacy, two discuss sex or intimacy (especially how sexuality declines with increased care needs) in the literature review sections only, failing to add relationship satisfaction measures to their studies.[17] Two do not relate sexuality to care-related stress.[18] And one conceptualizes the reports of low intimacy or love found in the study as the result of increased care-related duties.[19] Clearly, the positive force that sex or intimacy may play in the lives of caregiving disabled/nondisabled couples is undertheorized and under-researched in the literature.

Although there is a growing body of research on the sexuality of people with disabilities, much of it remains focused on sexual self-esteem, physical and psychological barriers to sex, and the problems disabled people face in finding sexual partners. There continues to be little about disabled people in sexual relationships, which explains why the sexuality and disability search yielded more results (179), but only 22 remained after review (most were about the disabled person outside of relationships). It is also interesting to note that nine (41 percent) of the twenty-two articles in the search were from the journal *Sexuality and Disability*.[20] Published by Springer, this international quarterly journal aims to provide "original scholarly articles addressing the psychological and medical aspects of sexuality in relation to rehabilitation."[21] To date, *Sexuality and Disability* is the only journal focused on this particular intersection. Thus, the sexuality of people with disabilities is relatively isolated in the applied fields. And, like the caregiving and spouse search, few researchers examining sexuality and disability have considered the ways in which disabled/nondisabled couples experience *both* care and intimacy. Eight (36 percent) of the articles from the sexuality and disability search do not address care or caregiving. Of the fourteen (64 percent) that do have some kind of discussion of care, only one suggests that sex and care are related and that, like care, "sexual expression is an interdependent activity."[22] The remaining thirteen articles discuss how care can be used to keep people with disabilities in abusive relationships,[23] the role of personal care assistants in the lives of people with disabilities,[24] the way in which parents providing care can impede people with disabilities in finding intimate partners,[25] how women with disabilities suffer because they are viewed as being unable to care for children,[26] and how partner care can lead to sex-related problems.[27]

Thus, when care is addressed in the sexuality and disability literature, it is predominately framed as a problem for people with disabilities and their partners. Because care is so frequently associated with burden and relationship problems in the literature, it is not uncommon for a study to attribute sexual problems to care burden even when no specific measure of care burden is used.[28] When sexual or relationship problems are found, researchers suggest that the source of the problem is the care-related needs of the disabled partner, and other social and psychological factors are ignored. In the next section, I explore the ways in which such underlying assumptions about the meaning and nature of care and sex influence research in the applied fields.

Research Design and Analysis

Negative assumptions about caregiving and receiving, as well as the sexuality of people with disabilities, are frequently built into the research. In this section, I will focus on four problem areas in the design and analysis of research in the applied fields: (1) a failure to conceptualize and account for the social dimensions of care and disability, (2) biased language, (3) instrumentation, and (4) a limited conceptualization of reciprocity in care relationships.

In most of the articles from the caregiving and spouse search, caregiving is conceptualized only as a negative activity that desexualizes the relationship and causes psychological and physical damage to the caregiver. Many of the studies hypothesize that care burden or care strain causes a variety of problems for the nondisabled partner (conceived as the caregiver), including increased psychological distress such as depression and anxiety,[29] decreased preventative health care behaviors,[30] and poorer physical health.[31] Representative statements include:

> Carers providing long hours of care over extended spells present raised levels of distress, women more so than men. Adverse effects on the psychological well-being of heavily involved carers are most pronounced around the start of their care episodes and when caregiving ends. Ongoing care increases their susceptibility to recurring distress, and adverse health effects are evident beyond the end of their caregiving episodes.[32]

> The care-related increase in depressive symptoms may result not from task-related burden, but from grief surrounding a loved one's illness, or from loss of relational reciprocity, for example.[33]

> It is evident that the older people's self-care ability is a key factor that influences caregiver burden; the more dependent the elder is and the more care they require, the greater the burden felt by the caregiver.[34]

> The increased dependence, especially on the partner—often with changing roles—can be a big strain on relationships.[35]

Most of the studies that framed care as a burden did indeed find that caregiving was a health risk to caregivers.[36] Their findings are suspect, however, because of inadequate or flawed measurements and research designs that set up care receiver and caregiver as antagonists. In addition, mediating factors, such as marital satisfaction, reciprocity, and social networks, are frequently omitted from care burden studies. For example, Michael Hirst set out to examine the relationship between psychological distress and caregiving by using longitudinal, population-based data. As the excerpt above highlights, Hirst found support for the hypothesis that caregiving increases psychological distress; however, the British Panel Household Survey that Hirst used as his study data is limited to the locus of care (e.g., coresident or care for someone outside of the home), level of involvement (i.e., hours per week), and relationship of the care recipient (e.g., spouse, child, or parent). Hirst excluded measures on perceived uplifts in caregiving, reciprocity, and marital satisfaction.[37] Thus, the study fails to consider care as a relationship. Similarly, Carolyn Cannuscio et al. found that high levels of care equal high levels of depressive symptoms for the caregiver (regardless of employment status and only slightly moderated by social ties); however, these researchers failed to consider the disabled partner's role in the relationship or the quality of the spousal relationship, both of which are factors that could affect the nondisabled partner's mental health.[38]

The language used in care burden studies helps illuminate why the research consistently fails to consider reciprocity; that is, to look at care as a relationship. Disabled partners are often referred to as "patients" and the nondisabled partner as "spouse."[39] The word "patient" brings to mind Talcott Parsons's sociological description of the "sick role" in which an ill or disabled person is exempted from normal social behaviors because he or she is supposed to focus on getting well.[40] Normal behaviors that are expected of the nonsick, such as caring for others, are actively discouraged by those placed in the sick role. The only duty that the person in the sick role has is succumbing to the technical expertise of doctors and other helpers. The sick role is the model of expected behavior in societies that are characterized by the medical model of disability, like the United States, in which the problem of the illness or disability can be overcome with science. Impairment is an individual's problem that he or she must seek help in overcoming, assuming the sick role along the way. Clearly, the sick role is a completely passive role. Patients, the epitome of the sick role, do nothing but receive help, guidance, and care from professionals and family. Researchers who use the word "patients" to describe the disabled partners in their studies reveal their assumptions that the disabled partners cannot give care or reciprocate in any way. From this perspective, the disabled and nondisabled partners are antagonists: the disabled partner can only take; the nondisabled partner can only give; and, eventually, this dynamic leads to burden, stress, and a desexualized intimate relationship.

The language of patient is symptomatic of the way in which the subjectivity of disabled people is undermined by professionals in the applied fields. People with disabilities are not quite whole persons. Data collection procedures and reporting practices also demonstrate this bias. For example, some of the researchers interviewed the disabled partner, or included data on the disabled partner, but reported consequences only for the nondisabled partner. Thus, the disabled partner's perspective was used merely to illuminate the nondisabled partner's situation. It was also quite common for researchers to gather data about the functional level of the disabled partner from the nondisabled partner.[41] Not only does this tactic literally silence the disabled partner, but it muddles the data because the nondisabled partner's perception of function may differ radically from what the disabled partner knows he or she is capable of doing. In other studies, researchers recruited couples, but reported only caregiver data.[42] For example, in Hennie R. Boeije and Anneke Van Doorne-Huiskes's study, both partners were interviewed, but the disabled partner's data were used only as a data check.[43] Doris Svetlik et al. used data collected from the Family Relationships in Late Life (FRILL) study to examine the perceptions of relationship loss (due to caregiving) and declines in satisfaction with physical intimacy.[44] FRILL collects data from both partners; however, Svetlik et al. used data from only the caregiver to conclude that increased care predicted perceptions of decreased intimacy and relationship loss. Svetlik et al. did not consider that the disabled partner's attitudes and behaviors may bear on the caregiver's perceptions of intimacy because the disabled partner is assumed to be passive. In one study, the omission of the disabled partner is so egregious that the study participants complained. Christina Hendrix and Charlene Ray tested an intervention that provided personal care training to the nondisabled partners of people being discharged from the hospital, and participants commented that the researchers should have included both partners to recognize that this is a "partnership" of care.[45] The norm, however, is to treat disabled and nondisabled partners as opponents: one needing care and one giving care.

Assumptions about disability popularized in the sick role influence research design and often set up the disabled and nondisabled partners as opponents. Thus, care measures, such as the Caregiver Strain Index, often contain only negatively framed items (see Figure 3.1). Rarely do studies ask the nondisabled partner to describe positive aspects of caregiving. For example, in their meta-analysis of the caregiving literature, Martin Pinquart and Silvia Sörensen found only 28 articles—out of 228—that mention perceived uplifts of caregiving (12 percent). Perceived uplifts included feeling useful, experiencing pride in one's own abilities to handle crisis, and appreciating closeness with the care receiver.[46] Physical or sexual intimacy, however, was not a perceived uplift, nor was sex a factor in the meta-analysis at all. In addition the care that the disabled partner provides to the nondisabled partner, or to other family members, is never factored into the analyses of caregiver strain. Such absences reveal the assumption that the disabled partner cannot give care or reciprocate in any way. Thus, measures of reciprocity—the ways in which the disabled partner may give back or care for the nondisabled partner—are often not included in care research.[47]

Even when a study does include reciprocity or caregiver gains, the notion of reciprocity operationalized is very limited and can influence study findings. The most common understanding of what the nondisabled partner gets out of providing care is a sense of pride or increased self-esteem.[48] These studies find that caregivers often feel good about being able to provide care to their loved ones. Sometimes this sense of pride is also related to a feeling of role stability because the caregiver knows what is needed and what to do.[49] And the caregiver may feel that he or she appreciates life more.[50] Although these are important gains, they are not strong examples of reciprocity because a sense of pride is not something that the disabled partner necessarily is directly or actively giving to the nondisabled partner in exchange for physical care. One can feel a sense of pride and increased self-esteem by taking care of a plant or raising

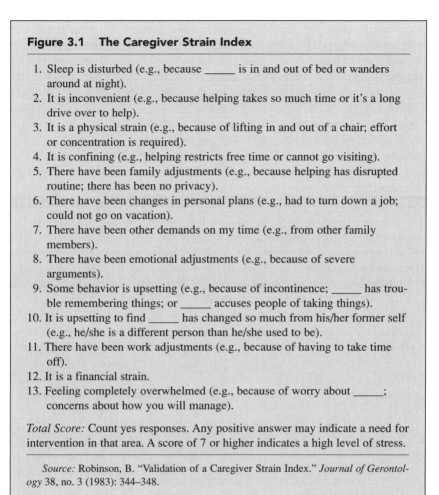

Figure 3.1   The Caregiver Strain Index

1. Sleep is disturbed (e.g., because _____ is in and out of bed or wanders around at night).
2. It is inconvenient (e.g., because helping takes so much time or it's a long drive over to help).
3. It is a physical strain (e.g., because of lifting in and out of a chair; effort or concentration is required).
4. It is confining (e.g., helping restricts free time or cannot go visiting).
5. There have been family adjustments (e.g., because helping has disrupted routine; there has been no privacy).
6. There have been changes in personal plans (e.g., had to turn down a job; could not go on vacation).
7. There have been other demands on my time (e.g., from other family members).
8. There have been emotional adjustments (e.g., because of severe arguments).
9. Some behavior is upsetting (e.g., because of incontinence; _____ has trouble remembering things; or _____ accuses people of taking things).
10. It is upsetting to find _____ has changed so much from his/her former self (e.g., he/she is a different person than he/she used to be).
11. There have been work adjustments (e.g., because of having to take time off).
12. It is a financial strain.
13. Feeling completely overwhelmed (e.g., because of worry about _____; concerns about how you will manage).

Total Score: Count yes responses. Any positive answer may indicate a need for intervention in that area. A score of 7 or higher indicates a high level of stress.

Source: Robinson, B. "Validation of a Caregiver Strain Index." *Journal of Gerontology* 38, no. 3 (1983): 344–348.

a puppy. Another form of reciprocity that is often employed in care studies is called "virtual" or "symbolic reciprocity."[51] The reciprocity is symbolic or virtual because the nondisabled partners explain that they give care because the disabled partner "would do the same for me," or "did the same for me in the past." The actual ways that the disabled partner gives care at the time of data collection are not addressed. Again, this is a limited notion of reciprocity that reflects the belief that there is nothing the disabled partner can currently and concretely give to the nondisabled partner.

In sum, care is often measured only in terms of burden (or other negative items), and when positives such as caregiver gains and reciprocity are added into the study, they are often limited by stereotypes of people with disabilities as passive, inactive members of the relationship (if they are considered at all). Instrumentation problems are not limited to notions of care and reciprocity in the literature. Measures of sexual satisfaction and sexual esteem used with people with disabilities are also typically framed in negative terms. For example, the ten-item Physical Disability Sexual and Body Esteem Scale[52] does not contain a single positively framed question about disability and sexuality (see Figure 3.2). Items include "I envy people with 'normal' bodies," "I feel that my disability is likely to prevent me from satisfying a sexual partner," "My sexual expression is limited by my disability," and "I would do a body swap with an able-bodied person if I could." Clearly, the framing of the questionnaire assumes impairment can have only a negative repercussion on sexuality, and it may reinforce sexual stigma. In addition, the questions place the locus of the "problem" in the disability itself, not social and physical barriers the disabled person may face. Ableist attitudes about sex and disability or the lack of privacy experienced by people with disabilities are not part of the measurement. By focusing only on the subjective experiences of disability, the social dimension of disability, which may indeed cause much of the psychological distress found in the research, is obscured.

For the past several decades, the social model of disability has been the dominant way to examine disability from within the interdisciplinary field of disability studies. The social model draws attention to the ways in which the

---

Figure 3.2   The Physical Disability Sexual and Body Esteem Scale

1. I feel that my disability interferes with my sexual enjoyment.
2. It is harder to find a sexual partner when you have a disability.
3. I would like to hide my disability as much as possible.
4. I feel sexually frustrated because of my disability.
5. I feel that my disability is likely to prevent me from satisfying a sexual partner.
6. My sexual expression is limited by my disability.
7. I feel that people are not sexually interested in me because of my disability.
8. I envy people with "normal" bodies.
9. I believe that I experience rejection from potential sexual partners because of my disability.
10. I would do a body swap with an able-bodied person if I could.

Items are answered using a 5-item Likert-type scale that ranges from 1 (*strongly agree*) to 5 (*strongly disagree*).

Source: Taleporos, George, and Marita P. McCabe. "Development and Validation of the Physical Disability Sexual and Body Esteem Scale." *Sexuality and Disability* 20, no. 3 (2002): 159–176.

built environment and discriminatory attitudes disable someone with an impairment. In other words, the social model places the problem of disability outside the individual. The solution is accommodation and education. The social model is also a critique of the medical model of disability, which continues to dominate the applied fields, that places the problem of disability in the individual. Most of the sixty-three articles that I analyzed in this chapter employ a medical model of disability and, therefore, fail to interrogate social aspects that may exacerbate (or even create) feelings of caregiver burden and declines in physical intimacy. For example, in Michael Raschick and Berit Ingersoll-Dayton's otherwise innovative study on the costs and rewards of caregiving, the researchers revert to care styles to explain why men experience less care burden than women.[53] They note:

> Men have more of a managerial approach that potentially provides them with "greater perceived control, the sense of being in charge, feelings of self-efficiency, as well as the ability to choose to act or not act"; women are bound by strong norms of nurturing responsibilities stemming from "an internalized model of caregiving based on a parent-infant model."[54]

Social and economic reasons that may account for women's increased care burden are not addressed. Similarly, Marie Louise Luttik et al. ignore social and economic factors that can create or exacerbate care stress, which they find is linked to decreased quality of life, increased illness, and stress.[55] There are many external factors that interact with the care relationship, including the affordability and availability of in-home care support or respite care, the cost of managing the impairment or illness, the stigma of disability, and the beliefs about care for partners that circulate in popular culture. As I noted at the beginning of this chapter, the experience of disability requires interaction with doctors, nurses, and other health professionals. The social and economic costs of these encounters can qualitatively alter the experience of care for a couple. As Linda Mona argues:

> Given the fact that many people with disabilities often need to structure their life plans around public and governmental supports (e.g., Social Security benefits, Medicare), it becomes impossible to conceptualize their sexual life experiences outside of societal influences and socio-cultural norms (e.g., societal belief systems about disability and sexuality) within which they are immersed.[56]

Researchers who study care and intimacy between disabled and nondisabled people must account for this reality and build the social dimensions of disability into research design and analysis. Such changes will allow for the possibility of alternative findings, including examples of disabled/nondisabled couples who care without experiencing debilitating levels of burden or strain and couples who are able to remain intimate in spite of (or because of) care.

Glimmers of Hope

Although the vast majority of the research emerging from the applied fields fails to conceptualize the care relationship as one in which the disabled and nondisabled partners can participate together and create new meanings about intimacy, sex, disability, and care in a social context, I did find some studies in the literature review that offered glimmers of hope. For example, several articles include instruments that measure social aspects of disability.[57] And some discuss social barriers in their implications and future research section.[58] Other articles focused on the relationship between the disabled and nondisabled partners because "disability does not just affect the individual but also his or her partner."[59] S. Feld et al. conceptualize care as a unit comprising both the disabled and the nondisabled individual as active participants, and discuss a history of reciprocity and current reciprocity in the care relationship (e.g., emotional care that the physically disabled partner may give the caregiver).[60] Similarly, Phyllis A. Gordon and Kristin M. Perrone argue that perceptions of equity are important to disabled/nondisabled couples, noting that

> Weinert and Long (1993) found that many participants in their caregiving study perceived their spouses to be the person they counted on the most for support even if the spouse was the ill partner. Consequently, although spouses may not be able to do the same chores or household tasks as they were prior to the illness, if they are perceived to be emotionally an equal partner, the relationship may be more satisfactory.[61]

Berit Ingersoll-Dayton and Michael Raschick suggest that helping behaviors—conceptualized as helping with chores, providing companionship, and giving money or gifts—can help mediate caregiving stress.[62] And Francine Ducharme et al. advocate that one way to improve services to older disabled/nondisabled couples is by reframing care for them by stressing benefits of care relationships, learning new things to do together, and so forth.[63]

Some researchers acknowledge that intimacy may be reframed for both the couple and the researchers. For example, Gordon and Perrone recognize that intimacy is an important aspect of the relationship, and that previous research has shown care to impede sexual intimacy in disabled/nondisabled relationships. They suggest, however, that "intimacy may be defined broadly, to include intellectual, spiritual, and recreational intimacy as well as sexual intimacy. In addition, Speziale (1997) reported that it may be useful for couples to examine prior beliefs about intimacy and sexual behavior.[64] Alternative understandings of intimacy may facilitate greater understanding of disabled/nondisabled couples as well as provide new frameworks for couples to negotiate their relationship.

Overall, the applied fields approach disabled/nondisabled couples with the assumption that the physical care that the nondisabled partner provides stresses the relationship. Thus, few of the articles that focus on care discuss sexuality or intimacy and vice versa. Prejudiced beliefs about disability are evident in the language that researchers use to describe the couple (e.g., "patient" and "spouse"), in instruments that include only negatively framed items, and in research designs that conceptualize the couple as antagonists. More researchers need to include social dimensions of disability, to include measurements of reciprocity (especially, active reciprocity), and to conduct couple-level research that examines the care as a relationship. By improving research, practitioners working with people with disabilities and their partners will have access to more nuanced understandings of care and sexuality in relationships. This, in turn, can improve the treatment that disabled/nondisabled couples receive in the applied fields.

Notes

1. Gordon and Perrone, "When Spouses," p. 29.
2. Galvin, "Researching the Disabled," p. 399.
3. Ibid., p. 397.
4. Ibid., p. 399.
5. Li and Yau, "Sexual Issues," p. 2.
6. Ibid., pp. 4–5.
7. See for example, Parritt and O'Callaghan, "Splitting the Difference"; Simpson et al., "Improving the Rehabilitative"; Tepper, "Providing Comprehensive."
8. See, for example, Singh and Sharma, "Sexuality and Women."
9. Li and Yau, "Sexual Issues," pp. 3–4.
10. Ibid., p. 4.
11. See, for example, Li and Yau, "Sexual Issues"; and Singh and Sharma, "Sexuality and Women."
12. It is now called Academic Search Complete.
13. Only Svetlik et al., "Declines in Satisfaction," appeared in both searches.
14. The three literature reviews were Campbell, "The Effectiveness"; Gordon and Perrone, "When Spouses"; and Wiegerink et al., "Social and Sexual Relationships."
15. Choi and Marks, "Transition to Caregiving"; Gordon and Perrone, "When Spouses."
16. Choi and Marks, "Transition to Caregiving," p. 1719.
17. Fultz et al., "The Impact"; Ruiz et al., "Does Who?" Ruiz et al. do have a marital satisfaction measure; however, it is unclear if this measure includes items related to sex or intimacy because the authors fail to publish the items. I place it with the articles that address sex or intimacy only in their literature review section because the discussion does not report any findings related to sex or intimacy; therefore, I assume that the measure does not include sex or intimacy.

18. Joseph and Bhatti, "Psychosocial Problems"; Giarelli, McCorkle, and Monturo, "Caring for a Spouse."

19. Boeije and Van Doorne-Huiskes, "Fulfilling a Sense."

20. According to ISI Web of Knowledge Journal Citation Reports, *Sexuality and Disability* is not a highly ranked journal (0.133 was the journal's impact factor in 2006). Indeed, the articles from *Sexuality and Disability* for this analysis had frequent grammar and spelling errors, and many articles had poor research design and analysis.

21. From the mission statement of the journal *Sexuality and Disability*, retrieved from http://www.springer.com/psychology/community+psychology/journal/11195.

22. Melby, "Facilitated Sex," p. 3.

23. Hassouneh-Phillips and McNeff, "I Thought."

24. Galvin, "Researching the Disabled"; Mona, "Sexual Options."

25. Wiegerink et al., "Social and Sexual Relationships."

26. Li and Yau, "Sexual Issues"; Zitzelsberger, "(In)visibility."

27. McCabe and Taleporos, "Sexual Esteem"; Murray and Harrison, "The Meaning"; Singh and Sharma, "Sexuality and Women"; Schmidt et al., "Sexuality in Multiple Sclerosis"; Taleporos and McCabe, "Relationships."

28. For example, Taleporos and McCabe, "Relationships."

29. For example, Choi and Marks, "Transition to Caregiving"; Druley et al., "Emotional Congruence"; Hirst, "Carer Distress."

30. For example, Kim et al., "Quality."

31. For example, Burton et al., "Transitions"; Lee et al., "Caregiving and Risk"; Luttik et al., "For Better."

32. Hirst, "Carer Distress," p. 704.

33. Cannuscio et al., "Employment Status," p. 1254.

34. Lin and Lu, "Hip Fracture," p. 725.

35. Cannuscio et al., "Employment Status," p. 1206.

36. However, it is important to note that a few found surprising results—increased care was not always associated with negative health and well-being outcomes.

37. Hirst, "Carer Distress."

38. Cannuscio et al., "Employment Status."

39. For example, Giarelli, McCorkle, and Monturo, "Caring for a Spouse"; Laursen et al., "Ongoing Pain"; Luttik et al., "For Better."

40. Parsons, *The Social System.*

41. For example, Bookwala et al., "Concurrent and Long-Term."

42. For example, Boeije and Van Doorne-Huiskes, "Fulfilling a Sense"; Kedde and van Berlo, "Sexual Satisfaction"; Svetlik et al., "Declines in Satisfaction."

43. Boeije and Doorne-Huiskes, "Fulfilling a Sense of Duty."

44. Svetlik et al., "Declines in Satisfaction."

45. Hendrix and Ray, "Informal Caregiver Training," p. 796.

46. Pinquart and Sörensen, "Associations of Stressors."

47. Robinson, "Validation."

48. For example, Ellenbogen et al., "The Impact"; Hash, "Caregiving and Post-Caregiving"; Kang, "Predictors of Emotional Strain"; Pinquart and Sörensen, "Associations of Stressors"; and Soskolne et al., "Caregiving Stressors."

49. As in Hash, "Caregiving and Post-Caregiving."

50. As in Kang, "Predictors of Emotional Strain."

51. See, for example, Boeije and Van Doorne-Huiskes, "Fulfilling a Sense"; and Boeije, Duijnstee, and Grypdonck, "Continuation of Caregiving."

52. Taleporos and McCabe, "Development and Validation."

53. Raschick and Ingersoll-Dayton's study is one of the few studies that looked at the disabled partners' helping behaviors, constructing the disabled partner as an active participant in the care relationship; Raschick and Ingersoll-Dayton, "The Costs and Rewards." See the section "Glimmers of Hope" for more on these studies.

54. Raschick and Ingersoll-Dayton, "The Costs and Rewards," p. 321.

55. Luttik et al., "For Better and Worse."

56. Mona, "Sexual Options," p. 212.

57. For example, Fultz et al., "The Impact"; Sakellariou, "If Not Disability"; and Singh and Sharma, "Sexuality and Women."

58. For example, Hirst, "Carer Distress."

59. Li and Yau, "Sexual Issues," p. 22.

60. Feld et al., "Expansion of Elderly Couples' IADL Caregiver Networks."

61. Gordon and Perrone, "When Spouses," p. 28.

62. Ingersoll-Dayton and Raschick, "The Relationship Between Care-Recipient Behaviors and Spousal Caregiving Stress."

63. Ducharme et al., "Older Husbands as Caregivers of Their Wives."

64. Speziale, "Couples," p. 30.

PART 2
Contesting the Mainstream

4

Flexible Gender Roles

As Chapter 2 on popular culture made clear, disability is intimately bound up with gender in our cultural imagination. Because of these gendered notions of disability, the experience of disability is considerably different for men and women. Masculinity connotes strength, independence, and protection; therefore, disabled men must reconcile their need for help with daily personal care and their masculine self-image. This crisis between disabled dependence and masculine independence is what fuels so many films featuring disabled men (e.g., *Born on the Fourth of July*, *The Men*, *Waterdance*).[1] Since femininity signifies dependence and passivity, it may at first glance seem as if femininity and disability are not at ideological odds with each other. However, the social roles of wife and mother hinge on providing physical, spiritual, and emotional care. Disabled women struggle with fulfilling these gendered expectations about women and caring.

Gender roles also impact the experience of providing physical care for a disabled partner. Women are typically viewed as natural caregivers and men as having to learn how to give care. Because caring is not perceived as innate to masculinity, men are also expected to struggle with the task for caregiving. This is the social landscape in which disabled/nondisabled couples must construct their realities. In this chapter, I explore how self-representations of people in disabled/nondisabled intimate relationships express gender roles and identities. Although all of the stories that I analyze used gender stereotypes as a reference point for their own understandings of giving and receiving care, almost everyone resisted, challenged, and subverted gender expectations. In fact, the ability of disabled/nondisabled couples to revise gender roles seems to be a primary factor in creating a successful intimate relationship across disability status. Those couples who were able to reconstruct gender seemed the most satisfied and fulfilled. Thus, contrary to dominant representations that suggest happiness comes through approximating gender norms, this research suggests that happiness is linked to rewriting gender scripts.

Masculine Caring: Nondisabled Men and Disabled Women

For the most part, the experiences of focus group participants differed markedly from popular culture representations. They were all in loving relationships that, in many ways, defied gendered expectations about caregiving. After all, ten of the twelve nondisabled participants were men who provided physical, personal care for disabled female partners. Although this sample is not necessarily representative, it does speak volumes against the notion that nondisabled men cannot or will not care for disabled female spouses. No caregivers disclosed gender role anxiety or expressed caregiver burden or burnout—not even in the private, follow-up journals. However, the nondisabled men did acknowledge the tension between being "a man" and taking care of their female partners. They knew that their caregiving violated gender role expectations, but they also expressed an internal acceptance of masculine caring. For example, Richard, the nondisabled spouse of Emma, who has cerebral palsy, discusses how he has had to resist the masculine impulse to control and take charge while providing physical care for Emma.

> RICHARD: Yeah. I decided that at one point, or once after taking care of her for a while, I would find myself arguing with her sometimes about her care. And I thought, "You know, you'd . . . you could . . . this would be a hell of a lot easier for you if you would just decide that you're her hands. Don't question anything she says about . . . how in the hell would you like it every time you wanted to do something somebody challenged you on it?" She knows how to take care of herself, she's . . . I mean she's had other people, instructed other people how to take care of herself for a long time. Just do what she wants, keep your own ego out of it, keep your own opinions out of it. You're still your own person—I haven't lost a thing—and I'm not losing my credibility or anything by doing what she wants me to do and doing it the way she wants it done. But I think it's very difficult to do that, especially when you're a guy! I think it . . . it's entirely different for a guy to take care of a woman than it is for a woman to take care of a guy. I mean that sounds—I'm more selfish than you are.
>
> OLIVIA: Women are more giving.
>
> RICHARD: It doesn't come automatic to me to, to do all these things. I have to think about it, and I have to have my own damn time.

I'm a boy. I have to have time during the day when I say, "Screw her, I want to go down to the computer and I want to write or I want to do this." And I tell her, "Don't call me. Don't call me! You gotta pee, let's go pee. Get it out because I want to be down there for two hours or three hours or four hours or whatever." For a while when I was working on a book and I would demand it: four hours a day, by myself, uninterrupted because I had to work.

EMMA: But he says that, but if I needed anything he would—

RICHARD: Yeah! If I heard a big rumble upstairs I'd go see if she's still alive! [*laughter*]

Richard describes being able to care for Emma, on her terms, as not "losing my credibility or anything." In other words, he can take instructions from his wife and provide physical care in the way she wants it performed without losing his masculinity. Although he is rewriting masculinity in this example, Richard and Olivia are also deploying gender stereotypes about care in the focus group discussion. They note that such care does not come naturally to men, and that men have to work against an internal drive toward selfishness. The belief that caring is somehow instinctual to women and not to men is used in this example to construct Richard's caregiving. In other words, the stereotype of men's uncaring nature is used as a foil to explain Richard's now caring nature.

Other men in the focus groups forgo references to traditional gender roles in their discussions of masculine caring. Instead, their stories focus on how caregiving has made them better men. For example, Kevin, the nondisabled partner of Ellen, who has MS, says:

KEVIN: There [are] things . . . talking to my buddies and stuff and other people at work and things . . . "well, my wife never lets me do this," or "we never do that," or just, I mean, other health care things. [*laughter*] I'm not talking just about. . . . [*laughter*] Hearing some of the wives talk that their husband won't go anywhere near them during certain times of the month and they're not allowed to touch them, they're not allowed to do this and no way and it just. . . . I help and I am involved in a lot more things than—I'm a therapist so I do this for a living as well—but just not only that, but with my wife I do things and we work together and we help with things. And I'm a lot more involved in things than any of my buddies or any other guys I work with other than with their patients that they're with, and so I think that is a wonderful thing because I know my wife a lot better than a lot of these guys ever will! And, I've—

ELLEN: That is true!

KEVIN: We're more involved and more . . . we've got more of a
trusting relationship . . . she trusts me to do things to help her
with stuff and to be around when things are going on. And that
carries over that much more because we've got two daughters
and the one thirteen is entering things and there has been different times where she is seeing that she knows that I help Mom
with things so she is a little bit more open. It's still, I'm sure
challenging to talk to a man. I'm Dad, about certain things. But
it had been, she said . . . made the comments other times, "Dad,
I'm glad you're a therapist, I'm glad you're my dad," because
she knows that no matter what happens I don't get upset or I
don't get mad. Well I do, but I mean, I mean with certain things
that I can be available and I can. It's not embarrassing, it's just
part of human nature, and the way the body works or needs to
work, so I consider that very intimate. The relationship I have
with my wife and with my daughters that, unfortunately from
what I hear from other people talk, they don't have with their
children or with their spouse.

Thus, caring for Ellen has helped facilitate Kevin's relationship with his
daughters. He is not scared off by supposedly embarrassing things about the
body. Kevin's daughters see that he is able to provide intimate, personal care;
therefore, he is marked as a trusting, reliable source and his daughters can
come to him with their own needs and questions. Consequently, Kevin's atypical male involvement has made his experience as a husband and father better.

In a similar vein, Jack, the nondisabled spouse of Rachel, seems to take
considerable pride in knowing and understanding things that are closed off to
most men. In his journal, he writes:

No sex, just snuggling. After the focus group, we went home. Once home, it
was bath time for Rachel, and on Fridays it's a shave night for her legs. How
many guys get to shave their wife's legs? So she trusts me, even though I
sometimes nick her. Doing pretty good on this point until the end. When dry-
ing her hair, I can hardly ever get her part right, and she knows it's hard for
me to do it. A lot of guys can't do hair and I'm really aware of it. We're only
talking a few strands on the wrong side, but she knows what she wants. So I
guess when it comes to care, there will always be some disagreement between
us, but it's not for lack of wanting to do it her way, just my inability.

As in the example with Richard above, Jack uses gender stereotypes to position himself and his abilities. But in his journal and in the focus group, Jack
was clearly proud of his closeness with his wife and he was quite aware that it

was this physical caregiving (that most men do not get to do for their wives) that facilitated such intimacy. Jack was satisfied with his ability to add care to his masculine repertoire.

In his autobiography *Saving Milly: Love, Politics, and Parkinson's Disease*, Morton Kondracke also expresses pride regarding his caregiving of his wife, Milly, who has Parkinson's disease. Kondracke says, "So far I think I have fulfilled my vow to do this one thing well—to 'take care of Milly.' In the process I've become a different, better person—someone I never expected to be."[2] Clearly, Kondracke is claiming that caring for Milly has enhanced his sense of self. In the book, he details how he prepares Milly's food, washes and dresses her, feeds her, and helps her with shopping and other activities.[3] But, he never writes about feeling emasculated. Instead, he provides a gender- and class-sensitive analysis of his and Milly's situation:

> I rarely resent this labor—mainly because I do not have to do it every day, all day. Always pressed for time, I get angry in traffic and yell at other drivers (with the windows up), but I do not feel enslaved by Parkinson's or sorry for myself. . . . Without Effexor, and without Fell and Grelanda helping, both my stoicism and my Christianity would be sorely tested. My love for Milly would also be tested. I think this because I finally did read Maggie Strong's book *Mainstay* and realized how lucky I am—that I am not a woman taking care of a chronically ill man, that I make enough money to hire people to help me, that my newspaper has excellent health insurance that has paid for Milly's surgery and wheelchairs without argument. . . . Other people are not so fortunate. They feel trapped, furious, oppressed, or depressed.[4]

Kondracke understands that men typically make more money or have better work-related benefits than their female partners. The loss of a man's job because of disability can financially devastate a family. In addition, paid outside help is frequently not offered through government-sponsored programs[5] or is financially out of reach for the family. A good income, benefits, and help make his life as a caregiver workable, and Kondracke is critical of the United States, which does not make family care reasonable for all people with disabilities.

In addition to providing physical care for their female spouses (e.g., bathing, shaving, doing hair), nondisabled men in the focus groups and published self-representations describe kitchen work (cooking, dishes, cleaning), child care, and emotional work. For example, Bob's wife, Connie, has MS. Connie used to be a high-powered executive in a Fortune 500 company, but she had to leave her position because of fatigue and memory problems associated with MS. Bob is very conscious of when Connie starts to feel like a burden. At those times, he asks for Connie's help with his own executive work, assigning tasks that she can do at home, to help her feel valued, needed, and appreciated. In this case, Bob helps manage Connie's fears and anxieties. Significantly, none of the men in the focus groups or published self-representations expressed any amount of resentment or consternation about performing these stereotypically feminine duties. On the contrary, most said they enjoy caregiving and insisted that it has become an integrated aspect of their masculine selves.

The women on the receiving end of this masculine care were typically appreciative that their husbands were not hung up on traditional gender roles. Connie remarks, "Isn't that amazing? We have great guys—they want to do stuff for us!" But this excitement was also tempered by mixed feelings regarding women's roles as wives and mothers. Many of the disabled women in the focus groups and published self-representations express anxiety about not being able to clean the house, prepare meals, run the kids to soccer, and other stereotypically womanly duties. The chapter titled "Taking Care" in Nancy Mairs's autobiography *Waist-High in the World: A Life Among the Nondisabled* describes her desire to take care of her husband and children the way she used to be able to do before MS. Mairs connects this desire to gender socialization, the way her nursing and caregiving were nurtured as a child.[6] Although Mairs acknowledges that care is a learned feminine behavior, she beautifully describes how it is a longing that has now cemented itself to her core. She says, "I yearn to act out my love, in the way that a dancer inscribes abstract movements on the air with hands and feet and torso and head in order to give her private vision public force. I want to *do* love. In particular, I want to love my husband in this dynamic way."[7] However, Mairs can no longer care for her husband in traditional ways. She is permanently in an electric wheelchair, and needs assistance with bathing, dressing, toileting, and preparing meals.

Women in the focus groups also express this longing to give care in physically active ways. For example, Jack, the nondisabled partner of Rachel, tells the group that Rachel "is always saying that 'I'm not a good wife; I don't take care of you.' I'm like . . . I didn't marry you just to do that." Rachel is upset that she cannot make a meal for her husband when he gets home from work, do his laundry, or perform other duties that women typically do for their husbands. In the following exchange, Ellen and Sabrina, who both have MS, discuss their desire to fulfill their ideals about being a woman.

ELLEN: I think it's a—being a woman. Personally, for my opinion, I'm a wife, I'm a woman, and I'm a mother and I have to keep up with all those quote "stereotypes"—

SABRINA: You're all those things before you're disabled.

ELLEN: Exactly.

KEVIN: I want to do the stuff my mom did.

ELLEN: Exactly. I have to be that 1950s mom that my mother was and I had to keep my house as clean as my mother did and get in the corners. . . . Why?

ADAM: Yeah, why?

SABRINA: Because my mom might come over and see it?

ELLEN: You know what, exactly.

ADAM: All the way from England? [*laughter*]

SABRINA: She'll know! [*laughter*]

ELLEN: [*inaudible*] I know what it took me two months ago. . . . I could not get down on my hands and knees anymore to wash my kitchen floors.

SABRINA: That's why we have husbands.

ELLEN: [*inaudible*] Oh my god, I got to the point, called the MS Society and said, "Do you have a cleaning service? We will give you $400 a year and they will come out and they will clean for you . . . and I did it. I had to bite . . . bite the bullet as the saying goes? And I had to do it. But you know what, that first time they came in to clean my house, [*inaudible*] so excited [*inaudible*] because—

SABRINA: We're calling the MS Society tomorrow! [*laughter*]

ELLEN: They do and you can do as often or however you can. And it was just like, I can take that energy and I can go with the kids, we can go to the pool today. And I found out the house is not important anymore. It took me awhile, but, a long time to get to that point.

Ellen and Sabrina connect being a good woman to being able to keep the corners of the floors clean. Like Mairs, they are aware that such desires come from social conditioning, from "stereotypes," but the desire persists nonetheless. However, this exchange also reveals alternatives that disabled women use to approximate their female roles and satisfy their needs to take physical care of home and family. Ellen uses the help provided by the MS Society to clean her house so that she has the energy to enjoy life. Although she struggled with letting someone else clean her house, she was able to finally realize that her own ability to get on her knees and scrub the floors did not determine her worth as a wife and mother.

Similarly, Mairs writes that she has learned other ways to express caregiving, including "permitting myself to be taken care of."[8] She writes that her mother, husband, and children like to be able to give back and take care of her, so that relinquishing her care monopoly ironically is a way she can care for those who love her. She goes on to state:

I have to improvise these alternatives to the traditional modes of tendering care, and I must learn to trust others to find them adequate. Since most physical acts are denied me, my efforts must take largely intellectual and emotional form. I've become a closer and more patient listener, and I spend time giving information, counsel, and encouragement, especially to people with cancer and MS, as well as to students and other fledgling writers. I also express appreciation and approval and affection much more readily: Once afraid of "gushing," I've turned into a positive freshet and to hell with Yankee reticence. Above all, I can still write, which for me has always been an act of oblation and nurturance: my means of taking the reader into my arms, holding a cup to her lips, stroking her forehead, whispering jokes into her ears. . . . With such gestures, I am taking all the care I can.[9]

Mairs is literally rewriting traditional notions of care. Writing, listening, encouraging, and even allowing oneself to be taken care of become ways of being a good wife, mother, and woman.

The nondisabled men receiving this modified care from their disabled female partners routinely express satisfaction. They do not think less of their partners because they cannot perform the traditional physical tasks. For example, in the documentary film *Shameless: The ART of Disability* (2006), directed by Bonnie Sherr Klein, Klein's partner Michael openly discusses why he stays with her after her stroke. In a voice-over Michael says:

The men of women who've had strokes leave their wives a shocking 80% of the time. Why didn't I leave? Oh, poverty of imagination, I suppose. [*Laughter*] No, I didn't leave because our relationship basically didn't change. I mean that's the major issue, that Bonnie takes care of me. And she took care of me when she was in the ICU and quadriplegic, she was taking care of Seth and me and Naomi.

As Michael says this, we see him help Klein across a rocky beach and into a canoe that they paddle together. This sequence highlights the ways in which Klein continues to take emotional care of her family, despite the physical care she now requires. Similarly, in his journal Kevin writes: "She [Ellen] cares for me and our family in ways that every mom does . . . making meals, laundry—in general making our house a loving home." Kevin and Michael value the emotional and physical care work their wives provide, and they do not view disability as erasing their wives' femininity.

So, both the nondisabled men and disabled women in this study were able to rewrite traditional gender roles to add new dimensions to femininity and masculinity. However, there are a few interesting consequences to nondisabled men caring for disabled female partners. For example, it was quite common for the focus group participants to discuss the way that male caregivers' "intentions" are often questioned by family, friends, and even strangers. For example, Rachel says:

[My parents] were scared. And my family, they would constantly, "Well, how is he with you? Well, what are you guys going to do? How does he act? Does he treat you OK?" "Yeah, yeah, it's fine. He treats me great." And they know that he does, but they're still afraid. And it's like—even now when we're married—now that we're married they're OK, but we were dating for a while. Um, we just got married like last year, so . . . now they're OK, but it's almost like they still need a constant—like, OK they're coming to our house—"Oh, you have a really nice house! Oh, and he does this!" They still need reassurance all the time that we're fine. Now my parents don't, my parents don't, but my like, indirect, immediate family, like aunts and uncles and cousins, they still are like, "Oh, is he OK? Is he good to you? Oh, OK, does he take care of you?"

Ted, the nondisabled partner of Sofia, has experienced similar questioning.

TED: My parents are very supportive. They love Sofia, and they're very supportive of everything that we do. I think her family was a little different. Like I had a great relationship with her father who passed away last year. But in the beginning, like when we first met and were dating, he, uh, he couldn't understand it, I think. Didn't he say somethin'?

SOFIA: They thought he had motives that aren't—motives to be with me and you know, I guess he feared I was gonna get taken advantage of or what have you. . . . And that faded.

SARAH: Once they got to know him longer.

TED: Mmmhmm. Well it faded with your dad for sure, and with the family a little bit. I think there's a couple members of your family that, they're still thinkin' something's up because, I don't know, I get a cold shoulder.

Although the participants did not chalk this distrust for male caregiving up to gender norms, beliefs about men as incapable caregivers contributed to the intention questioning that Ted and Jack (nondisabled male participants) receive. Based on the belief that men are not naturally caring, family and friends start looking for reasons that a nondisabled man would want to be with a disabled woman. None of the nondisabled women in the focus groups or self-representations encountered questioning of their intentions to be with disabled men. On the contrary, it was typically viewed as a natural extension of the femininity. Masculine caregiving violates gender expectations and, thus, invites critical questioning.

For Richard, being involved in a relationship with a disabled woman meant the loss of friends.

RICHARD: Well, when I first met her, um, people thought I was crazy. We met on the Internet and I told them I was dating, later moving in, later getting married and so forth. And they just

thought, You're absolutely nuts! Do you realize what you're
doing? Do you know what you're doing? So, I . . . my set of
friends changed a lot 'cause there were a lot of people who were
not very supportive. They just thought I was just a little crazy.

EMMA: You were in the academic community.

RICHARD: Yah, and [the university] is a pretty stuffy place. It's truly
pretty stuffy. They were not very supportive.

Although Richard's experience is not typical (no other male participants mentioned such explicit shunning), it does exemplify how gender expectations can so negatively impact disabled/nondisabled couples. Richard's decision to enter a relationship with a severely disabled woman violated the norms set for him by his friends and colleagues.

Many of the nondisabled male partners in this study also brought up being glorified by friends, family, and strangers for providing physical care. Instead of being questioned or shunned, their masculine caregiving was elevated to sainthood. Victoria says that, when she and Gene go out, people always say, "What a good guy he is," "He's just a wonderful guy," and "He takes such good care of you." Such exorbitant adulations were less common for nondisabled female partners and, when it did happen, the praise was for being such a "good person," not such a "good woman." Thus, glorification is the flip side of intention questioning. Both are rooted in ideas about masculinity, femininity, and care.

Mairs's husband, George, also experiences excessive praise for taking care of Mairs; however, George revels in the limelight. She writes, "He tells me he is no more eager to relinquish his caregiving role—which he finds 'seductive, because the world esteems me for it'—than I am to hire outside assistance."[10] Kondracke also enjoys the admiration. He writes:

> Some people tell me, "You're a saint." I admit that for years I used to inwardly exult in that. I feigned modesty, but I was not modest. I wanted to be Saint Mort, and I wanted to be known as Saint Mort. When Milly and I go to wedding receptions, we always dance a few numbers because I know that she loved dancing and desperately misses being able to do it. But part of my motivation used to be the knowledge that people would say to one another, "Look at them. Isn't that great!" When I wheeled Milly into a room and treated her in the loving way that is normal for us, I couldn't do it without also thinking about how admirable people would think I was. I was using Milly, in effect, to secure respect from people that I feared I couldn't achieve otherwise. I do not know why I stopped doing this. In truth, I haven't entirely stopped.[11]

Thus, Kondracke both loves and feels guilty about mobilizing masculine caregiving to gain acclaim.

Frequently, physical caregiving made the nondisabled male particularly appealing to other women. Female strangers frequently made sexual advances.

EMMA: I don't know if it's because I'm a woman and disabled and he's a man, but it seems like women are more attracted to him because he is taking care of me.

RICHARD: Oh, yeah. [*laughter*]

EMMA: It makes me mad! [*laughter*]

RICHARD: Yeah, they'll come over and put their head on my shoulder, "Oh, you're so beautiful."

EMMA: "You're so sweet."

RICHARD: "So sweet." And I'll say, "Yeah, well you've been watching a little too much Lifetime television."

In these cases, the man's apparent sensitivity makes him more desirable. In each case, the man's nonhegemonic gender performance—his caring and attentiveness—gets positive notice. Walking a dog or carrying a baby produces similar results. It is tempting to interpret such reactions as a positive indication that gender norms may be changing in ways that encourage male expressiveness and attunement to others; however, this change is at the expense of disabled women. Indeed, Emma notes that often the sexual passes persist even when her relationship with Richard is made obvious.

EMMA: We were in a bar once and I still haven't figured out if this lady thought he was my dad or my boyfriend—can't remember if he was my boyfriend or my husband at the time. Anyways, we were together, we were engaged. Anyways, I was out of my wheelchair because I had to walk up steps and sit in a chair, so couldn't move my arms, lucky for her! I would have . . . that is the only time I would have decked somebody. But, she was like hugging him and—

RICHARD: Yeah, it was embarrassing! I mean it was— [*laughter*]

SARAH: That's funny—

EMMA: And she was asking to pick him up and we had a bunch of friends there who were trying to—I mean she was drunk, OK she was drunk. But—they were really trying to explain to her that he was with me, but she—

OLIVIA: She wasn't listening! She had those beer glasses on! [*laughter*]

RICHARD: Right. Beer goggles.

Drunkenness aside, Emma was not perceived as a real barrier. In these public encounters, she is literally no different from a puppy—a prop that makes the man more desirable. Thus, such incidences are far from progressive.

The nondisabled men and disabled women resisted and challenged these negative consequences of gender expectations; however, both the intention questioning and excessive glorification of masculine caring left their marks. Nevertheless, for the most part, nondisabled men were able to add caregiving to their masculine identity, and disabled women were able to revise traditional ways of expressing feminine care.

Disabling *Leave It to Beaver*:
Nondisabled Women and Disabled Men

In the male disabled/female nondisabled couplings, care can appear to conform to traditional gender roles; however, I argue that the presence of disability puts gender into play, adding new dimensions to both masculinity and femininity. In some arrangements, the nondisabled female partner may perform in stereotypically female ways, and the disabled male partner in stereotypically male ways. Yet since disability is perceived to render a man less masculine, performing in traditionally gendered ways is a way to dismiss ablest assumptions about disability and gender. It also can have the effect of making obvious the constructed nature of gender roles. For example, John Hockenberry is a famous newscaster who became paraplegic in 1976. He and his wife, Alison, have four children. Before Alison had the children she was a producer (that is how she and John met), but now she is a full-time homemaker and mother, and he works full-time away from the house. In one sense this arrangement conforms to gender expectations, but it resists such easy labeling because the person with the disability works full-time. Alison's choice to stay at home allows John to roll out into the world and destroy stereotypes about people with disabilities.

Focus group participants Olivia and Randall have a similar arrangement. Randall has cerebral palsy, but he is the one who works outside the home and Olivia stays at home with the children. Olivia even plays the role of housewife with pleasure:

> I did. I, I . . . in my house the women always take care of the men and that is how it is when I was raised. Um, to this day, um, my mom and my stepdad— well, they're not together anymore—but my mom would make his plate and take it to him. And I do the same thing and I've always done the same thing even for our son, which is my stepson, but that's my baby. I make his plate, and they sit down and I bring their food to them. And it's just been how I was raised, and just the fact of how I like to do things. And I would see the aid come in and I'm like, you know, why is she giving him a bath? That is my husband, that is something personal that I enjoy doing.

Although it is rooted in her own upbringing about what a woman should do for men, Olivia knows that performing such a role for her husband also allows him to defy stereotypes about disabled men. Thus, gender and disability are played against each other. In addition, Olivia is anything but passive. She may like to make Randall's plate and serve him dinner, but she is also clearly a dominant person.

In these types of disabled/nondisabled couplings, there is usually a sense of subversive joy in defying ableist beliefs. For example, in Focus Group 3, Kay and Dan have the following exchange:

> KAY: Yeah, and like with Dan and I, I feel we have two children and he works full-time, I work full-time, and, um, you just get caught up in life. You know, the kids gotta get up and go to school. Lisa's in Girl Scouts, I help with Girl Scouts. They both play soccer so then we're running, we're takin' them to soccer and, in the meantime, dinner needs made and the house needs kept and the lawn needs mowed. And at the end of the day you're—and I, and more of that falls on me just for the nature of what it is. And when I speak to able-bodied people they are jealous of me for the fact that Dan cleans. I mean— [*laughter*]
>
> DAN: I grew up in a family that . . . everything had its place.
>
> KAY: I mean I have had a lot of people say, "Yeah my husband's completely able-bodied, but you wouldn't see him runnin' a vacuum cleaner," and I tease Dan about his obsessiveness with the floors. He's like always, well—
>
> DAN: I'm a floor man.

Here, Kay revels in the irony of having a more egalitarian relationship than her nondisabled coupled peers in spite of Dan's disability status (he has a spinal cord injury and is paraplegic). The dialogue starts with expressing a gender normative division of labor that may seem heightened because of Dan's care needs. However, the end of the conversation points out the ways in which their relationship is perhaps further from stereotypical gender arrangements.

Similarly, Alison Hockenberry, quoted in Robert C. Samuels's article, says:

> "There is absolutely no question . . . that he is more involved and more of an equal partner in parenting than any of my friends' husbands." He changes diapers and gets up in the middle of the night. He potty-trained the girls. "People tell me, oh, wow, it must be tough on you. There's an implication that [I have it tough] not only because I have four kids but also because my husband uses a wheelchair. They have no idea how good I have it."[12]

Again, what appears to conform to expected gender norms (stay-at-home mom, working father) flies in the face of gender and disability stereotypes.

Providing physical care for a male partner can also put the female partner "in charge" in ways not available to nondisabled couples. On one hand it looks like she is serving him, but on the other she has much more physical power and freedom. Robert Frances Murphy writes at length about the way power has shifted to his wife, Yolanda, as his paralyzing condition spreads through his body. He says, "In the first two years of our marriage, dominance was important to me, for it was part of the assertive masculinity of young men."[13] However, as he became older and more physically impaired, he relinquished this type of hegemonic masculinity. Murphy writes, "In the subtle politics of the household, by a series of steps too small to be described, we have passed parity to a point where the balance of power rests with her. Our mutual dependencies are no longer equal, her increased authority is justified by her added responsibilities, and I accept this as fitting and proper."[14] For Murphy and many disabled men, "disability is a great leveler."[15] It forecloses an ancient power struggle and puts an end to "male superiority." But neither does disability inherently emasculate men. It may destroy masculinity that is associated with superiority, physical strength, and potency, but it can also be a way for men to have other, perhaps better, ways of expressing masculinity. This is certainly the case for Murphy. He describes his fall from masculine superiority as enhancing his relationships with his students, children, wife, friends, and colleagues. He learned how to be an empathetic listener, to put the other's needs before his own, and to provide for his family in nonphysical ways.

John Hockenberry describes a similar process of learning humility through the experience of disability. In *Moving Violations: War Zones, Wheelchairs, and Declarations of Independence*, Hockenberry openly discusses his struggles with trying to meet notions of hegemonic masculinity after his injury. He wants to do everything on his own, yells at people that try to push his chair, rides the subway alone, and uses a "jock wheelchair" (one without armrests). Although he achieves much and proves to himself and others that a man in a wheelchair can cover international news affairs, even in a war zone, he also learns that some efforts at independence are ultimately silly, meaningless markers of American male independence that are harmful to all people. He writes that "separating oneself through personal triumph over some physical limitation is an act of isolation that repudiates the influences of family and community; openly acknowledging limitations binds and draws people together, as an emblem and reminder of just how similar we all are."[16]

On a much more explicit level, Bob Flanagan and his nondisabled partner Sheree, featured in the film *Sick: The Life and Death of Bob Flanagan Supermasochist* (1997), used disability to add to their gender role play. Flanagan, who had cystic fibrosis, was a famous performance artist. In his relationship with Sheree, he was her 24/7 "slave," and she was his "Mistress."[17] She took care of him, especially at the end of his life when he was very ill, but she was literally and figuratively dominant. As part of their gendered, sadomasochistic play, she would cage him, put him in a collar, have him perform humiliating tasks for her, and inflict (consensual) pain on him. Flanagan and Sheree obviously represent an extreme, but their relationship is also a good example of the way that power in female nondisabled/male disabled intimate relationships is not necessarily as traditional as the power relations epitomized on the 1960s television series *Leave It to Beaver.*

Of course, learning how to relinquish control and retain a masculine sense of self is not easy in this world. A sense of ambivalence or tension between traditional masculinity and alternative forms is typical. In his journal, Dan writes:

> As a male with a disability and not able to perform as an able body, it is mentally difficult to have sex. There are many things I wish I could do, but am limited in my mobility. I think this frustration has built up over the years and has led to a decrease in sexual activity. This is strictly on my part and I know it affects my wife. She feels I don't desire her anymore. I feel less than satisfied.

> My wife says I haven't adjusted to my disability and she is right. I see so many things I wish I could do. Also it keeps getting harder as I get older and my body changes. There is always something new to deal with. She says she understands my frustrations, but until you experience it you can't know.

> One thing she suggested was I help coach my daughter's softball team. I told her you have to be able to show the kids what to do as to telling them. I can't show them how to stand at the plate and hold a bat or how to field a ball.

Dan has learned to do the floors and other non-gender typical behaviors, but he also struggles with the way that disability seems to interfere with his ideas of masculinity. Thus, disability can be freeing in the sense that men can learn masculine submissiveness and the limits of masculine independence. But it can also be frustrating. No one goes unaffected by gender stereotypes, and even the most enlightened disabled male can experience dissonance between gender norms and realities.

For couples in female nondisabled/male disabled relationships, gender roles may look like those in *Leave It to Beaver*: women care for men, allowing men to work in the public sphere while they reproduce the labor power in the home. However, as I have argued in this chapter, disability upsets such gendered expectations. Disabled men also learn how to submit to nondisabled partners, and nondisabled women learn how to take charge and be in control. In doing so, these couples make obvious the way that gender roles and beliefs about disability are socially constructed. Disabled/nondisabled couples who are able to make it work, then, are also part of a queer sexual culture in that they expose gender as a performance, as something that is not so neatly tied to the biological positions of male and female.[18] Judith Butler, one of the foundational queer theory philosophers, famously asserts that "there is no gender identity behind the expression of gender; that identity is performatively constituted by the very 'expressions' that are said to be its results."[19] In other words, there is no inherent, essential, original way of being a masculine male or feminine female. These gender identities are social constructions. In the case of disabled/nondisabled couples, these gender identities are not particularly useful; therefore, new identities are crafted—always in relation to the dominant gender identities circulated in mainstream society, but altered and revised nonetheless.

Notes

1. *Born on the Fourth of July*, directed by Oliver Stone, 1989 (Universal City, CA: Universal Studios, 2000), DVD; *The Men*, directed by Fred Zinnemann, 1950 (Santa Monica, CA: Republic Pictures, distributed by Artisan Home Entertainment, 2003), DVD; *Waterdance*, directed by Neal Jimenez and Michael Steinberg, 1992 (Culver City, CA: Columbia TriStar Home Video, 2001), DVD.

2. Kondracke, *Saving Milly*, p. 127.

3. Ibid., pp. 122–124.

4. Ibid., p. 124.

5. Personal care assistance is not paid for by the government except in a few areas that have secured grant funding to provide support to people with disabilities. There is no federal program and most of the local programs are geared to individuals born with cognitive or developmental disabilities—not people who become disabled due to spinal cord injury, MS, Parkinson's disease, and so forth.

6. Mairs, *Waist-High*, p. 79.

7. Ibid.

8. Ibid., p. 83.

9. Ibid., pp. 83–84.

10. Ibid., p. 74.

11. Kondracke, *Saving Milly*, p. 126.

12. Samuels, "The Hockenberrys."

13. Murphy, *The Body Silent*, p. 215.

14. Ibid., pp. 216–217.

15. Ibid., p. 129.

16. Hockenberry, *Moving Violations*, p. 257.

17. Bob Flanagan and Sheree were public figures who were open about their consensual bondage, discipline, dominance, submission, sadism, and masochism (BDSM) relationship. People involved in BDSM relationships take pleasure in exchanging consensual pain and pleasure, and often enjoy explicit roles in their relationship; *Sick*.

18. Biological categories are also not so neatly divided, but that is for another book. The point here is simply that the expression of one's biological assignment is a performance.

19. Butler, *Gender Trouble*, p. 33.

5

Pride and Resistance

Not surprisingly, experiences of discrimination and prejudice were shared in the focus groups and commonly portrayed in published self-representations. Although racism, sexism, homophobia, and classism are frequent topics in public discourse, ableism is rarely discussed and often misunderstood. Many people believe they are saying the right thing when they express pity for a person with a physical disability, or say things like, "I hope they find a cure." There are confusions over language (e.g., "disabled" vs. "special," "differently abled," and "handicapped"), whether to help or not, and how to interact with a person with a disability. As a society, we are simply far behind when it comes to disability awareness. Although some of the experiences of ableism discussed in the focus groups or portrayed in published self-representations were not specific to their love relationship, the *dailiness* of such incidences can significantly influence the lives of disabled/nondisabled couples. Regular confrontations with prejudice elicited reactions of dismay, frustration, anger, and sadness. It could also lead to avoiding public events out of fear of discrimination and struggling against internalizing ablest attitudes. Despite the barrage of ableism, the couples in my focus groups had not crumbled from the social pressure and stigma. Thus, in this chapter, I examine the strategies of resistance that these disabled/nondisabled couples employed to stay sane and together. These strategies of resistance include pride in the face of prejudice, disability humor, and becoming political. In what follows, I will illustrate the kinds of discrimination that the couples experience and provide examples of resistance. The ability to resist internalizing ableism is important to disabled/nondisabled couplings because, without such resilience, these atypical relationships would surely fail.

Discrimination

The published self-representations are replete with examples of discrimination. Both Bonnie Sherr Klein and Nancy Mairs talk about the nightmare of flying with a power wheelchair. Air travel is not covered under the Americans with Disabilities Act (1990) but under the less strict Air Carrier Access Act (1986) that permits airlines to refuse to board people whose disability may endanger the health and safety of passengers. What counts as a health and safety risk is up to the individual airline. In addition, there are no universal guidelines on how to work with people with disabilities, so treatment from airline and airport staff can vary widely. Thus, Klein runs into problems with her power wheelchair battery,[1] and Mairs runs into problems with seating and the handling of her wheelchair by airport employees.[2] John Hockenberry writes about the perpetual problem of catching a taxi when in a wheelchair. In one instance, Hockenberry is stranded in New York City on Christmas Eve. Cab after cab ignores him and, when one cab finally does stop, the driver refuses to get out of the cab and put Hockenberry's wheelchair in the trunk after he has transferred to the backseat.[3] Fed up, Hockenberry takes out his rage on the cab driver's car, breaking the window and headlights.[4]

Because of the group atmosphere, focus group participants shared particularly rich experiences of discrimination. Frequently, after one incident of discrimination was shared, similar stories from other couples were also aired, demonstrating the feminist consciousness-raising function of the group interview. For example, several participants shared horror stories about restaurants. Olivia, the nondisabled partner of Randall, who has cerebral palsy, relays, "I know a lot of times, we have people who at restaurants or just out in the public will ask what nursing home we're from or something like that. We'll be at a restaurant and they'll ask me what nursing home we're from and Randall always tells them, 'I'm paying your tip! You're not starting off too good!' That happens a lot." Richard, the nondisabled partner of Emma, who also has cerebral palsy, responds with a similar story:

> We were in a restaurant and there was a woman who was facing us—she was with another person so she was facing us—and I heard her drop something about why does she, why do they bring her out and upset everybody and ruin your appetite or something. And then she turned around and turned her back to us and the other woman sat on the other side so she wouldn't have to see.

In both of these stories, the routine activity of going out to eat becomes a site of confrontation with prejudice. Asking what nursing home one is from and changing seats to avoid seeing disability are both explicit ways to segregate the disabled from the nondisabled world.

Staring is another way in which the nondisabled segregate the disabled. Rosemarie Garland-Thomson writes that

> staring at disability choreographs a visual relation between a spectator and a spectacle. A more intense form of looking than glancing, glimpsing, scanning, surveying, gazing, and other forms of casual or uninterested looking, staring registers the perception of difference and gives meaning to impairment by marking it as aberrant. . . . Staring thus creates disability as a state of absolute difference rather than simply one more variation in human form.[5]

The person staring has the power to differentiate and define the disabled person as an object; thus staring distances the nondisabled from the disabled. All disabled people with visible impairments can share stories of being stared at, and the persistent presence of staring can lead to anger and frustration. In the focus group, Olivia, Randall's partner, says:

> And we'll be sitting there [in a restaurant] and I'll see him, you know, I'll look up every now and then and we're talking or something and he'll be sticking his tongue out at somebody. I'm like "What are you doing?" [*laughter*] Well, one day he was sitting there eating and he said, "Hold on, I'll be back." And he got up and went and sat at their booth, he said, "Is your food good?" And they're like, "Yah." I'm like, what is he doing. He says, "Are you enjoying your meal?" And they said, "Yeah." He said, "Well if you quit staring at me, I'd enjoy mine." And they left. I was so—my face was so red. [*laughter*] He doesn't care, he'll tell you. [*inaudible*]

As this story makes clear, Randall had had enough. The toll of being stared at in public reached a breaking point and he had to talk back. Staring registers disgust, contempt, and fear, and functions to distance the disabled person from the nondisabled. This desire to distance and separate is rooted in ableism. Robert Francis Murphy writes:

> We [the disabled] are subverters of the American ideal. . . . And to the extent that we depart from the ideal, we become ugly and repulsive to the able-bodied. People recoil from us, especially when there is facial damage or bodily distortion. The disabled serve as constant, visual reminders to the able-bodied that the society they live in is shot through with inequity and suffering, that they live in a counterfeit paradise, that they too are vulnerable. We represent a fearsome possibility.[6]

Thus, staring helps keep the specter of disability at bay.

Although reactions of disgust or distancing may not be directed at the couple per se, such incidences do impact the relationship because their status as a couple is denied. Frequently, participants reported that strangers interpreted the nondisabled partner as a paid caretaker. For example, Kay, the nondisabled partner of Dan, who has a spinal cord injury, tells the group about the couple's experience on an airplane.

> KAY: We were flying to see my brother and they put people with disabilities on the plane first so you have plenty of room to get around and stuff, and the stewardess comes up and asks, starts—
>
> DAN: I'm in the aisle.
>
> KAY: He is in the aisle seat and I'm sitting next to him, starts to ask in case of an emergency, what kind of procedures or whatever do we need to go through. But she stops midsentence, leans over him, and says to me, "Can he speak?" [*laughter*]
>
> SARAH: Oh, no!
>
> KAY: I just kind of laughed and said—
>
> DAN: And at that moment, I couldn't. [*laughter*]
>
> KAY: I said, "Yeah!"
>
> GENE: And probably a good thing, huh?
>
> KAY: I just kind of like, "Why couldn't he speak?" And she said, "Well, you just never know." I thought, wouldn't you have first assumed that someone could speak until someone stopped you and said—
>
> GENE: If they don't respond to a question, then it's appropriate to ask the question, "Can he speak?"

Addressing the nondisabled person accompanying the person with the disability sends a clear message: the disabled person is not perceived as a subject, but as a ward of the nondisabled person that he or she is with. This message is also relayed when strangers praise the nondisabled partner for helping or simply being with the disabled partner. When asked how strangers react to the couple in public, Gene, the nondisabled partner of Victoria, who has muscular dystrophy, simply states, "God bless you for taking her out." Kay confirms, adding, "I've gotten some of the 'That must be hard,' or, 'You're a very special person.'" These comments demonstrate that it is common to view physical impairment as a burden on the nondisabled. The nondisabled person is doing a favor or a good deed by accompanying the disabled person in public.

Hockenberry writes about how difficult such ableist assumptions were for his first wife, Alice. He says,

Our best moments were when we were alone. Our worst moments were out among people. The assumptions people appeared to make about me spilled over onto her. Like on "Oprah," she felt people cast her as the nurse, or as the martyr, or as the person who needed to take care of someone else. Upon meeting us, people would ask her how many years we had been married before my accident. This was something I would never get asked; she always did. No one ever assumed that she might have chosen to be with me regardless of the wheelchair. No one considered the possibility that she did not think my accident was a tragedy. The decision I had made to "persevere" and not commit suicide was infinitely more comprehensible to those around us than her decision to choose me as a husband. The question stung her. Each answer, that we had met and gotten married well after my accident, was greeted with a surprise that hurt even more.[7]

These types of questions and stunned responses tell the nondisabled partner that she or he is weird to be with a disabled person; there must be something "off," some other reason that a nondisabled person would ever subject themselves to such a lifetime of drudgery!

Another all too common form of disability discrimination was surveillance. Based on the ableist belief that people with disabilities are schemers who are trying to manipulate the system, insurance companies periodically check on the disabled person to ensure he or she is still disabled enough to receive benefits. Typically, this means required doctor appointments, but sometimes it means secret surveillance, as Bob and Connie relay in the following conversation:

BOB: Well, we had an interesting experience not too long ago. Connie is, um, collecting social security as well as long-term disability—

CONNIE: Insurance, from the insurance company.

SARAH: Right.

BOB: From our previous employer. And, uh, to make a long story short we were, we had some family business and ended up traveling across town. And as we're nearing our destination, our daughter's house, I said, "Connie, I think there is somebody following us."

[*gasps*]

CONNIE: It was on a Friday. Before Labor Day.

BOB: Yeah, before Labor Day. I said, I think there is somebody following us. Now, for us average Joe Blow, to pick up on the fact that there is a vehicle behind me that is making every turn that we're making seemed a little unusual. [*laughter*] So, we pull into the neighborhood where our daughter's house is and sure enough this vehicle follows us in there. And I said, "I'm not stopping at [our daughter's] house, I better keep going." I did a circle with this guy right behind. I stopped, this guy stops back there. I said, we went by a cop up by the [*inaudible*] and I'm going to go back to the cop.

CONNIE: We live in [city], she lives in [other city].

BOB: So, I go back to the cop and I said, "This is going to sound screwy and we're not nuts, but there is somebody following us." Well, about that time, that vehicle went on by, and turned on further down the road. We went back to our daughter's house, and we had called the police, and they came over and we told them what was going on. Connie had a doctor's appointment later that day, 2:30 or so, and this was earlier in the day. We went to the doctor's appointment. By now I'm looking [*looks around*], what's going on? We go into the doctor's appointment, we come out, pull out of the parking lot where the doctor is and this guy is behind us again. So, I pull into the next parking lot, he follows us. I get out of my truck like wait a minute buddy, who or what, we end up chasing this guy halfway through the city. Make a long story short, find out it's the insurance company.

SARAH: Oh, my gosh.

CONNIE: They [*inaudible*] we didn't know at the time.

BOB: We didn't know.

The other participants in the focus group were horrified by this level of surveillance, but I had already heard or read many similar stories. In an effort to weed out the fakers from the real disabled, insurance companies and the Social Security Administration are permitted to send you to their own doctors and to hire private investigators to make sure you are still disabled enough to receive benefits. On the one hand, this right is understandable. No one likes the idea of someone living off the government when they can actually be supporting themselves. But on the other hand, it also points to the general distrust of the disabled and the way the system is set up to suspect the disabled no matter what the cause of the impairment. After all, Connie had MS. There is no cure for MS, nor are there any medications out there that reverse the damage from demyelination. In Connie's case, it seems like more of a waste to pay a private investigator to track her; she is not going to suddenly be cured.

Floyd Skloot, a writer who becomes brain injured from a viral attack, tells a similar story of surveillance in his essay called "A Measure of Acceptance." Because his impairment is caused by an organic problem resulting in damage to his brain, Skloot, like Connie, is not going to get better. Nevertheless, the

Social Security Administration informed him that he must submit to an evaluation by a psychiatrist and two days of physical tests, eight years after his disability claim was originally approved. Skloot writes about the mix of anger, fear, and paranoia that results from these periodic inspections designed for "weeding out hypochondriacs, malingerers, fakers, people who were ill without organic causes."[8] He says:

> The patient, or—in the lingo of insurance operations—the claimant, is approached not only as an adversary but as a deceiver. *You can climb more stairs than that! You can really stand on one leg, like a heron; stop falling over, freeloader! We know that game.* Paranoia rules; here an institution seems caught in its grip. With money at stake, the disabled are automatically supposed to be up to some kind of chicanery, and our displays of symptoms are viewed as untrustworthy. Never mind that I contributed to Social Security for my entire working life, with the mutual understanding that if I were disabled the fund would be there for me. Never mind that both my employer and I paid for disability insurance with the mutual understanding that if I were disabled, payments would be there for me. Our doctors are suspect, our caregivers are implicated, and *we've got our eyes on you!*[9]

In addition to the paranoia that such an interaction can cast, these tests are physically and emotionally taxing to the disabled person. Skloot writes that one of the last tests he was asked to perform was to get on his hands and knees and crawl. He considered refusing such a degrading act, but did it because he also needs to be able to continue to qualify for benefits.[10] His physical symptoms also worsened after the testing.[11]

Everyday people have also adopted this critical gaze and take it upon themselves to make sure that disabled parking spaces are used by those who need them. Several participants mentioned hostile or investigative looks when they used disabled parking, especially when they were not using a scooter or cane or other marker of legitimate disability. This daily surveillance was particularly upsetting to the participants with MS who did not regularly use a walking aid, but needed the closer spaces because distance walking could cause fatigue and worsen the symptoms of MS. Although the nondisabled people who monitor the parking spaces believe they are doing a good thing, their actions are based on the erroneous belief that you can detect real disability by examining how someone walks or gets in or out of a car. It is also based on the belief that many people who get handicap placards or plates are just faking it to fool the system, and it is up to the people on the street to protect and monitor. However, all disabled people pay for this surveillance; being viewed as suspect by doctors, insurance companies, the Social Security Administration, and strangers in the grocery store parking lot can take a psychological toll.

Family members and friends were usually much more supportive of the couple; however, many participants reported early or ongoing concerns expressed by immediate family and close friends. For a variety of reasons, nondisabled partners are often viewed with suspicion.[12] Because physical disability is perceived to be a burden, the nondisabled partner's motives for entering such a relationship are questioned. Friends and family may worry that the nondisabled person is looking for someone to control and manage. This may be especially true when the impairment is congenital and the family has cared for the disabled person all of his or her life. For example, Rachel, who has spinal muscular atrophy type 2 and is married to Jack, relates that "my parents, you know they're very open-minded, but they're very protective on the same side. So my dad's like, 'Wow, what is this guy's intention? What does he want? How is he going to hurt you?' You know, they were very protective, my entire family."

Rachel's parents were wary of a nondisabled man's interest in their daughter, particularly because she is severely disabled and needs total care. Their concerns are not entirely unfounded because spousal abuse between disabled/nondisabled partners does appear to be all too common.[13] Thus, Jack had to prove himself to Rachel's family. Nevertheless, Rachel indicates that concerns remain. Although her parents may have finally accepted Jack, she notes that her extended family remains worried. Jennifer reports similar family concerns:

> As far as Frank's family is concerned, they were very accepting of me being in a wheelchair. And after a while, they actually redid their bathroom with a higher toilet seat and everything and kind of made it accessible for me even though they're older and they kind of considered me in their remodeling, which is very nice and unexpected. And my mom has pretty much accepted our relationship and I think my brothers and her ask a lot if he's helping me. "Is he helping you? Is he doing the laundry? Is he doing, you know? Is he vacuuming for you?" And sometimes I say yes, sometimes no, but I think they're—they, you know, want him to be helpful and always make sure that I'm getting the help I need.

Family members and friends are clearly concerned that the nondisabled partner is taking adequate care—doing what is needed without controlling or micromanaging his or her loved one. As I discussed in Chapter 4, some of these fears are based on gendered beliefs about men's inability to provide care. Regardless of the source, distrust and suspicion of the nondisabled partner was a common experience.

Fear that the nondisabled partner will abandon the disabled partner may also be a source of worry for family and friends. Again, this fear is rooted in reality. Numerous studies of people with disabilities report divorce after disability.[14] Even within this small sample, participants had experienced rejection from partners. Partners Adam and Sabrina both have MS.[15] They recount:

ADAM: My first wife, you know, she didn't want to be around me because I had MS and the same with Sabrina's first husband. He's basically—he said, "I didn't sign up for this."

SABRINA: Three months after being married, I got diagnosed and, or, I was in the midst of being diagnosed. We were pretty sure what it was and, uh, he was like, "this wasn't what I signed up for" and he left!

OTHERS: Oh.

As Adam's and Sabrina's experiences indicate, it is not unreasonable for family and friends to worry that their loved one will be abandoned. Regardless, this wariness and distrust of the nondisabled partner can stress the relationship.

One way that friends and family members temper this fear is by suggesting that the nondisabled partner should not be the disabled partner's caregiver. According to Emma and Olivia, this advice was given to both of the couples in Focus Group 2.

EMMA: Everybody warned me against having my partner or my husband as a caregiver.

OLIVIA: Hmm, they did us too.

EMMA: They said that's a big mistake because its gonna get all mixed up. You're not going to know when he's your attendant or when he's your husband. It's not like that at all, for when we're together it all kinda, it doesn't matter if he's giving me a shower or feeding me, I can say anything I want because he's my husband and don't feel any kind of [embarrassment].

Emma clearly prefers care from her husband, and as I explain in Chapter 6, Emma does not feel as if the care interferes with their love relationship. Since Olivia and Randall said that they received the same advice, I probed further.

SARAH: Why do you think people recommended that you didn't let your able-bodied partner care for you?

RANDALL: Just because of the simple fact that— . . . some people would tell me that it would take away from the relationship because they won't think of you like a partner. They will look at you like a, a— . . . you know, I got to do this, I got to do that. It won't be equal, you guys won't be equal.

Randall does go on to say that he feared that a sense of inequality would develop or that the physical caregiving activities would complicate their sexual intimacy. But his partner, Olivia, was the one who insisted that she do all the care—primarily out of a sense of feminine duty and privacy. (Olivia states throughout the focus group that she feels it is a woman's role to care for her man.) Randall explains:

> It took her and my mom forever to get me to get rid of my PCA [personal care assistant] because that was my comfort zone. All the other girlfriends that I've had, they usually walk away. You can walk away, I don't care, but to get rid of those PCAs, I can't say you can walk away because I'm stuck! But I had to really trust, I had to trust her and that is part of getting married is to trust. The only difference, she trusts me to provide for the house, it's the trust thing. [Olivia gets up to check on baby] When I did get rid of my PCAs, I was scared to death. I was afraid that she, you know, I . . . she explained to me that I'm not going to have another woman come in my house and bathe you. I'm going to be the one to do that. I'm not going to have another woman come to my house and see you naked. I'm not going to do that. I didn't really understand it because I didn't look at it like that. I just said, "It's not like that." But the more I . . . it bothered her, the more I said, "Alright, we'll try it. But if it doesn't work, then we're going to go back." But, but, I think that's when you know that you're in love . . . when you can trust that person with every ounce that you have, and I just don't, you know, some people don't do it that way. But at my house, that's how we're . . . because she assumes me is no different than her, if she is hungry, she eats!

Randall was reluctant to stop the use of a personal care assistant because it would make him more dependent on his wife; however, Randall and Olivia were able to maintain a sense of equality within their relationship.

Nondisabled partners reported that friends and family were worried that they were "getting in over their heads," especially when the nondisabled partner was doing all the care. Olivia says:

> A lot of people, when we first got together, his family as well as mine . . . we have a lot of different barriers with I'm white and he's black and he's disabled and I'm not. So, everybody, I don't know if it was just the disability, but they questioned, "Are you sure you know what you're doing?" "Are you sure this is what you want to do?" But, you know, once everybody says that we're more in love than anybody that they've ever met. So, I think once they met us and, um, got to see how we are together, we've been married for six years now and it seems like, I mean, nothing's, I think we're more in love now than before, but everybody is really supportive of us. They just wanted to make sure that we knew what we were doing, what we were getting ourselves into.

In this instance, the families wanted to make sure Olivia understood the physical and emotional stress that care can cause—they wanted Olivia to avoid caregiver burnout. At times, however, this concern developed into rejection. For example, as I mentioned in Chapter 4, Richard received a negative response from friends when he announced his relationship with Emma. Richard's friends and colleagues—professors at a medium-sized university—rejected his relationship with Emma and ceased the friendship. In this case, concerns that Richard was making a bad decision to be in a relationship in which he was also a caregiver were likely complicated with outright ableism. Although smart and successful, Emma has a speech impairment and has difficulty controlling her bodily movements. Richard's former friends may also have been uncomfortable with his new partner. Ultimately, however, both Olivia and Emma were happy that they did not follow the advice of friends and family members. They preferred that their partners provide care and they did not feel that this arrangement harmed their relationship.

Although it may often be less explicit than concerns over care, friends and family may also be afraid that the nondisabled partner is sexually deviant.[16] As Mitchell Tepper states:

> The person attracted to someone with a disability automatically gets labeled as having a fetish or his or her motives are called into question. The partner with the disability is assumed unattractive, suggesting one must be imbalanced to be attracted to us. And the person who is actually sexually orientated to some aspect of a disability—whether it be a brace or a stump or a leg bag—is automatically assumed to be deviant in all aspects of his or her sexual relationship.[17]

None of the participants had friends or family come out with such fears, but I argue that discomfort with disabled sexuality shadows the other reasons for discomfort outlined above. Thus, especially when the reasons for the dismissive attitudes are unclear to the couple, it is possible that at least part of the suspicion is rooted in a belief that people attracted to people with disabilities are sexually "sick." As I discussed in Chapter 4, Sofia's family clearly has ongoing concerns about Ted's sexual or other motivations. Although most couples report "problems with in-laws," the participants felt as if a lot of their problems were related to ableism from friends and family or concerns about blending care in intimate relationships. In other words, they reported the same personality or political conflicts with family members that nondisabled couples face, but the presence of impairment added an extra dimension that they had to negotiate. For the most part, however, participants felt that their close friends and family supported the relationship. This support often took time to develop, but all participants were happy when it was finally there (or expressed a wish that family members would learn to support them). Especially since reactions from strangers are almost always negative, it is particularly important to have support of friends and family.

Discrimination can come from many sources. Parents, friends, family members, doctors, government bureaucrats, and strangers on the street create a web of prejudice that is difficult for people with disabilities and their partners to maneuver. Ableist attitudes and inaccessible environments are demoralizing and can definitely take their toll on a couple. However, the disabled/nondisabled couples in this study combat the various forms of discrimination—staring, surveillance, judgment—with a mixture of strategies, including laughter, political critique, and pride. In the following section, I will detail how couples use humor to ward off and manage discrimination.

Disability Humor

As with many marginalized communities, the disability community has developed its own form of "crip humor." This may seem odd to nondisabled people for several reasons. First, most people view disability as a tragedy, something to pity, not laugh about or celebrate. Second, most people have been told not to stare or laugh at the disabled. The disability scholars that have begun to look at this phenomenon suggest that humor functions in several ways, including community building,[18] bridge building between the disabled and nondisabled experience,[19] and morale building by turning tragedy into comedy.[20] In my own research on disabled/nondisabled couples, disability humor took two main forms: community building and morale building. In this section, I present examples of each, focusing especially on the way the body functions in disability humor. By turning the leaky, unpredictable, and excessive disabled body into a joke, disabled/nondisabled couples help manage negative experiences like stares and discrimination. Thus, being able to laugh at disability is essential to the psychological health of the disabled/nondisabled couple.

Almost all of the autobiographies that I analyzed relay stories of incontinence in humorous ways. For example, Hockenberry writes wittily about making "broadcast history" when he wet his pants while telling America about John Belushi's death.[21] In her essay called "Plunging In," Mairs writes about the joyous spectacle of her weekly water exercise class sponsored by the MS Society in which "urine floated in its sealed pouch on the blue surface."[22] None of these tales are meant to elicit pity. On the contrary, the tone of all the stories about bodily fluids is acceptance of the body's physical limits, perhaps even a reveling in the ludicrousness of it all. Tom Shakespeare writes that this kind of disability humor centers on "shared meanings" between disabled people because such taboo topics are part of the daily conversation for people with disabilities, but they are so shocking to the nondisabled. In other words, it is funny because the nondisabled do not "get it."[23] Physical disabilities like spinal cord injury, Parkinson's disease, MS, and many others often impact urinary and bowel functions; therefore, dealing with poop and pee is a common ordeal for many disabled people. Intermittent catheterization, indwelling catheters, colostomy bags, digital penetration of the bowel reflex, suppositories, adult diapers, and other aids and techniques become a regular part of life for many people with disabilities. Thus, in the case of disabled/nondisabled couples, I believe this humor also signals the nondisabled partner's group membership, his or her solidarity with the disability partner. As the person that helps manage the bladder and bowels, the nondisabled partner is intimately connected to this disability reality. This "below the belt humor" functions to build community and solidarity. Below the belt humor, then, is also part of the burgeoning alternative or queer sexual culture in disability circles. Private body parts and processes that are not so private for people with disabilities are re-rendered as sources of strength, connection, and group identification.

In the focus groups, laughter was frequently cited as the salve that healed wounds and kept relationships together. Humor could neutralize uncomfortable or embarrassing situations. Therefore, many participants felt that humor was an adaptive strategy, a better alternative than getting mad, frustrated, or discouraged by impairment. For example, in this conversation from Focus Group 1, the participants discuss the advantages of laughter:

RACHEL: I think a lot of it too is humor, I mean—

SARAH: Yes!

RACHEL: [*inaudible*]

SABRINA: Yes, I think that is how we deal with a lot, with disability, is with humor.

TRACY: Oh, yeah, absolutely.

SABRINA: Otherwise, you'd go nuts.

RACHEL: And you get people, you get family members that are like, "Oh, I can't believe you guys are laughing about that!" I'm like, it's so funny!

ELLEN: You have to otherwise, I just, I, I always have told Kevin we have had experiences, I have had experiences. One of my friends said, "You know what, Ellen, if you talked to people, they would never believe your stories, you need to write an MS humor book because I think it's the only way you could get through some of the situations." I mean, we have been through [experiences] where batteries have died in the middle of Walmart, where we went to a park with the girls and he had my whole scooter and forgot the seat at home! [*laughter*] And it was a forty-five-minute [drive back home]. Now, the girls are wanting to go to a water park, I mean it's just, how am I gonna go to a water park when there is no seat on my scooter? And you have to laugh at things or just, you wouldn't believe the things you do. But like you said, it's humor, people would sit there and go, "You're laughing about that?" Well, we have to.

RACHEL: Yeah, I mean my aides sometimes, I'll be telling them
what we're laughing about or we'll be joking and they're like,
"What are you two talking about now?" We're like, "Oh, this
happened!" They're like, "Oh, we don't want to hear about it,
we don't want to hear about it, it's bad, you guys are gross."
I'm like, "Well, hey, it happens, you know." And then our
famous thing is with the aides we do, um . . . we have a lot of
caregivers that are pretty wacky, and where they find these people! They come to my house and I'm like, oh, my lord! Um,
they come in and we kind of rate them. [*inaudible*] And I, we
rate them and we do a whole skit, we like do voices of them
and things they do. We're like, "Oh, we're going to be Trudy.
OK, look, we're going to mess up the toilet! And break this,
and . . ." [*laughter*] It's funny, and it's hilarious, it's like our
own little entertainment.

JACK: You have to keep a—

RACHEL: You have to be able to at least laugh, otherwise you're just
going to be angry and you're going to throw things and cry. So
you have to just laugh.

In this excerpt, the participants are primarily using laughter to make fun of the
foibles that living with impairment can bring (e.g., running out of batteries in
Walmart), including poking fun at the professionalized support system set up
for people with disabilities (e.g., aides). Rachel and Jack were not the only participants that made fun of the system or people in the system. Inadequate
resources and poor aides are frequent complaints; however, in the example
above, Rachel and Jack use humor to relieve tension. The system is frustrating, but humor can help one stay sane and can be an effective way to point out
the system's flaws. Personal care assistants need better pay, training, and benefits; without these provisions in place, Rachel is unlikely to ever get good
help. In the meantime, Rachel pokes fun at the system's failures and, as I elab-
orate in the next section, tries to change the system by working in disability
rights and support organizations.

Disability humor was also used in self-deprecating ways, not as a way to
express self-hatred, but as a way to make fun of negative aspects of the impairment and to take back control. For example, an MS symptom that Connie deals
with is short-term memory loss. One of the ways in which Connie and her husband Bob manage her brain's "failure" is to joke. For example, while discussing
movies, Connie quips that she can never remember movies and then follows the
comment by saying "At least I'm a cheap date," implying that she can be shown
the same entertainment over and over and be happy. Instead of being sad or feel-

ing sorry for herself, Connie takes charge and makes this "flaw" a funny personality characteristic. In the following exchange, Bob joins in the joking.

CONNIE: Yeah. You see my pad of paper—

FRANK: I do, I've been making notes too.

CONNIE: I have books and books and books at home—

SARAH: So you remember—

CONNIE: Because I don't remember things so I write everything down.

BOB: Including the pad of paper that says where the other pad of paper is [*laughter*].

Both of these jokes—about the movies and the pads of paper—work in part because they are told by the impacted person or with her approval. She is part of the jokemaking, not the hapless object of the joke.

Who makes the joke and in what *context* are key for differentiating acceptable disability humor from ableist jokes. For example, within disabled circles, it is often acceptable to refer to oneself and each other as a "gimp" or "crip." Mairs, for instance, prefers to use the word "cripple" when talking about herself and she often uses it amusingly, as when she catches a glimpse of herself in a full-length mirror and screams, "Eek . . . a cripple!"[24] In Focus Group 4, the participants also discuss the dynamics of in-group language.

ALLISON: It's interesting because if you, I think if someone brings up a disability-related joke and they have a disability it's okay. But if someone brings it up that doesn't have a disability then it's like, it's taboo.

BOB: Oh, yeah.

ALLISON: Like, I have a lot of friends that are visually impaired and we talk about like, oh ran into a sign, or we try we joke around. But if someone else brings it up, I think we get a little touchy. It's like, "you can't joke about that because you haven't experienced it" kind of a thing and so, um . . .

SARAH: Similar to race.

ALLISON: Yeah. You can't make a joke about someone who is Jewish unless you are Jewish. So, I think that, you know, is a kind of thing. I don't know how you guys take that, but I know when people make blind jokes that aren't blind, I get a little irritated. But I can think of blind jokes all I want, so—

As Allison notes, words like "gimp" or "crip" and related disability jokes are usually acceptable in disability circles but, outside those groups, they are offensive.[25] Disability humor can be a way to build community, to share in-group knowledge and humor. In addition, joking about impairment can be an effective way to regain control over the disabled body and turn tragedy upside down. In the next section, I turn to expressions of disability pride as another form of resistance to discrimination.

Disability Pride

Just as disability humor is connected to sadness, disability pride is intimately connected with shame. In other words, pride is born from the struggle with shame, and it always, inevitably, carries a little of its origins with it. This does not mean that physical impairment unavoidably causes shame. The origins of shame lie in the social dimensions of disability. However, in today's society, prejudice and discrimination are so widespread against the disabled that I do not know of a single disabled person who has not, on some level, internalized ableism. For example, almost all of the participants in the focus groups were connected to activist organizations and the disability rights movement. These people were full of disability pride; however, a few also shared worries about the viability of their relationships or themselves as sexual subjects. Since their concerns were not shared by the nondisabled partners (not even in the private, follow-up journals), I believe these fears are the result of internalized ableism. Disabled participants sometimes had a difficult time believing that their nondisabled partners were truly happy in the relationship and that they wanted to stay together. For example, Ellen, who had been married to Kevin for only one year when she was diagnosed with MS, says:

> That was the hardest part— . . . I mean we're— . . . I mean everybody has different situations, but when we got married we were married "normal"—as normal as you possibly could be! And then you find out that one spouse has MS. I think when I found out . . . do you still want to be married? That was the biggest thing. Why would you stay with me? Do you really want to stay with me? I mean this is before kids or anything and . . . and that was a scary, I think a scary thing, not knowing where your relationship was going.

Connie, who also was diagnosed with MS after her relationship with Bob began, expresses similar sentiments:

> No matter how many times I've told him . . . I said you deserve somebody who's much more active, better in everything than I am. You know anybody that grew up, if you were in control, you were the one who drove the kids

[*inaudible*] and you were the one that did all the organizing and could do all the stuff standing up in the house. The sexual stuff, could initiate or whatever. If you can't do it anymore, if you don't have somebody that's constantly saying "I don't want to leave you," I couldn't find anybody better. It does make a big difference.

In society, women are expected to be able to drive the kids, clean the house, and be sexually available. And as Connie explains, when these gendered tasks become complicated by (or even made impossible by) physical impairment, it is easy to feel like a failure. Both Connie and Ellen note that having a supportive partner who insists on staying in the relationship and constantly reminds them that they are loved helps them maintain a positive sense of self. Nevertheless, as citizens subjected to dominant culture values, they have internalized ablest ideals; therefore, they must constantly work at seeing themselves as worthy partners.

Participants with congenital disabilities, as well as those who became disabled later in life but met their current partners after they had become physically impaired, expressed similar worries. Neither a lifetime of living with impairment nor meeting their partners postdisability spared them from feeling like a burden or internalizing ablest assumptions about sexual relationships. In her journal, Rachel writes:

Sometimes in our relationship I feel that Jack does not get to do what he used to do before he met me because of my disability and me needing care. I hope that our relationship won't become strained because he feels that he is missing out. He doesn't at all make me feel this way, it is just a fear that I have deep inside. I guess it stems from feeling like a burden when I lived at home with my parents. Sometimes in doing care, my parents and my brother would complain about things. Now that I don't live with them anymore, they have a newfound freedom. They go out every weekend with their friends and even go on vacations.

Even though Jack frequently tells Rachel that he does not feel any amount of burden, her fear remains. Similarly, Allison worries that Jason will get tired of the amount of responsibility that he takes on in their relationship:

I was diagnosed with macular degeneration before . . . when I was nine, so it was preexisting and I think Jason had some idea of what he was getting into when we started dating, but I don't think he really realized it. [*laughter*] Especially, you know, we started dating when we were seventeen, which is really young for, um, I think for him to have to deal with some of the stuff that he has to deal with. And I think he has taken on more responsibility once we moved in together and we've been living together for over three years now. But I know that sometimes like going out, and when we go shopping and me needing help to look at sizes or prices and things like that.

Jason helps Allison with looking at sizes and prices, reading menus, crossing streets, and other daily visual tasks; however, according to Jason, the only area that ever feels a bit like a burden is the perpetual driving duty. Nevertheless, Allison worries that the accumulation of these tasks will eventually be too much for Jason, especially if and when they decide to have children. Because caregiving is typically framed only in negative terms in society, and because people with disabilities are at increased risk of divorce and abandonment, it is sometimes difficult for disabled partners to trust that their nondisabled lovers are not building resentment or on the brink of care burnout.

In *Waist-High*, Mairs tells readers about the contradictory feelings she has about disability. Early in the book, she writes:

> Here I am now, a quarter of a century later, prime well past, hunched and twisted and powerless but for two twelve-volt batteries beneath my ass. Woe is me! Except that, on the whole, woe isn't me. . . . I feel—and feel fully— the ordinary complement of negative emotions in response to specific trig- gers: anger and frustration at my clumsiness; embarrassment about my leaky bladder; wistfulness for the dancing and hiking and cycling I'll never do again; guilt that my helplessness burdens family and friends; anxiety about further deterioration. I simply don't feel especially sorry for myself. Neither do most of the other people with disabilities I know, so I'm neither unusually brave nor exceptionally thick-skinned. Self-pity is simply one of those senti- ments more likely to be projected onto one from the outside than generated within. That is, because nondisabled people pity us, they presume that we must also pity ourselves. This supposition may actually function as a power- ful antidote, inasmuch as almost every cripple I know, sensing it every day, resents and actively repudiates it.[26]

On the one hand, Mairs admits to being distressed over disability and later, even "appalled by my own appearance."[27] But on the other hand, her book is full of moments of pride and claims of satisfaction, even delight. As she notes, part of the pride she feels may be the result of rebelling against the prevailing attitudes about disability. In other words, amidst so much pity, Mairs thumbs her nose, carving out a space in which she can enjoy her body and the disabil- ity experience. She writes, "Relaxed and focused, I feel emotionally far more 'up' than I generally did when I stood on two sound legs. Nondisabled people, I find, tend to be skeptical of such contentment. . . . For the most part—and you can believe this or not as you choose—I consider my life unusually priv- ileged."[28] Later in the book, she even claims that the disabled body may be "better off" than the nondisabled body: "The body in trouble, becoming both a warier and a humbler creature, is more apt to experience herself all of a piece: a biochemical dynamo cranking out consciousness much as it generates platelets, feces, or reproductive cells to ensure the manufacture of new dynamos."[29] Mairs argues that the disabled can experience more mind and body integration, more self-awareness, than the "perfectly healthy person," whose body "may impinge so little on her sense of well-being that she may believe herself separate from and even in control of them."[30] Thus, in the kernels of shame and distress, Mairs finds new ways to conceive of the disabled body as a source of pride and strength.

Another marker of the pride/shame struggle was the use of overcoming language in the focus groups. For example, in Focus Group 4, Connie and the other participants all express outrage when strangers act as if their disability is tragic; however, the participants themselves sometimes frame impairment as bad fortune. Notice how Allison and Connie construct Allison's predicted vision loss in the following exchange:

ALLISON: It's supposed to, but it's been stable since I've been nine, um, which—they don't know, I mean, it usually happens in adults over sixty-five so they, when I was diagnosed there was only forty kids in the state that had my condition. So they were kind of looking at me like I was a pin cushion instead of like a person and, um, so it's supposed to get worse, but it hasn't and I'm twenty-three now, so knock on wood, so . . .

CONNIE: Congratulations.

ALLISON: Thank you.

Likewise, Kevin and Adam, from Focus Group 1, use metaphors of overcoming (see emphasis added in their dialogue):

ADAM: I'm Adam, Sabrina's husband. Um, I'm doing this because anything we can do to help MS and its research and help people that is going to help *put the disease behind us*, um, easier for them, the better.

KEVIN: I'm Kevin, I'm married to Ellen. I'm able-bodied, and we've been through everything together and then some so, also the more we can do to help ourselves, help other people—I'm afraid there is a reason that we are here, *this has been entrusted to us*, so I figure, well, *march forward* and help and do whatever we can to help other people as well. . . . There is times, I know she's had some rough times with things and, well, it doesn't matter. We'll figure out what to do, we'll get through this, we'll survive. We always have. We're Catholics, we're quite religious, and *the Lord gave us a test for a reason*. He's led us this far, he's not gonna let us go now, so. . . . There is always some support somewhere.

In both of these excerpts, the disability is constructed as a problem to move past, to get over. The metaphors of overcoming are used to frame disability as something outside themselves, an external, negative force that they must contend with and beat. The use of these metaphors contrasts with the integration of disability and pride that the participants discuss in other parts of the focus group. I read these contradictions as symptomatic of the struggle against internalized ableism, but also as evidence of successful coping. Drawing on religious and other meaning-making discourses provides a language for people to make sense of their situations. These phrases help the participants create useful myths to tell themselves and others. All the participants in the study paint themselves and their relationships as positive. Regardless, the language of overcoming is used as a stock narrative to frame aspects of their lives. Overcoming is the language that the dominant elicits from the disabled—these are the narratives the nondisabled want to hear. Therefore, it is not entirely surprising that people in disabled/nondisabled intimate relationships would, at times, resort to such language and even internalize, on some level, the desire to be rid of disability.

Significantly, however, negative feelings about their disabled bodies and worries about their relationship were overshadowed by disability pride and the strength of their love relationships for all the participants. Dan may struggle with his sexual self-image, but he is also a disability rights advocate and, in general, feels like a competent citizen and worthy partner and father. The struggle between disability pride and shame is evident in Dan's discussion about cures with the other participants.

DAN: I mean I often feel, jeez, if I could just have one thing easier, like if I had my hands and stuff like that. But again I have to count my blessings because I've got friends who I can do more than they can. But it, you know, in all the stem cell research and stuff like that and it, if they can make me walk again, as much pain as I'm in now that I can feel, I would hate to know what that pain would be like, if I had full sensation.

KAY: But you would take it if you could get it.

DAN: I, I, well, yeah. I don't know, it would depend on what they could offer me.

KAY: He would take it if he could get it.

DAN: I mean even, if they could say I could, I could, make you have full use of your arms, I'd be tickled. But then I'm sure after I got that I'd say, OK, let's go to the next step.

KAY: Yup.

GENE: Hey this is pretty cool! What else you got! [*laughter*]

KAY: I can, he stumbles, but I can tell you pretty assuredly he'd take it if he could take it.

Dan "stumbles" because he had contradictory feelings about disability—it is both a source of pride, a marker of difference that defines his identity (and career), and, in his experience, something that limits his physical activities.

Participants in the focus groups and authors and filmmakers of published self-representations were always quick to point out that this struggle would be less difficult if society valued disabled bodies. While discussing his own frustrations about his physical limitations, Dan says, "Well, society dictates that this is normal, this is what normal people do." So, Dan may not always feel full of disability pride, but he is well aware of the source of his negative feelings. Furthermore, the messages that participants received about disability were also shaped by gender norms. Dan is most upset about his "failure" to approximate specifically masculine norms around fatherhood and male sexuality. But, at least, Dan has received some positive messages about disabled male sexuality—he reports that he was told in rehabilitation that he could still have sex and father children. Sofia, however, received no information about sex or sexuality during rehabilitation for her spinal cord injury. Indeed, previous studies of sex education in rehabilitation facilities report a marked gender bias.[31] Since women's sexuality is constructed as passive and receptive, they often do not receive information about how to be sexual agents with physical disability. Disabled men and women both receive negative messages about their worth and attractiveness, but it is important to recognize that these messages are always gendered.

Disabled/nondisabled couples may experience moments of shame, but feelings of pride are stronger. Sometimes the source of this pride was being able to see the benefits and beauties of disability, as Mairs does when she writes about well-integrated disabled bodies.[32] At other points, the source of the pride is clearly political. Participants and authors and filmmakers alike offered insightful critiques of the representation of people with disabilities in popular culture and the myth of independence and autonomy dominant in the United States. Thus, this next section delves further into the political analysis offered by disabled/nondisabled couples. It is their acute awareness of discrimination and their ability to critique social structures that perpetuate prejudice that form the backbone of their disability pride.

Political Critique: The Need for Visibility and Revaluing Interdependence

As I argued in Chapter 2, popular culture can affect individuals by defining what is socially imaginable and by describing culturally acceptable ways of being. For disabled/nondisabled couples, the messages most often relayed position care as a burden that desexualizes their relationship, the disabled body as shameful, and the disability experience as painful and pitiable. Of course, disabled/nondisabled couples can impact popular culture by producing alternative representations (such as the autobiographies that I analyzed in this study) and by selecting what to, and what not to, watch. It would be impossible, however, to claim that popular culture has no influence. As Shakespeare, Gillespie-Sells, and Davies note, "disabled people themselves are socialized within the dominant culture, and therefore hold conflicting views about desirable partners, and can have negative views of themselves."[33] This pervasiveness of the dominant popular culture makes negative imagery one of the "main problems faced by disabled people attempting to assert themselves as independent adults and positive sexual beings."[34] In my conversations with the disabled/nondisabled couples in the focus groups, participants singled out popular culture as key to dismantling negative stereotypes.

When we first started discussing representations in the focus groups, participants often claimed that disabled/nondisabled relationships were simply absent in popular culture:

> SARAH: In terms of media, TV, do you ever see representations of
> disabled/nondisabled intimate relationships?
>
> ALL: No! [*laughter and other cries of "No"*]
>
> UNKNOWN: No, never have.
>
> ADAM: You're not supposed to!

But in each group—through discussion and group brainstorming—participants began thinking of numerous examples. For the most part, however, these examples were largely negative or inaccurate portrayals of disability.

Participants were especially upset by representations that were blatantly inaccurate. For example, Connie, who has MS and is married to Bob, brings up a problematic episode of a popular television show.

> CONNIE: MS is not a— It's not like you hear that you have cancer.
> That you're going to die.
>
> SARAH: That you're going to die. Well, people still think that
> though.
>
> CONNIE: But, have you watched on TV, that program we saw on TV
> and the guy died of MS, and it was like, I was so indignant. I
> said I'm writing the producer of this television show. MS is not
> a terminal illness or whatever.
>
> SARAH: Right.

FRANK: You can't catch it either. I'm not going to catch it sitting next to you.

SARAH: Right, you can't catch it.

FRANK: I've seen people do that: "You have MS?" [*shrinks away, as if scared of catching a disease*]

ALL: [*laughter*]

SARAH: Really.

CONNIE: I was really upset.

SARAH: Yeah, I think I saw that show, I've seen it before 'cause . . . or have seen similar takes.

BOB: There have been several programs and movies where that sort of, that pronouncement has been a death nail.

SARAH: Right, you're dead.

BOB: You know, it's like, like Connie said. And the following pause is always that, "Oh, it's the worst thing that could happen."

SARAH: Right.

In the television episode, the perpetrator's excuse for his criminal behavior is that he is going to die soon (from MS) anyway—a sentiment that provides audiences with erroneous information about the disease. At one point in time MS was indeed a disease that could progress quickly and one could die; however, today there are many treatments that slow or even stop the progression for most people. Representing MS as a disease with a rather quick and inevitably fatal end perpetuates ignorance that can, in turn, negatively impact people with MS by treating them as if they are "terminal," that MS is the "worst thing that could happen."

Participants also felt the Mothers Against Drunk Driving commercial (discussed in Chapter 2) perpetuated inaccurate stereotypes of disabled people as being isolated.[35] This conversation among the participants in Focus Group 3 is representative of all participants' reactions to that public service announcement.

SOFIA: Insulting.

GENE: Yeah, definitely.

DAN: And they view the person with the disability as locked away, and that's where they should be.

SARAH: Absolutely.

KAY: I mean, I see the point that they're trying to make, but they did it in a rather uncaring way. I mean there is definitely that . . .

yeah, there's just definitely that impression of "Oh yeah, you lose your abilities and your life is basically over."

GENE: And you'll never have love.

KAY: Yeah.

TED: That's the big thing. I mean, having done my clinicals in a nursing home, I mean that does happen. You can get in an accident and you can end up in a nursing home and not be able to enjoy the things you once used to do. So I can see that end of it. But then showing that relationship going on outside and portraying that you can't have one or whatever, that's pretty wrong.

The young man in the Mothers Against Drunk Driving commercial generates the image of people with disabilities being forced to live in institutions. Although many people with disabilities do indeed live institutionally because they have no other viable options, this is certainly no longer standard. More and more people with disabilities live in the community, and have loving partnerships and families (as evidenced by the focus group participants). This reality, however, continues to be absent in popular culture. Some participants also noted that when a disabled person is portrayed as sexual, it is not a loving relationship. Kay says:

> They are a couple, but they're not positive. I mean both in *Forrest Gump* and in *Born on the Fourth of July*, I think. But they were both like prostitute or one-night-stand-type anger. You know, the man was just angry about his disability and, I mean, it wasn't a loving situation at all.

There is a dearth of realistic or positive portrayals of people with disabilities and their partners. For the couples in the focus groups, these absences contributed to the prejudice and discrimination they experienced, as outlined above, in their daily lives. A lack of models also made it difficult to resist internalizing ablest attitudes.

Participants were eager to point out a need to portray different kinds of bodies and different kinds of sexual possibilities. For example, Allison noted that, even when disability is portrayed, the bodily difference is often minimized or erased completely.

ALLISON: What about the, uh, *An Affair to Remember*? Doesn't she get hit by a car and she's, she's like supposed to meet him at the top of the Empire State Building and then she gets hit by a car and she becomes paralyzed and . . .

CONNIE: Right, she hides it from him.

ALLISON: She couldn't, she hides it and she is sitting on the couch, and he comes in and she can't get up.

SARAH: Right.

ALLISON: And, then, he realizes it or whatever. I don't know.

FRANK: That is why she never called him.

ALLISON: And that is why she never called him.

SARAH: Mmm . . . right, OK. But then at the end they do get together.

ALLISON: They do get together, yeah.

SARAH: So, that is a good point.

ALLISON: But I don't think they ever actually show her in a wheelchair. [*laughter*] I think that she is just sitting on the couch with a blanket on her.

Although the example is dated, the erasure of bodies that do not fit normative ideals remains.[36] Twisted limbs, atrophied legs, and other deformities are the stuff of horror films. When mainstream film and television call for a disabled character, his or her physical difference is covered up or neatly contained. Such erasure makes it difficult for the nondisabled to become used to disabled bodies and movement; therefore, in addition to more real people with disabilities, more attention needs to be given to real bodies.

Many of the published self-representations also critique the invisibility of the real disabled body. For example, after pages of details on how she uses the restroom, Mairs confronts readers and says, "About now I can imagine you saying you don't know why I'm dwelling on this indelicate subject again."[37] She explains that, if she keeps quiet about the ways in which public restrooms fail to truly accommodate the disabled body, then nothing will change. Nondisabled people will go on thinking that the needs of the disabled have been miraculously solved by the Americans with Disabilities Act and no further work is necessary. Talking about bowel movements and urination may not be pretty, but "somebody has got to talk about toilets."[38] Later Mairs poignantly writes, "If I want people to grow accustomed to my presence, and to view mine as an ordinary life, less agreeable in some of its particulars than theirs but satisfying overall, then I must routinely roll out among them."[39] By refusing to hide her bodily differences, Mairs is attempting to socialize the nondisabled, which can in turn help the disabled live less marginalized.

It is significant that the body present in the self-representations that I analyzed is not always a pleasurable and contained body. Sometimes the bodies of both the disabled and nondisabled alike are in pain, exhausted, violated, exposed, and uncontrolled. These may not be the bodies that the disability rights movement has traditionally privileged as spokesbodies; however, the authors let them loose in the texts to expose the angst and joy of physical disability and care. This provides a new model of disability politics that acknowledges both the needs of the disabled body and the potential it gives in return. These bodies are part of the "new realism" paradigm shift (outlined in Chapter 1) that exposes the nitty-gritty, painful realities of disability, but does not render such narratives "politically impotent."[40] The realism of individual pain and pleasure is connected to a critique of cultural norms that establish body hygiene as private and self-performed.[41] By connecting complicated body images to social/political realities, the new realism of the body adds teeth to making the body visible. New realism mirrors Cheryl Marie Wade's plea, nearly two decades earlier, for disability activists and scholars to talk about disabled bodies, especially those aspects that "ain't exactly sexy." As Wade argues:

> If I can't talk about the need [for personal care], then I can't talk about the choices, either. And yes, even the weak, vulnerable cripples have choices. But if our shame tells us that our needs lack dignity, that we lack dignity, then the next thing we hear our shame say is that it is more dignified to die than to live with these basic needs that take away our privacy and seem like such a burden.[42]

Thus, it is politically vital to expose the realities—both the pleasures and pains—of the disabled body.

Shameless: The ART of Disability and *Want* also expose the disabled body and the need for care.[43] In *Want*, there is a sequence in which Loree is cared for by various friends. We see them pull down her pants, hand her toilet paper, and lift her from the toilet to the wheelchair. This sequence, combined with the emphasis in the sex sequence on Loree's body and wheelchair, makes visible the differences of the disabled body. In the final sequence of the film, Loree and her lover are having sex and her lover accidentally turns Loree's power chair on. The two laugh it off, but including this moment in the film demonstrates Loree's commitment to full visibility—body, chair accidents, and all. Similarly, moments in which the excesses of the disabled body and its need for care become obvious are not edited out of *Shameless*. Early in the film, the five friends are having a movie night, watching examples of Hollywood representations of disability. Suddenly, McMurchy's legs have a spasm and his bowl of popcorn falls off his lap. It would have been easy to leave this moment out of the film, to minimize the difference disability does make, but Klein chooses to include it, as she does her own fall in her bedroom later in the film. *Shameless* is also reflexive about the tension in the disability community to present only strong and able images to the public. When Frazee suddenly falls very ill and has to be hospitalized, Klein talks openly with Frazee about how hard it is to see Frazee—a pillar of strength in the community—so frail and sick. And Frazee notes that her own denial of her body sometimes results in these moments of extreme illness. This conversation highlights the realities of illness and the need for medical attention and care from friends and lovers while maintaining control over one's life, autonomy, and serving as a source of strength for others.

In addition to the focus on the realities of the disabled body and its need for care, all of the self-representations that I analyzed critique dominant notions of autonomy and independence by emphasizing the value of connection and interdependence. The focus group participants and the authors of the published self-representations are very aware of the progressive political potential behind relational lives. For example, many of the writers explicitly connect their lives and writing to disability rights. Murphy critiques at length the value that Americans place on independence and self-reliance. He writes that "lack of autonomy and unreciprocated dependence on others bring debasement of status in American culture—and in many other cultures. . . . It is for these reasons that escape from dependency has been a central goal of the disability political movement."[44] Although all people are inherently interdependent, and all subjectivity relies on the others that participate in their lives, Murphy is up-front with the fact that physical impairment helped him fully understand this social reality. As an able-bodied, white male academic, Murphy had failed to register his intrinsic involvement with others. Disability, however, made the play between separation and connection obvious. He notes that the "oscillation between involvement and withdrawal" had "bedeviled me all my life," but that it "grew stronger in my illness."[45] Although Murphy initially becomes depressed, suicidal, and withdrawn because of his physical disability, Yolanda confronts him and explains how his retreat from life would impact herself and their children: "It was not my private affair, for, although our lives in theory may belong to us, they are mortgaged. My life belonged to my family, primarily, and also to many others."[46] Murphy's physical body made his own intersubjectivity palpable and helped inform his critique of social relations in general. Toward the end of his book, Murphy eloquently summarizes:

> There is, then, a constant process built into all our endeavors in which we must reach out, relate, and love, while taking care not to lose ourselves. . . . In the final analysis, social life is made possible by keeping a delicate balance between falling inward and falling outward. The structure of all our moments is that we are constantly being pulled apart between the two. It is also the story of our lives.[47]

Thus, it is through the experience of disability that Murphy is able to articulate the fundamental intersubjectivity of all social relations—a radical political position indeed.

Similarly, Morton Kondracke writes at length about what his wife's illness has taught him. He says, "Milly's diagnosis changed me. When it became clear in 1988 that she had Parkinson's, I said to myself, 'This is one thing in your life you are going to do right.' I meant that I was determined to be a loving husband and to help Milly fight the disease."[48] Part of helping "Milly fight the disease" was to become political. Kondracke uses his role as a journalist to access politicians and lobby for their support of research funding, especially controversial but promising research on stem cells. He also politicizes his experience with caregiving. Kondracke details how he prepares Milly's food, washes and dresses her, feeds her and helps her with shopping and other activities.[49] But he also acknowledges that he is able to give such good care because his gender and class status allow him to employ outside help and take respites when needed. His family is not burdened with the additional stresses of absent or inadequate insurance, work concerns, and other outside factors that can make care in intimate relationships difficult.

Kondracke and Murphy understand how relational selves undermine myths of autonomy, and they are quick to connect their personal experiences with disability to social and political issues. In her video *Want*, director Loree Erickson also provides an insightful critique of social and physical barriers that she faces. She tells viewers that her personal care needs are met by a collective of friends from her community because public funding for personal care is inadequate and many of the paid personal care assistants are homophobic. Care from friends and community members enable her to "express myself as a sexual being without fear of abuse or denial of care."[50] Then, while filming from her wheelchair point of view, Erickson rolls along the streets of Canada, visually demonstrating the physical barriers she faces. While in voice-over, she states:

> I want to be recognized, not only as a good friend, but also a good fuck. I'm sick of being seen as impotent, childlike, and inspirational simply because the environment wasn't constructed with people who have disabilities in mind. I'm tired of waiting for the next bus, and possibly the bus after that one, because the lift on this one is either not working, or it's not accessible to begin with. And by the way, I can think of a lot better things to do with my time than waiting just five more minutes, just ten more minutes, just twenty more minutes for something that should have been accessible in the first place. I'm tired of fighting off the internalization of mainstream society's fucked-up perception that I am not sexy. I'm tired of your ableist standards of beauty keeping me from getting as much action as I want. Most of all, I'm tired of having to think about all of this when I just want to have fun, and laugh, and love, and fuck.

Combined with the visuals of Erickson watching nondisabled people walk up bus steps, facing coffee shop counters made for standing people, and seeing people staring at her on the street, this manifesto is effective.

Klein too critiques inaccessible toilets, travel, buildings, and so forth in her book, but she also writes about the moment she embraces "disability pride" when she and her family happen upon a Disability Pride Day event in Boston. Klein was a feminist, who had spent the past few decades critiquing the construction of female difference, and an antiwar activist. However, she had never considered disability as something socially devalued—something that activists need to revalue and be proud of—until listening to the speakers on that fateful day.[51] Although shocked and dismayed at first, Klein had a political awakening that permitted her to reframe her life, to think about the ways in which popular culture's emphasis on autonomy masks interdependence that all people have and need. Through the disability community, Klein is also able to begin to accept and feel good about her different body.

Not surprisingly, almost all of the couples in this study participated in disability activism, which helped strengthen their sense of community and pride, much as the authors of the self-representations describe. Rachel, from Focus Group 1, ran a support group for people with disabilities like herself. The rest of the participants in Focus Group 1 were members of the MS Society. Before they were even together, Jeff (Tracy's husband) participated in MS walks. Participants from Focus Group 2 and Focus Group 3 worked at the Centers for Independent Living, helping people with disabilities live in the community. In addition, Rachel and Allison were pursuing careers that would allow them to work with people with disabilities, presumably helping them in ways they wished they would have been helped by social workers and occupational therapists. Connection to the disability community was important to all the participants because it affirmed their lives and relationships. Additionally, the political power of the various organizations helped participants shape the world they live in, making it more accessible and friendly for people like themselves.

Although politically active (sometimes even aggressive, when needed), the disabled/nondisabled couples in this study were aware of the need to make their lives and realities familiar or relatable to the nondisabled. As already noted, the physical realities of impairment can make the disabled experience quite alien, and the fear of becoming disabled oneself often leads nondisabled people to distance themselves from the disabled through staring, joking, and so forth. Aware of this reality, disabled authors and directors use strategies that position the familiar with the unfamiliar in order to facilitate audience identification across the difference that disability makes. For example, as Mairs does in writing, Bob Flanagan employs a "strategy of layered (un)familiarity," frequently coupling scenes that "evoke a flash of shock and pity" with scenes that encourage spectator identification.[52] Flanagan's primary method of encouraging engagement was humor. Dawn Reynolds writes:

> Laughter created collaborators: Those at Flanagan's exhibit who understood his humorous touches were conspirators in his quest to open up conversations

about and connections to sexuality, illness, and death. The artist's use of humor served to disarm and put at ease even the most squeamish audiences. During one particular performance, in which Flanagan sewed his penis inside his scrotum, his monologue included jokes, which he believed put his audience off guard and distracted them from what he was actually doing. He argued that people would "accept it better if I'm sitting there telling jokes like I'm working on some macramé or needlepoint—well, this [scrotum-sewing] is a form of needlepoint!"[53]

Thus, Flanagan's performances could deal with heavy issues—bondage, discipline, dominance, submission, sadism, and masochism (BDSM) sexuality; death; the physical pain of cystic fibrosis—without completely alienating his audiences. *Sick: The Life and Death of Bob Flanagan Supermasochist* recreates this layered (un)familiarity by juxtaposing scenes in which Bob and Sheree are mundanely talking with scenes of BDSM.[54]

Similarly, *Want* and *Shameless* mix strategies that encourage spectator identification and distance.[55] For example, in *Shameless,* to see Klein fall in her bedroom, to see McMurchy struggle with grasping and handling a set of springs, and to see Roche's disfigured face all may provoke a sense of distance from nondisabled audiences, but each of these scenes stands next to images and acts that emphasize how similar people with disabilities are to the nondisabled. Roche is loved and massaged by his able-bodied wife, Klein talks about wanting to "look good" for the camera and put on makeup, and McMurchy talks about enjoying his independence. Thus, over the course of the film, *Shameless* shows filmmakers and subjects as both different and similar to nondisabled audiences.

Want uses the different channels of expression available to a filmmaker to simultaneously layer the familiar with the unfamiliar. For example, during the care montage sequence in which Loree's friends help her with toileting, on top of the music Loree is heard in voice-over saying, "I want to be a girl you laugh with . . . a girl you have fun with . . . a girl who cares for your heavy heart . . . a girl you respect . . . a girl who makes you stop and think about the world around you . . . a girl you can be real with . . . I want it all." Everyone, regardless of disability, can identify with Loree's desires. The image channel, however, is showing an experience that is likely to be alienating to nondisabled audiences. By coupling the two, image and sound, Loree increases the chances that audiences will be able to adjust, continue to engage the film, and perhaps begin to understand the disability experience.

Layering the familiar with the unfamiliar theoretically increases the openness of the audience toward difference. It invites looking, not staring, that can potentially bridge the gap between the nondisabled and the disabled. Thus, in *Want, Shameless*, and *Sick*, audiences can take in the difference of disability and sexuality, including the need for care between intimate partners. This technique can make readable the political critique offered by disability self-representations.

Although the focus group participants and the authors of the published self-representations all experienced various forms of discrimination and prejudice, they weathered this storm by employing strategies of resistance such as disability humor, pride, and political/social criticism. I believe these forms of resistance help disabled/nondisabled couples ward off the pressures from the outside world to view themselves as weird, unworthy, and inferior. It could be that, even without these strategies, their love alone would help them survive. However, humor, pride, and political/social criticism featured so heavily in all the stories I collected and analyzed that I doubt love is enough. Love is a strong emotion; however, it is rarely, if ever, the only thing that makes a couple work. In the next chapter, I will turn to how disabled/nondisabled couples express love.

Notes

1. Klein and Blackbridge, *Slow Dance*, pp. 317–319.
2. Mairs, *Waist-High*, pp. 192–194.
3. Hockenberry, *Moving Violations*, p. 298.
4. Ibid., p. 299.
5. Garland-Thomson, *Extraordinary Bodies*, p. 217.
6. Murphy, *The Body Silent*, pp. 116–117.
7. Hockenberry, *Moving Violations*, p. 131.
8. Skloot, "A Measure of Acceptance," p. 195.
9. Ibid., p. 202.
10. Ibid., p. 205.
11. Ibid., p. 206.
12. Asch and Fine, "Nurturance, Sexuality and Women with Disabilities," p. 245.
13. See, for example, Olkin, "Women with Physical Disabilities."
14. Singh and Sharma, "Sexuality and Women," p. 29.
15. Adam was considered the nondisabled partner in my study because he was largely not symptomatic. Sabrina was the disabled partner because she did need help with one or more activities of daily living as a result of the MS. As is the nature of the disease, Adam will also likely need help with activities of daily living as the MS progresses.
16. It is quite possible that Richard's former friends also saw the relationship, and now Richard, as sexually deviant.
17. Tepper, "What Does?"
18. Albrecht, "Disability Humor"; Shakespeare, "Joking a Part."
19. Stronach and Allan, "Joking with Disability."
20. Albrecht, "Disability Humor"; Stronach and Allan, "Joking with Disability"; Shakespeare, "Joking a Part."
21. Hockenberry, *Moving Violations*, p. 197.
22. Mairs, *Waist-High*, p. 16.
23. Shakespeare, "Joking a Part."
24. Mairs, *Waist-High*, p. 46.
25. Shakespeare, "Joking a Part," 50.
26. Mairs, *Waist-High*, p. 32.

27. Ibid., p. 46.

28. Ibid., p. 38.

29. Ibid., p. 42.

30. Ibid., p. 41.

31. See, for example, Li and Yau, "Sexual Issues"; and Singh and Sharma, "Sexuality and Women."

32. Mairs, *Waist-High*, pp. 8–10.

33. Shakespeare, Gillespie-Sells, and Davies, *The Sexual Politics*, p. 49.

34. Ibid., p. 68.

35. "Girlfriend," Mothers Against Drunk Driving Canada (2005).

36. *An Affair to Remember* was released in 1957.

37. Mairs, *Waist-High*, p. 96.

38. Ibid.

39. Ibid., p. 104.

40. Siebers, "Disability in Theory," p. 746.

41. Ibid., p. 747.

42. Wade, "It Ain't," p. 90.

43. *Shameless: The ART of Disability*, directed by Bonnie Sherr Klein, 2006 (Montreal, Quebec: National Film Board of Canada), DVD; *Want*, directed by Loree Erickson, 2007 (Toronto, Ontario: Femmegimp Productions), DVD.

44. Murphy, *The Body Silent*, p. 201.

45. Ibid., p. 74.

46. Ibid., p. 66.

47. Ibid., p. 227.

48. Kondracke, *Saving Milly*, p. 109.

49. Ibid., pp. 122–124.

50. *Want*, directed by Loree Erickson, 2007 (Toronto, Ontario: Femmegimp Productions), DVD.

51. Klein and Blackbridge, *Slow Dance*, p. 349.

52. Mintz, "Transforming the Tale," p. 266.

53. Dawn Reynolds, "Disability and BDSM," p. 47.

54. *Sick*, directed by Kirby Dick, 1997 (Santa Monica, CA: Lion's Gate Home Entertainment), DVD.

55. *Want*, directed by Loree Erickson, 2007 (Toronto, Ontario: Femmegimp Productions), DVD; *Shameless: The ART of Disability*, directed by Bonnie Sherr Klein, 2006 (Montreal, Quebec: National Film Board of Canada), DVD.

6

Love

Love is by far the most significant theme to emerge in my research on disabled/nondisabled couplings. All of the focus group participants and the authors of published self-representations discussed in Part 2 of this book claim to be in love. But what does that mean to these couples, and how do their versions of love speak to the existing literature about love? Is love expressed differently in disabled/nondisabled intimate relationships? If so, why? In this chapter, I will analyze what disabled/nondisabled couples say about love and how they express love to each other. I argue that disability does make a difference for these couples. In other words, disability affects how love is experienced and expressed. However, contrary to what may be expected from popular representations of disabled/nondisabled couples, the disability seems to strengthen or clarify love. Disabled/nondisabled couples are hyperaware of the need for respect, trust, and reciprocity in love relationships and, because of the physical impairment, they work vigilantly to nurture these qualities. They are conscious of the need to work at love and, in this sense, disabled/nondisabled couples may be better tooled for love than nondisabled couples.

Studying Love

Romantic or companion love is a notoriously different phenomenon to define, particularly from a feminist, disability perspective. It seems necessary to insist that such love between adults is characterized by sexual passion and concern for each other's well-being, but these traits alone do not confer the sense of union that anyone in love has experienced. Nor does the addition of union differentiate what feminists would define as harmful relationships from healthy love. Feeling too much concern for the other can have the effect of eclipsing personal autonomy so that my concern for you could cause me to act in ways that are bad,

115

even life-threatening, for me. Conversely, feeling too much concern for myself in our relationship could mean that I control our relationship. You may consent, but only because I have exhausted you, or because I have made it clear that the consequences of not consenting are far worse than just giving in to begin with. What is too much and what is too little is sometimes difficult to define. Nonetheless, we *love* love; most of us want to be in love if we're not already, and work at keeping love if we have it. But it is also messy and complicated.

It is for these very reasons that there has been so little said about love in the formidable body of feminist literature (and the growing body of disability literature).[1] Most of what is written about love in the feminist literature is about bad love, abusive love—what love should not be. There are, however, a few feminist scholars who have described the positive aspects of love. To understand what love should be, I have drawn primarily from Andrea Westlund's work on marriage, Jessica Benjamin's concept of intersubjectivity and Gail Weiss's related concept of intercorporeality, and Marguerite La Caze's analysis of Immanuel Kant and Luce Irigaray.[2] Using these feminist thinkers, I cobble out a sketch of "healthy" romantic love that I use to compare the expression of love in disabled/nondisabled intimate relationships. In addition, I map out how these concepts are visible in the study of narrative and identity. Although not concerned with the expression of love per se, autobiographical scholars like Paul John Eakin and Susanna Egan provide useful frames for seeing relationality in self-representations.[3]

Critical of what she calls "union" theories of love, Westlund sets out to forge a rehabilitated, feminist understanding of companion love that "neither threatens the autonomy of the individual parties nor erodes the boundaries of their own identities."[4] According to Westlund, union theories emphasize a oneness or merging that, understandingly so, makes feminists wary. For far too long, the idealized version of love for women has been absorption into the other, the erasure of self-identity. Yet Westlund does not want to abandon the project of theorizing the togetherness of love. After all, it is possible to be in love and experience union, yet retain one's distinct sense of self. Westlund suggests that it is helpful to think of lovers "united in the ongoing process of forging a *shared practical perspective*," a collaborative way of prioritizing and planning, evaluating and remembering.[5] She goes on to state:

> Because building a shared practical perspective is an ongoing process that requires ongoing reconciliation of distinct practical perspectives, I'll argue that union in marriage is best understood as a kind of *re*union. As such, it depends on the persistence of dialogue between distinct individuals, whose efforts to build a shared perspective are at the same time efforts to achieve and sustain the reciprocity of mutual recognition.[6]

Thus, instead of complete merger or absolute separateness, the shared practical perspective focuses on what is created between joined individuals.

Westlund's focus on interaction between subjects and the need for reciprocity and mutual recognition in love relationships evokes Benjamin's concept of intersubjectivity, a psychologically ideal state of subjectivity in which "the individual grows in and through the relationship to other subjects."[7] As an alternative to ego psychology, which emphasizes separation and individuation as healthy self-development, intersubjectivity theory focuses on "the need for mutual recognition, the necessity of recognizing as well as being recognized by an other."[8] Benjamin explains, "The need for recognition entails this fundamental paradox: at the very moment of realizing our own independence we are dependent upon another to recognize it."[9] Thus, our subjectivity is intimately connected to others. There would be no "I" without another to care for, recognize, and be affected by it.

Because the selves of the self-representations that I analyzed are marked by physical impairment, the role of the body in the process of intersubjectivity is paramount. The body becomes the "corporeal substratum of identity"; it shapes and is shaped by other bodies and environments.[10] The caregiver's sense of self is affected by the disabled body it cares for; likewise, the disabled body's sense of self is affected by the body that moves it. Since bodies are so important in the relational lives that I analyzed, Gail Weiss's concept of intercorporeality is a useful way to conceptualize the intersubjective moments in the texts that take place through bodies.[11] As Weiss notes, "the experience of being embodied is never a private affair."[12] It is an unconscious, "ongoing exchange between bodies and body images."[13] By "body image," Weiss is referring to proprioception, the sense of one's body in space, how it looks, feels, and is bounded. Individuals have many different body images (although relative stability is needed for reliable movement and response) and these body images adjust in response to physical changes within the body, the physical environment, and the other bodies one encounters. Intercorporeality "implies that body images are in continual interaction with one another, participating in a mutually constitutive corporeal dialogue that defies solipsistic analysis."[14] Thus, intersubjectivity and intercorporeality emphasize the "dialogue between distinct individuals" in Westlund's shared perspective.[15]

The actions of each individual in the dialogue are critical to maintaining the sense of relationality that Benjamin and Westlund outline. La Caze, using Kant and Irigaray, helps parse out the role of the individual in love relationships. Kant is particularly useful because of his emphasis on respect for the other as an essential duty in love. He argues that love implies that the loved one is obliged to offer something in return.[16] Failure to, at a minimum, show gratitude for love will lead to the ultimate demise of the love relationship. This sense of obligation to return love is extremely important in disabled/ nondisabled intimate relationships. There may be times in which one partner contributes more than the other because of the physical impairment; however, if this imbalance persists, love begins to wane. Thus, care relationships based on romantic love are distinct from other care relationships because of this need for concrete reciprocity.[17] Giving some kind of return for physical care, whether it is in the form of gratitude, emotional care, or other forms of physical care, is key to showing respect. However, for Kant, respect is essential to love because it helps keep it in balance. As love draws you closer to the other, you risk absorbing the other into you, erasing differences between yourself and the other. Respect encourages you to keep your distance. It repels love, keeping love in check. La Caze argues that Kant overemphasizes the conflict between love and respect.[18] I agree, and I add that, particularly in disabled/nondisabled love relationships, respect is not (and should not) always be expressed as a pulling away or distancing.

La Caze argues that Irigaray offers a more nuanced place for respect. For Irigaray, respect is not an opposite duty to love, but an essentially integrated component, perhaps even a condition for love, because "for love to exist between two people, both must be independent beings who are not subsumed in love. Love must accept difference and specificity in the other."[19] In other words, love is not possible in the first place without the ability to like and respect the other person. La Caze uses Irigaray's discussion of wonder to explain how respect for the other may also be a pulling toward (not necessarily only a pulling away, as in Kant). She says, "Wonder is a nonjudgmental openness to difference."[20] The other's difference from oneself, his or her individuality, is what fuels wonder in love relationships. If a lover becomes too controlling and subsumes the other, wonder disappears because there is no longer a difference. Wonder is a particularly good way to explain desire and love in disabled/nondisabled relationships. In addition to all the typical ways in which lovers may be different from each other, disabled/nondisabled couples have a corporeal variation. Accepting that difference is the first step to interdisability love; maintaining that difference is key to their ongoing love.

Wonder for the other is also an ongoing process. Whereas Kant argued that love cannot be demanded, Irigaray says that love can be "cultivated or is 'governable.'"[21] La Caze goes on to say, "Since love, like other passions, involves understanding, it can be cultivated or educated . . . we can bring about the conditions for loving relations, we can educate people to be loving, and we can nurture loving feelings in ourselves."[22] Framing love as something that needs supplemental education is particularly useful in the context of disability because physical demands and capabilities change over time, necessitating experimentation and communication. In other words, the couple can never stop learning about disability if their love is to continue. Part of this learning is also learning to love oneself, which, as both Irigaray and Kant acknowledge, is fundamental to loving others.[23] In our context, then, love must be connected to disability pride. Disabled partners must be able to love themselves, to see themselves as a being worthy of love and intimacy, if they are to be in a meaningful, lasting, romantic relationship. This can be a particularly difficult task since social and cultural circumstances impact one's self-image. Thus, self-love is something that must be continually worked on for love relationships to continue.

Individuals in love, then, have several duties to self and other that are necessary to maintain the balance characteristic of intersubjectivity and sharing a common perspective. Each lover must love himself or herself, be willing to learn about new dimensions of both self and other, express wonder at the other's difference, and show respect through reciprocity. In the focus groups, these tasks were often explicitly discussed. These love duties were less explicit in the autobiographical self-representations because I could not ask the authors about tactics to probe for ways in which they balance self and other in their love relationships. However, narrative theory provides some useful ways to see this balance between self and other in the style and form of the text. So, before I turn to the analysis of love in the self-representations, it is helpful to briefly outline some of the relevant work on intersubjectivity in autobiography.

In autobiographical studies, Eakin uses the term "relational life" to describe the intersubjective identity model. Eakin says that the "relational life" is the "story of a relational model of identity, developed collaboratively with others, often family members."[24] The relational life makes connection very obvious. The lives of others figure prominently in the autobiographies of relational selves, so much so that the text becomes part biography of the proximate other(s) or ethnography of the proximate community.[25] Physical impairment can facilitate the saliency of relationality because the disabled person needs the other in atypical ways. Indeed, the disability rights movement puts forth the concept of interdependency[26] to emphasize how the disabled and nondisabled alike are dependent on others for daily survival. The authors whom I analyze below are aware of the way in which caregiving and receiving can help them see their connection to others, and they mark this connection by using a variety of strategies.

One way that intersubjectivity is marked in the texts is through what Egan calls "mirror talk": the dialogue between two characters, the dialogue between reader and author, and the internal dialogue of the narrator in autobiographical texts.[27] Mirror talk includes all the dialogic moments that create the relational self. Egan argues that this mirror talk exemplifies intersubjectivity because it stresses the need for a subject to be recognized by another subject. The dialogic moments in autobiographical texts enact intersubjectivity, producing a self in relation to an other, producing a narrator always in the process of subject formation. In other words, through dialogue with the writer, with the reader, and between characters, the narrator emerges into subjectivity.

Because I am particularly interested in the author's relationship with romantic partners, I will focus on the mirror talk between the author and his or her lover in the texts that I analyze. By paying attention to literary strategies, it becomes possible to see the way that authors of self-representations articulate intercorporeality, their connection to other bodies. The intersubjectivity of the couples in the focus groups was direct. Focus group participants could articulate their sense of relationality more explicitly, and they were particularly adept at doing so. Disability had forced all of the participants and the authors to recognize the ongoing struggle between connection and separation. They were familiar with talking about their love as a balance, and they were keenly aware of the roles of respect, trust, and reciprocity in the maintenance of love. This ability and willingness to acknowledge the struggle and work of love is one of the advantages that interdisability couples have over nondisabled couples. Following idealized notions of romantic love, many people believe love is organic and effortless. Disabled/nondisabled couples know better. They know that keeping connection and separation in play, and maximizing reciprocity, are the hallmarks of good love. In the sections below, I will show how disabled/nondisabled couples express these two characteristics of love— intersubjectivity and reciprocity—and fulfill their duties to love themselves, continually learn about disability, express wonder, and show respect.

Intersubjectivity: Balancing Self and Other

Intersubjectivity—the way in which the self and other engage in mutual recognition and construct a shared perspective—is highly evident in all the published self-representations that I analyzed.[28] Bonnie Sherr Klein and Persimmon Blackbridge's *Slow Dance: A Story of Stroke, Love, and Disability* is intersubjective in content and form, and there are points in the texts where it is difficult for readers (and for Klein) to clearly discern her voice from the voice of others. Largely, this is because Klein, who became disabled through a stroke, refuses sole authorship in a variety of ways. First, she uses a coauthor, feminist writer and performer Blackbridge, to construct the text. As Klein explains in the preface, Blackbridge helped her assemble and edit the journal entries that form the backbone of the book, but also asked her questions about her memories to help narrate the story, adding depth and texture to the account. Even though Klein did most of the writing and Blackbridge did most of the assembling, Klein says, "To say I 'wrote' the book and Persimmon 'edited' it would not acknowledge the reality of our collaborative process. . . . The manuscript moved back and forth between us until we stopped knowing whose idea was whose."[29] Klein's story emerges, literally, from the exchange between Blackbridge and herself. Thus, it is impossible to know for sure what is Klein and what is Blackbridge in the text, and that is precisely Klein's point. Her life and work are so relational that the self/other distinction is lost.

In addition to using Blackbridge as coauthor, she includes the writings of friends, doctors, and family members along with hers. Most prominent are the writings of her husband, Michael, and children, Naomi and Seth. Frequently their words are set off in blocks with the speaker's name like the text of a play. Doctors' and nurses' chart reports appear throughout in a different text font than the rest of the book. And, in sections of the story in which Klein was unable to speak (because of the stroke she experienced a period of being "locked-in"), she represents her internal thoughts with italicized text. The block quotes, chart reports, and italicized text intermingle among the regular voice of the narrating Klein/Blackbridge to create a truly dynamic reading experience. Sometimes these voices disagree, complicating the picture for readers. For example, during Klein's locked-in period, she experienced terrifying nightmares and panic attacks. A portion of the text at this point reads:

> MICHAEL: The phone was next to your bed so that if you got particularly anxious, the nurses could call me and put the phone to your ear and I would talk to you. You couldn't talk to me, but you could hear my voice.
>
> *I was afraid to sleep because that's when the film loop would start. But I wouldn't get well unless I slept. It went around and around. Michael was gone.*
>
> It took me a long time to get the nurse's attention, and a long time to tell her what I needed. She refused to call Michael. She told me I was being a baby, that he had to eat and sleep and play tennis, so I would have to wait until he came back. She smiled and patted my hand. "He needs some time for himself." "No," I wanted to yell, "I don't care what he needs. If he knew how desperate I am, he would want to be with me and save me."[30]

In this selection, the multiple voices—Michael, Klein's memory of internal thought, Klein's present voice, and the nurse—create a cacophony. At other points, the voices overlap, so much so that Klein asks, "Which memories are mine and which are Michael's?"[31] Together, these voices narrate Klein's experience with becoming disabled through a stroke because, as she notes, "we are living this together."[32] For Klein, telling her story with a singular voice would pervert the way in which her experience of disability has been interdependent. Her disability identity has been formed through the reactions, emotions, and thoughts of those important to her; thus, their voices are central to her story. Klein shows respect for Michael and her family through these representational strategies.

For Marion Deutsche Cohen, living with disability—and writing about it in *Dirty Details: The Days and Nights of a Well Spouse*—are also a family affair. Cohen is the nondisabled spouse of Jeff, who has MS. Although Cohen is Jeff's primary caregiver, their children—Marielle, Arin, Bret, and Devin—help out frequently. Even when not actively involved with the physical care, Cohen is conscious of how Jeff's disability affects the whole family. Instead of thinking of the disabled individual in their family, Cohen thinks in terms of the "disabled family" because "Jeff's MS makes the entire household disabled."[33]

Everyone is impacted, in both positive and negative ways. Cohen worries that the children will resent the way in which Jeff's disability tied them to home much of the time. She also notes that Arin and Bret, two of the children who performed a lot of physical care, became emotionally and physically burned-out with caregiving. When Jeff was living in the home (he was eventually placed in a nursing home), family time was frequently interrupted with requests for toilet assistance and other needs. Nonetheless, in-home care also meant that the family was together more often and that care, fun, and work became integrated. Cohen writes:

> If it was a scary home, it was also loving. Jeff's illness meant we were together more; we often had to be. Sometimes we resented it, but what I remember is lounging on the big bed—Jeff, me, and the two youngest. I remember reading or drawing with Bret while nursing Dev. I remember Jeff helping Bret with physics. Or all of us parallel playing or parallel working—Bret drawing, Dev playing UNO or Lego, Jeff doing physics, me writing. We also spent some nights together on that big bed; that is, we had what's known as "the family bed," all of us sleeping together.[34]

Care and disability were stressful, but they also glued the family together, making their connections explicit. Work, play, and care became intermingled activities; therefore, Cohen's identities of academic, writer, mother, wife, and caregiver are often impossible to tease apart in the text. "Family bed" was a positive aspect of her relational life; stress and burnout when she was pulled in too many directions at once formed the negative. By revealing both, Cohen is able to provide a complex critique of home care in a society that devalues care, both socially and financially.

Nancy Mairs is explicit that her intent is to bring her interconnected, embodied disability experience into the light, to make it public, "through the lens of my own experience and those of people I know well."[35] Describing her life with MS as "a project, in which others must participate if it is to prosper," Mairs's narration from what she calls "a crippled female body" clearly connects her body to the bodies (and experiences) of others (especially her husband, George).[36] Thus, the detailed descriptions of other people's stories, such as the stranger, Jenny, who calls Nancy to discuss possible symptoms of MS she is experiencing, as well as the intimate details disclosed about George and their children, function to emphasize Mairs's relationships to friends, family, and acquaintances. These voices help situate Mairs's embodied subjectivity and make visible the lives of other people with disabilities.

Yet Mairs is careful to draw attention to her own specificity. She says, "At the outset, I want to make clear that I speak as an individual and not as a representative of 'my kind.'"[37] People with disabilities form a large and diverse group, and Mairs does not claim to speak for or represent all disabled people. Mairs's preference to call herself "cripple" reflects this specificity of representation: "Because it is a word that many people with disabilities find deeply offensive, I apply it only to myself, and so it reminds me that I am not speaking for others."[38] This acknowledgment of separateness is paramount to the intersubjective self because recognition is meaningful only from other subjects. As Benjamin notes, "In the balance between self and other, disengagement (open space) is as important as engagement."[39] In other words, the other must also be a subject in his or her own right, distinct from Mairs's self, in order to enter into mirror talk.

To help make the voices of others more salient and thus emphasize the other's subjectivity, all of the authors, except for Murphy, frequently reproduce conversations they have had with others, sometimes even using quotation marks to authorize their words. For example, in her essay titled "Taking Care," Mairs uses quotation marks around her husband's comments about caring for Mairs.[40] And in "Freeing Choices," quotation marks are used around her daughter's concern over having a child with a disability. In both of these cases, quotation marks are ways to mark off and emphasize another's subjectivity. Interestingly, Mairs also seems to be quoting from written texts at points. For example, "The Wider World" includes what appears to be a journal entry from George about their travels in England.[41] And, in "Ups and Downs," Mairs provides snippets from Anne and Matthew's written response to the prompt "on being raised by a cripple."[42] It is important for Mairs to represent the other as a subject, separate—but connected to—her own subjectivity. Direct quotations help emphasize that Mairs is "narrating an individual (but affiliated) life."[43]

Morton Kondracke also uses quotation marks to emphasize Milly's separateness, and Milly's speech via the computer (which she employs when she is unable to use her voice) is represented in capital letters in the text. In addition, Kondracke includes Milly's reaction to the book's publication in the 2002 afterword, emphasizing both her relation and distinctiveness to her husband's text.[44] Similarly, Marion Deutsche Cohen states that she waited to share her poems and prose about dealing with MS until Jeff was ready to "come out."[45] She also includes Jeff's response to having someone take photos of their life for the book, noting that he limited access to above the belt photos. Including such permissions and responses is important for both Kondracke and Cohen because they are sharing private details about their partners. Without their partners' voices in the text, they would risk objectifying them. Including their voices and responses emphasizes that Milly and Jeff are subjects in their own right. Such literary tactics demonstrate how respect for the other's individuality is important in disabled/nondisabled love relations.

However, the other's distinction is not complete from the author's in these texts. For example, in Mairs's text, the quotation marks draw a rather permeable boundary around the bodies and voices of those to whom she is connected. After all, citations do not accompany these quotations; thus, the authenticity of these words is not concrete. And quotation marks are not used consistently to mark another's subjectivity. Often, Mairs takes the liberty of paraphrasing another's words. This is done, for example, with the patients of Don and Joyce in the essay "Getting Byned." Their comments are paraphrased instead of quoted. Similarly, George's opinions and thoughts often go unquoted, even when the content seems highly intimate and personal. Like other main characters, George's own words are often set apart, but he also occupies much of the text outside of the quotations, quite literally mingling in and out of the essays. For example, readers learn that George is impotent and has accepted his body and its functions outside quotation marks.[46] By intermittingly using and refusing direct quotations, Mairs seems to be emphasizing both the separateness and connectiveness inherent in embodied subjectivity.

Balancing separation and engagement is an ongoing struggle in relational lives, especially when engagement is necessary for basic physical needs like eating, toileting, and dressing. Care relationships can collapse when there is inadequate differentiation or inefficient connection. As mentioned above, Marion Deutsche Cohen ultimately becomes overwhelmed with in-home care and has to place Jeff in a nursing home. As Jeff becomes more physically impaired, Cohen writes, "I was too busy doing nights, lifting, and toilet, or worrying or tantruming about them. I was also busy sorting things out, protecting the me in me (finding time and space for writing, teaching, thrift shopping, singing) and protecting the mother in me, for the sake of both the kids and me. . . . I was, in short, fighting for my life."[47] The balance between self and other in Cohen's relationship with Jeff begins to tip and she starts to feel consumed. Kondracke, too, is aware of this possibility for caregivers, but he has the race, gender, and class privilege to protect him from this fate.

Balancing self and other was also a central theme in the focus group discussions. Unlike the written self-representations, however, the focus group participants emphasized the initial and ongoing need to build trust in order for intersubjectivity to flourish. Whereas the authors discussed above used quotation marks and voice to indicate the distinction between self and other, focus group participants discussed testing to discern and monitor their loved one's commitment and self-survival.

"Testing" involves the use of distancing maneuvers that the disabled partner hurdles at the nondisabled partner to see if he or she can stay in the relationship. From an intersubjective standpoint, it is literally the way in which the other's survivability and distinction as a separate self are formed. As Benjamin notes, a baby learns that the mother or breast is not simply an extension of his or her self when the mother refuses to do what the baby wants.[48] The baby is connected, but separate from the mother. Likewise, the nondisabled partner's refusal to give in to the test shows the disabled spouse that he or she will remain connected, but separate. Sometimes this testing periodically continued into the long-term relationship to ensure that the nondisabled partner would stay, but generally it seemed that this testing was most pronounced during the early parts of the relationship. For example, Randall and Emma both used their speech (both have speech impairment from cerebral palsy) as a test early in their relationships:

> OLIVIA: —'cause we talked online for like three months before we met, and I loved him before I met him. And then when I kept bugging him, like, "Why won't you let me call you?" he said, "You know, I'm different from everybody else." And I said, "So I am too, you know, I'm from the country." He said, "No, you don't understand." And that funny story, that, it always cracks me up. He always says, "You know, to describe how I talk, go drink a six-pack of beer and then listen to yourself talk and that is how I sound." And so, he told me to call his pager—at the time, that is so long ago he had a pager. . . . He said, "Call my pager. If you can understand my message on my pager, leave a message and I'll call you back." So, when I called his pager, I repeated what he said on his pager and then we talked after that.
>
> EMMA: We kinda had the same experience. I was trying to discourage him from calling because I, um, I told him up-front that I was disabled, but that can mean anything. I didn't tell him what my disability was or how severe it was or anything. [*inaudible*] And then he said, "Why don't we meet in the zoo or at the park or somewhere public?" And I'm like, "OK, it's time to discourage him!" [*laughter*] So I just tell him every bad thing I could think of so . . . [*inaudible*] He said, "Oh, I can put your wheelchair in my car. Help you in the car. That is no problem." And I thought when he heard my voice on the phone—we had to connect for some reason, you wanted to tell me something or . . .
>
> RICHARD: I don't remember.
>
> EMMA: We were forced to talk on the phone. [*inaudible*] I thought after hearing my voice, he'll make up an excuse not to. [*inaudible*]

Of course, Richard and Olivia passed Emma's and Randall's respective tests, but it is important to remember that the disabled partners set up these tests in the first place because nondisabled people have failed in the past.

Frequently, the testing continued in the relationship. Rachel explains that she continues to test Jack:

> Yeah! I'm like, all right, and I kept testing him, remember I kept testing you? [*laughter*] I even to this day kinda do! Like, I think of some crazy thing, like,

would you . . . —with your situation catheter or something? [*to Sabrina*]
Would you do IV fluids [*inaudible*] on me if you had to? Yeah. Would you do
a PICC line [peripherally inserted central catheter]? Yeah. Okay. And I just
constantly test him, you know, and, um, I did all through our relationship.

Rachel's continual interrogation of Jack's limits helps assure her that he can
handle anything he may have to do as a result of her disability. Because care
is associated with burden in popular culture, and because participants had
either had firsthand experience with abandonment or knew a friend that had,
the fear is real. The testing that most of the participants talked about was an
attempt to weed out the potential flight risks. As Emma explains:

Yeah. Getting to—when he's gone, he's gone. So at the beginning of the relationship, like the first two years, I would tell him to go away, get lost. I don't
want you. I would say all kinds of horrible things just to get him to leave
because I knew eventually if he did leave I'd be on my own again and I didn't
want that shock factor to happen . . . you know what I mean?

Testing is a form of protection, and it is integral to developing trust in the dis-
abled/nondisabled relationship and establishing the balance between self and
other. This is particularly important in disabled/nondisabled relationships because it takes an enormous amount of trust on the disabled partner's part to
rely on the nondisabled partner for activities of daily living.

Once the nondisabled partner had passed all the tests, the couple continued to work on maintaining delicate balance between self and other. In the
focus groups, couples often articulated this tension as maintaining balance
between care and self-reliance. Almost all of the disabled participants noted
that it was important that they be able to do some things on their own, to be
independent in some areas of their lives. But they also understood that the
need to be self-reliant one minute, and then need physical help the next, could
be confusing to their partners and loved ones.

ELLEN: Our family's wonderful, they're great. Um, being a person
with MS, I want my independence and I want to take care of
my children and I want to take care of my household and do
what I can possibly do. . . . There is things I've learned that I
can't, but it's hard when they see you struggling to do simple
day tasks. . . . This is how I get through, this is how I do the
dishes or how I do the laundry or whatever the case may be. To
me, it's not a struggle, this is what I do and the overprotective-
ness . . . wanting to jump in can drive you a little batty at times.
It's nice to have that compassion and to have closeness, but it

gets [*laughter*] a little bit—, even from a spouse too—, it sounds very protective. And he's learning. [*laughter*]

KEVIN: Yes, dear. [*laughter*]

To feel like a full adult, Ellen needs to be able to do the laundry—even if it takes her twice as long and exhausts her. In this sense, Ellen is asking her family to suspend judgment and experience wonder at the different way she now accomplishes household tasks. This space also requires Kevin to learn how to read Ellen, a considerable challenge since MS is an impairment characterized by change. What Ellen could do one day, she may not be able to do the next. As her body changes, both partners must adapt, learning new ways to express love and complete tasks of daily living.

Ellen's desire to do things independently as her body permits speaks to the duties of learning and wonder required of love relationships, and her desire to do things "on her own" was a common expression. Allison and Connie in Focus Group 4 discuss similar desires:

ALLISON: Like the other day, we were at dinner and Jason's like, "You're holding [the menu] upside down so why are you even holding it?" But I don't know, it's just something I do . . . you know what I mean, like I just . . . I don't know. I mean he's really, really helpful. I think that, as we've grown up together, he just knows when he can step in and knows when to step out. He knows how to be helpful, but he also knows when I should do things for myself and I never want it to be a relationship where he felt like he had to do things for me. . . . Like I want to still try to do things for myself and so we're still working and building on that but . . . 'cause if it was up to him I could still do everything and I know that there are things that I can do and I can't allow him to do all of that for me so . . .

CONNIE: Isn't that amazing? We have great guys. They want to do stuff for us, but I'm the same way. It's like I can walk up the stairs by myself.

ALLISON: Well, it's like the biggest thing is that like my parents did everything for me when I was in high school, like all my cooking and laundry and everything. And then when I get to college, we had dorm food or whatever, but then when we moved in together he does all the cooking like all the time. And he's just afraid that maybe I would hurt myself or whatever, but I really want to start trying that. And I'm like . . . he'll be like, "Oh, let me just do that." And I'm like, "No, stop it. I want to try to do it myself." So, I think that's the thing right now is like I just want to try to be more independent . . . at least in the kitchen and things like that. But I mean I do most of the cleaning, I do most of the laundry and independently, and I feel good when I can do something for the benefit of both of us but . . . 'cause I know that driving he has to do, and helping me at the store he has to do, and things like that, so I feel like this is something I can contribute.

The balance between self-reliance and receiving help was an ongoing struggle that each couple had to negotiate. While this is true of all couples, the presence of impairment makes disabled/nondisabled couples hyperaware of the need to do things on one's own while in a relationship. When successful, the couple was able to develop a sense of interdependence that allowed the disabled partner to give back or reciprocate for all the physical care received from the nondisabled mate.

A common barrier to the self/other or self-reliance/care balance was the need for outside help. About half of the participants also used some form of outside help.[49] This was in the form of both respite care and personal care assistants in addition to the partner.[50] Outside aid helped the couple by providing relief, but it also hindered by creating a source of stress for most of the couples. In the following conversation from Focus Group 1, several key problems with getting help emerged:

ADAM: Did you ever notice that you guys, when they have somebody from the outside come in, that you fight more often then?

RACHEL: Yeah.

ADAM: The arguing is more.

RACHEL: Yeah.

SARAH: It's like you guys were saying . . . it's easier to handle, sometimes it's easier to arrange the care between yourselves.

ALL: Yeah.

SABRINA: You almost feel like you have to entertain that person that is there to help you too.

ALL: Right.

SABRINA: Interact with them when, if you don't feel good and you're tired anyways, that is the last thing you want to do.

ALL: Right.

SABRINA: You feel they're in your home, so it's your responsibility.

Feeling the need to tend to the helper defeats—to a point—having a helper in the first place. In addition, aides were a source of tension between lovers. Many of the less disabled couples used this as the reason that they were avoiding outside help.

Some participants, however, had to use aides because their level of impairment required twenty-four-hour care. Rachel, for example, used personal care assistants when Jack was at work. For the people who had to rely on personal care assistants, lack of privacy and the instability of workers were two major struggles. In fact, problems with aides dominated both Rachel's and Jack's follow-up journals. At one point Jack explains that "the only reason I keep bringing the aide issues up is because that's where most of any friction between me and Rachel develops." Rachel and Jack talk about aides being lazy, treating Rachel poorly or abusively (e.g., refusing to feed her), being late or not showing up at all, and other transgressions. The irony of the situation is that Rachel and Jack are doing what most professionals recommend—they are using outside help so that Jack is not always Rachel's caregiver. Writing about maintaining love and intimacy after disability, Elizabeth McNeff recommends that health professionals help couples "address the balance in the relationship between partner and caregiver roles. Couples' expectations for a shared, balanced role within the relationship may become impossible with a disability. Both partners need to be aware that sustaining intimacy predominately depends on creating viable caregiving boundaries."[51] Indeed, as the literature in Chapter 3 demonstrates, professionals in the applied fields almost unanimously recommend that partners not function as caregivers in disabled/nondisabled intimate relationships.

The professional advice, of course, is based on the assumption that care is only a burdensome activity and that caregiving will desexualize the relationship. The participants in the focus groups, however, begged to differ. Outside help was most often *the* source of stress. In addition, the presence of that third person prevents alone time for the couple, time for the pair to be intimate and relaxed. Gene explains: "Going back to sex for a second. [*laughter*] Something that she said in the frustration that the, um, that the nurses present and generate some frustration and some tension with us. There's, you know, we're too tired at night and we have somebody else in the house in the morning when we're not tired and we're refreshed." The lack of privacy, and how that affected their sex lives, were mentioned by all participants who used a significant amount of outside help. Nevertheless, some participants had no choice but to employ outside help. Both Gene and Jack worked full-time and could not care for Victoria and Rachel, respectively, full-time.

For other participants, outside help was a choice and one that they felt was worth it, even with all its flaws. For example, Emma insisted on keeping her aides, even though Richard is retired and technically could care for her twenty-four hours a day. For her, aides provided a safety net and the respite was a way for her to care for Richard.

> EMMA: When I talk about caring, I think the way that I care for Richard, my husband, is by having attendants come in once or twice a week because of his age and because I need to keep connected with the agency 'cause if something ever happens to him, I still need to go pee. [*laughter*] I still need to poop. And my dad gets so mad at me that, "How can you think of such a thing?" 'Cause it's a reality of our life. I'm not being mean. I don't want, I don't want anything to happen to him. I'm not planning on it, but—
>
> RICHARD: Right, she said to me, I said . . . she said, "You know what the first thing I would think about if you died? Who's going to wipe my ass?" And I said, "Oh, my God." [*laughter*]
>
> OLIVIA: You can call me, Emma!
>
> RICHARD: That is how close I live to my body, that is how close I live to this reality of disability . . .
>
> EMMA: You know, I would feel—before we talked about it, I felt so bad like, "How can you even think of that?" You know, like, "How can you even think of that?" But the reality is that, if something does happen to him, I still need help then, I still—
>
> RICHARD: Yeah, that day! Maybe twenty minutes from then.
>
> EMMA: Yeah, yeah.

Because Emma must live so closely to the realities of the disabled body, as Richard so aptly puts it, she knows that if Richard ever leaves (or dies), she needs care immediately. Aides are her safety net for that situation. In addition, using aides is a way for her to take care of Richard, to give him a break. In fact, the couple builds in weeklong respites in which Richard goes away several times a year to a cottage that they own.

Emma's use of outside help as a way to give care to Richard brings us into the second major theme about love in the focus groups: reciprocity. As I outlined above, trust and respect are prerequisites for creating a balance between self and other in love relationships. Integral to establishing this level of trust is a willingness to continue to learn about disability and about each other, and to develop new routines that accommodate changing bodies. This type of trust and respect brought the couples closer together, facilitating what La Caze describes as a "coming closer."[52] However, reciprocity—giving back and creating distinct roles for each partner—was key to helping love flourish and last. Ideally, all love relationships are characterized by reciprocity. Disabled/nondisabled relationships are no different; however, they do stand out from more typical romantic love relationships in the explicitness of reciprocity. As I will detail below, reciprocity was something actively discussed, negotiated, and reassessed by the disabled/nondisabled couples in the focus groups. Such consciousness should be a model for all love relations.

Reciprocity

Reciprocity between caregiver and care receiver was quite clearly the key to maintaining balance between self and other in disabled/nondisabled intimate relationships. Mutual care and exchange emerged as a common theme across all the texts and focus groups, demonstrating that care was not a binary relationship, that the disabled partner gives care and the nondisabled partner receives care and vice versa. Mairs's essay called "Taking Care" highlights the reciprocity of care relationships. The argument throughout the chapter is that it is just as psychologically and physically important for Mairs to be able to provide some form of caregiving to the people she loves as it is for them to care for her. Although she has had to change the way that she takes care of others, she insists that she is more than a body cared-for. Primarily her caregiving takes the form of intellectual and emotional efforts. In addition, she writes that "permitting myself to be taken care of is, in fact, one of the ways I can take care of others."[53] On a larger scale, writing is the crucial way that Mairs gives back to those connected to herself, including readers. Describing her desire to fulfill a moral duty to community, Mairs says that, "above all, I can still write, which for me has always been an act of oblation and nurturance: my means of taking the reader into my arms, holding a cup to her lips, stroking her forehead, whispering jokes into her ears. . . . With such gestures, I am taking all the care that I can."[54] Mairs's discussion of care emphasizes the need for mutuality, echoing Benjamin's statement that "her recognition will be meaningful only to the extent that it reflects her own equally separate subjectivity."[55] She must be able to both give and receive care, although the reciprocity can come in different forms. Mairs's embodied and relational subjectivity highlights the need to be a separate self that is distinct, but connected, to others.

In *The Body Silent*, Robert Francis Murphy also uses his brain to give back: "My brain was the only part of the central cortex that still worked well, but that also is where I made my living."[56] Thus, as Murphy's body slows and becomes completely immobile from an inoperable spinal cord tumor, he has to rely on his wife, Yolanda, students, and aides at work to help him move, eat, dress, and bathe. Such an extreme level of care means that Yolanda's freedom has been limited. Murphy writes that, "in a very real sense, we are both held in thrall by my condition—we are each other's captives."[57] He is totally dependent in terms of physical care; however, he is still able to talk, think, write, listen, and interact with the world. He says that, "in light of this position of passivity and dependency, my role as the chief financial support of the family has acquired greater symbolic importance in my mind; it became a mainstay of my ego."[58] Thus, his income and benefits as a professor continue to support his family. He also provides advice and feedback to Yolanda, who is also an anthropologist. And he acknowledges that Yolanda is dependent on him, albeit in different ways and to different degrees.

> Throughout our ten-year siege, Yolanda has clung to me as I to her, for she has her own forms of dependency, and our need for each other has protected our bond in trying times. We have built around ourselves a universe; we have become extensions of each other; we have absorbed each other. But in some ways we have remained strangers, for in all our thirty-six years together, we have negotiated the tricky game of holding on to one another while not losing ourselves. There is always that residual inner self where we store private moods and memories, and where we dream strange things. And so Yolanda remains a mystery to me, but this is why the magic remains after these many years.[59]

Thus, Murphy's relationship with Yolanda is characterized by mutual care. They are able to sustain the reciprocity by ensuring each has a role, that each experiences caregiving and care receiving, and that there is also space for disengagement from one another.

Even Marion Deutsche Cohen, the one author in the sample who ultimately does burn out on care, acknowledges that she did receive (not just give) in the relationship—just not frequently and substantially enough to prevent collapse. As already noted, in-home care allowed a blending of roles that was suitable for Cohen's writing, parenting, and partnering. In addition, Jeff remained Cohen's emotional and intellectual support regardless of how disabled he became. Like Murphy, Jeff still had his mind to share with his wife. Cohen relates:

> I wrote a poem, "That Room," about our bedroom, where, beginning two or three years ago, Jeff sat in the trike [wheelchair] almost all day, the room from whence "Mar!" issued. I didn't want to be there, and I got out of there whenever I could, but when something bad happened to me, or something good, I'd go zooming right back in. Jeff was the one I wanted to tell, especially if it was a math problem or solution, or some incident with my calculus students. And he was the one who would say, "You're great, Mar," or "Don't worry, Mar"— just as he had when I was laboring with each of the babies.[60]

As this passage indicates, Cohen relies on Jeff for recognition and support, care tasks that he is able to continue despite his physical disability. In addition, like Murphy, Jeff is able to help the family financially, even from the nursing home he eventually resides in, through physics research.[61]

Reciprocity was also one of the main themes in the focus groups. Couples consistently explained that they are careful to figure out ways in which the disabled partner can give care to the relationship. For example, Emma needs help with activities of daily living. Despite this level of physical care, she and her partner Richard insist that their relationship is characterized by mutuality and reciprocity.

> EMMA: I guess you can't look at physical care as something that's
> unequal in the relationship because I care for him by taking
> care of the bills and making a budget and remembering our cal-
> endar and, um—
>
> RICHARD: Yeah, we try to maximize everything, maximize her par-
> ticipation in everything just by letting her . . . when she can do
> something it's hers!

Emma and Richard are aware of the need for Emma to participate and give back in the relationship. Because Emma's impairment limits what she can do physically, her form of care takes the shape of brainwork. In fact, nonphysical care such as brainwork or emotional care was a common method of reciprocity for the couples dealing with more severe levels of physical impairment.

> OLIVIA: I think my husband takes more care of me than I take care
> of him, and he needs more help than I do physically. But, I
> don't know, I mean—
>
> RANDALL: Our marriage, I mean— . . . there is no such thing as a
> perfect marriage, but we really feed off of each other. I mean,
> it's obvious that, um, the physical . . . she helps me more than I
> help her physically. But on the other hand, mentally I think we
> are equal.
>
> OLIVIA: I'm going to have to disagree. [*laughter*]
>
> RANDALL: Just like issues that I have, that she [*inaudible*] it's gonna
> be OK. Like bills . . . I get worried about bills, she—
>
> OLIVIA: I could care less.
>
> RANDALL: She says don't worry about it, it will be OK. But and
> then the house, I got to make sure that bills are paid, she is still
> happy, and my son is still happy, and now my daughter is still
> happy. And so it's, it's a lot. But, if you look from the outside
> [*inaudible*] people just say she takes care of him, but I try so
> hard to be there for her mentally and I don't go and brag about
> it. It's just between me and her. If somebody wants to say that
> it's all on her, I mean I don't, I don't think . . . she knows what

I'm doing, she knows how much I help her. At first I was worried . . . I used to hear that a lot, but I don't hear that as much now. My in-laws are probably the best in-laws I could have because I rarely hear them talk about my disability. My sister-in-law is more jealous because her sister has more going on than she does and she's the younger sibling, and I think that because when she goes home to see her family I think our marriage is so . . . I don't know the word to use, but—

OLIVIA: Inspiring.

Randall's mental help, in exchange for Olivia's physical help, makes the couple feel like equals. They are even the envy of their peers.

Similarly, Gene credits Victoria for keeping him focused, composed, and "together." When asked how she cares for Gene, Victoria says, "I do the cooking, that is about it!" But, Gene quickly corrects her:

GENE: No, that is not nearly it! There have been some things that have gone on in life over the past ten years that I'm not sure that I would have known how to get through without her, both from listening to me and talking me through things, but also in being around her. And I'm not saying that you're an inspiration to us all [*laughter*], um, the courage, um, that just kind of rubs off on me. I'll put it that way, it's not her, not just the courage, but the example that I was just talking about in her tolerance of other people where I would just like freak out. "Get your ass over here and do this now!" She is very tolerant, she lets people do things, that has taught me a lot, and that is not really responding to your caring question, um—

SARAH: Yeah, it is.

GENE: Um, the . . . there is and I can't even believe that these words are about to come out of my mouth. There, in some circles I might say the nagging, but it's not nagging, it's reminding and kind of bringing me back to reality. She knows how I am about things and I am focused on what I'm doing, when I can focus it is on what I'm doing. She helps me, remind me, helps to remind me that there are other things that I need to draw into the picture a little better, so she definitely watches over me.

Victoria's watchfulness is what permits Gene to be successful. In fact, they are a particularly dynamic team in their local disability rights organization.

Teamwork was one of the ways in which couples framed the care and reciprocity in their relationships. As Allison notes:

I mean I feel like, like, I try to do most of the cleaning and the laundry independently because that is something that I can do for us together. Because I know that the driving and the cooking a lot of times that he takes over. So, I feel like when we do it together, we're doing it together for us and our household and not just for me doing for him and him doing it for me kind of a thing. So, I feel like we're kind of working together as a team rather than him having to do stuff for me because I'm visually impaired and me just feeling like I have to do it back just to feel like we're equal. I just feel like we kind of work together as a team.

When imbalances of power did arise, or when the disabled partner began to feel like a burden, couples were quick to find remedies.

CONNIE: And that is where Bob is brilliant about . . . I will say something exactly like that, along those lines to him, I feel like that is all I, I need, I need, I need. There is times that you never say to me, "Well, you do this for us and you do this for us," things around the house, cleaning the house, cooking, that kind of stuff. But I just sometimes, besides the everyday run-of-the-mill stuff, I need to do something that I feel like I'm contributing to stuff, and he will give me something that he needs done.

SARAH: Right.

CONNIE: If it's work that he could have done at home, you know on the computer, he'll put on there and stuff because he knows I'm good at figuring stuff out on the computer from my old job. He'll make, he'll give me something to make me feel important.

FRANK: Oh, I don't believe that.

BOB: No, it helps me, if that is a by-product. [*inaudible*]

SARAH: Right, it's not just . . . [*inaudible*]

FRANK: She's saying it makes me feel good . . . you don't do it for that reason.

BOB: No.

SARAH: Right.

FRANK: I want to defend him for that. I think he does it because he really does need the help.

CONNIE: I think, in part, he genuinely appreciates the help, I'm not say [*inaudible*], but he genuinely ap . . . But there's times where he knows that, if I got really down in the dumps because I don't feel important, I don't feel like I'm needed in any way, he will give me something. It will make me feel . . . he could do the job himself . . . OK?

FRANK: [*inaudible*]

SARAH: Right.

FRANK: Somebody else could do it then.

CONNIE: Oh, he's got a ton of people working under him, he could give it to one of them, but if he gives it to me at home to do, OK. I could take my time at home and it makes me feel good because I'm doing something for him.

BOB: The flip side to that is, that, um, and a lot of couples say this and it sounds corny, but she truly is my other half. And for me with stuff like that I know she thinks the same way I do, so I can ask her to do some of these things and I know darn well it would be done the same way that I would do it because we think along similar terms. It's the same with . . . my position is HR related and so there will be times where there are people issues that come up at work and Connie is my sounding board.

SARAH: Right.

BOB: I go to her and I'll say "OK, here is what's going on. How am I going to handle this?" And, um, there have been times where I've changed the direction I was going because of something that Connie said, um, so, I . . . she appreciates it, yes, and you're right [to Frank], I'm not doing it just for those reasons, but it does help her and I can tell when she appreciates it.

Thus, part of the work of the disabled/nondisabled couple involves assessing what the disabled partner can do and ensuring that he or she becomes responsible for those activities. As Dan, who has a spinal cord injury, explains, "I do those things because those are the things that I can do." Dan cannot mow the lawn or do house maintenance, but he can vacuum the floors and do the laundry. Ways in which the disabled partner can reciprocate and give care to his or her nondisabled partner are actively sought and acknowledged in order to maintain a sense of equality.

Negotiating reciprocity and roles in the relationship is an excellent example of Westlund's "shared practical perspective."[62] Instead of merging personalities or extreme separateness in the relationships, the members of the couple work on a joint understanding of what counts as reciprocity and what their union means. Randall returned Olivia's care by providing emotional support and helping her center, and this was openly recognized by both of them. Similarly, Richard readily acknowledged the ways in which Emma returned his physical caregiving by managing their calendar, paying bills, and making sure Richard took respites.

Disabled/nondisabled couples work diligently on maintaining their shared practical perspective so that individual autonomy, respect, and wonder can continue to flourish in their relationships. Reciprocity helped them maintain that delicate balance between self and other that fuels intersubjectivity, allowing couples to forge a shared practical perspective about their lives, hopes, and dreams. Based on the representations that I analyzed in Part 1 of this book, it would be reasonable to assume that physical impairment makes many aspects of love more difficult. The burden of physical care may lower respect for the disabled partner, shifting the balance between self and other. However, this research suggests that, in all of these aspects of love, impairment seemed to facilitate, even strengthen, love. In fact, many of the participants in the focus groups felt that their love was better than the love relationships their nondisabled peers experienced. For example, Gene says:

> I think some of the things that we deal with in our relationship prevent us from getting hung up on things that really don't count that screw up other people's relationships. Does that make sense? That, that, um, because we're dealing with things that essentially really matter, uh, the more significant things, the superficial things that I've had tear apart other relationships. Um, the not really dealing with real problems . . . they become problems, but they aren't really problems. But whereas you're dealing with things and you're getting through things together, it makes a relationship stronger, and it's not the tearing apart that some of those other problems that end up coming up in other relationships. Does that help clarify it all?

Because Gene and Victoria have to deal with suctioning (Victoria has a tracheotomy), positioning, and toileting, they are less affected by trivial issues, such as what to wear to a dinner party, that seem to plague nondisabled couples. Impairment helped them keep focused on the more important parts of being a couple. In addition, managing physical impairment in an intimate relationship requires conversations about alone time, duties and tasks, respect, and balance that often go silently assumed in nondisabled relationships. I believe that this hyperawareness of self/other balance and reciprocity helps strengthen love in disabled/nondisabled relationships.

Kevin, the nondisabled spouse of Ellen, who has MS, expresses a similar "better than" sentiment. In his journal, he writes:

> Another typical Tuesday: work, school, karate at night. . . . We make sure we get on each other to make sure we each take care of ourselves as well as taking care of the family. I helped Ellen get her legs up into bed tonight . . . seemingly an ordinary task. But I care for her and she doesn't feel dependent . . . just . . . closer between us. Things "normal" couples don't *get* to do for each other. We get to spend more intimate time together.

> Looking over the past two weeks . . . I think we both show each other caring
> and enjoy intimacy . . . not like other couples . . . but maybe even better. We
> have developed a trust between us that has allowed us to experience a close-
> ness that I don't think many "normal" couples would ever experience. We
> have our ups and downs like all couples . . . but I think we're doing alright.

Impairment requires an intimacy with each other's physical bodies that goes far
beyond the carnal knowledge typical of nondisabled relationships. Thus,
disabled/nondisabled couples that successfully manage the balance between
self/other, reciprocity, respect, and trust may experience a better love than most.

Notes

1. Jackson, "Love and Romance," p. 39.

2. Westlund, "The Reunion of Marriage"; Benjamin, *The Bonds of Love* and *Like Subjects*; Weiss, *Body Images*; La Caze, "Love."

3. Eakin, *How Our Lives Become Stories*; Egan, *Mirror Talk*.

4. Westlund, "The Reunion," p. 566.

5. Ibid., p. 560 (emphasis added).

6. Ibid.

7. Benjamin, *The Bonds*, pp. 19–20.

8. Ibid., p. 23.

9. Ibid., p. 33.

10. Eakin, *How Our Lives*, p. 26.

11. I suppose that all intersubjective moments take place in bodies; however, I am reserving the term to describe moments in which the authors are foregrounding their or their partner's body in the relationship.

12. Gail Weiss, *Body Images*, p. 5.

13. Ibid., p. 3.

14. Ibid., p. 33.

15. Westlund, "The Reunion," p. 560.

16. La Caze, "Love," p. 95.

17. For example, in *Caring*, Nel Noddings explains that the caregiver does not necessarily receive any form of concrete reciprocity and that the cared-for's flourish-ing is an adequate return for the care relationship to continue.

18. La Caze, "Love," pp. 94–95.

19. Ibid., p. 101.

20. Ibid., p. 102.

21. Ibid., p. 99.

22. Ibid., p. 99.

23. Ibid., p. 96.

24. Eakin, *How Our Lives*, p. 57.

25. Ibid., p. 86.

26. Although I will use both the words "interdependence" and "intersubjective" to signify this fundamental connectivity, I prefer intersubjective because it foregrounds subjectivity.

27. Egan, *Mirror Talk*.

28. Although all the authors of published self-representations in my sample emphasize relationality, the female authors seem to take relationality to a different—perhaps deeper—level. The selves that emerge in Kondracke's and Murphy's texts are relational, but they also look and feel as expected (relatively linear, bounded histories). In other words, they do not defy some of the "certitudes" that readers of autobiography expect. Kondracke's narrative *Saving Milly* unfolds in a linear manner: he begins with his and Milly's childhoods, tells how they met, and then describes their experience of Parkinson's disease. He uses "old Milly" and "new Mort" to describe fundamental and radical shifts and their personalities and roles in the relationship, but readers can easily trace a discernable Mort throughout the text. Likewise, Murphy's voice is clear throughout *The Body Silent*. He is changed by disability and his life is intimately connected to Yolanda, but he—and readers—can always tell where he begins and others end. The self/other distinction seems a bit more slippery for the female authors.

29. Klein and Blackbridge, *Slow Dance*, p. xv.

30. Ibid., p. 143.

31. Ibid., p. 95.

32. Ibid., p. 329.

33. Marion Deutsche Cohen, *Dirty Details*, p. 111.

34. Ibid., p. 76.

35. Mairs, *Waist-High*, p. 12.

36. Ibid., p. 71.

37. Ibid., p. 12.

38. Ibid.

39. Benjamin, *The Bonds*, p. 42.

40. Mairs, *Waist-High*, pp. 74–75.

41. Ibid., pp. 207–208.

42. Ibid., p. 34.

43. Wong, "First Person," p. 174.

44. Kondracke, *Saving Milly*, p. 215.

45. Cohen, *Dirty Details*, p. xiv.

46. Mairs, *Waist-High*, pp. 48–49.

47. Marion Deutsche Cohen, *Dirty Details*, p. 87.

48. Benjamin, *Bonds of Love*, pp. 34–35.

49. Two couples reported that they self-pay for in-home care (this may include housecleaning or other assistance), and five couples said that they used personal care assistants paid for by outside sources (e.g., state funding).

50. "Respite care" is care provided to the person with a disability while the regular caregiver (in this case, the partner) takes a break. The break may range from a few hours to several weeks.

51. McNeff, "Issues," p. 597.

52. La Caze, "Love," p. 95.

53. Mairs, *Waist-High*, p. 83.

54. Ibid., p. 84.

55. Benjamin, *The Bonds*, p. 24.

56. Murphy, *The Body Silent*, p. 66.

57. Ibid., p. 199.

58. Ibid., p. 212.

59. Ibid., p. 219.

60. Marion Deutsche Cohen, *Dirty Details*, p. 94.

61. Ibid., p. 7.

62. Westlund, "The Reunion," p. 560.

7

The Sexual Pleasure of Care

Disabled people are not supposed to be sexual or sexy. Historically, people with physical impairments have been institutionalized—hidden
from the nondisabled. Often, disabled people were forcibly sterilized or forbid-
den by law to have intimate relationships or reproduce. Although most disabled
people are no longer forced into institutions or prohibited from having adult
sexual relationships, attitudes have not changed that much.[1] As reflected in
popular culture (see Chapter 2), and confirmed by numerous attitudinal studies,
it is still quite common for nondisabled people to assume that sex is not important to people with disabilities, that disabled people have lower sex drives or
more important things to worry about, or that the physical impairment means
they are unable to have sex.[2] Conversely, some people believe that disabled
people are hypersexual and need their relationships and fertility monitored.
These attitudes can make it difficult, if not impossible, for people with disabilities to develop positive sexual self-images and find sexual partners.

Our cultural beliefs about what counts as sex are another set of obstacles
that people with disabilities face. When one's body is different, sexual activity and intimacy may also look different. The "normal" sexual position—
missionary position—may be impossible, for example, for a man with a spinal
cord injury. Depending on the disability, genitals may not work properly, stam-
ina may be impaired, and appearance may deviate greatly from what is culturally endorsed. Unfortunately, such functional and physical diversity is rarely
represented in popular culture. In addition, it is rare for sex health educators
or for professionals in the applied fields to offer alternative models of sexuality to people with disabilities. Thus, education, popular culture, and the
applied fields all contribute to sustaining heteronormativity, affecting the lives
of *all* people, including the nondisabled. Miriam Kaufman, Cory Silverberg,
and Fran Odette candidly write:

141

> Watch any one of the thousands of mainstream porn films (or even regular
> films with sex scenes) released each year and you'll get some idea of how
> sex is "supposed" to work. "Real" sex progresses from light activities like
> kissing to the "real" thing, penis-in-vagina intercourse, to simultaneous
> orgasm in ten minutes or less. You should also be able to have sex in a vari-
> ety of different positions all in the same night. Everything we do sexually is
> supposed to progress toward that goal, and none of it is as important as the
> result itself. Thus "foreplay" is nothing more than a prelude to the main
> event. Oral sex is hot, but it's still not as good as the "real" thing.[3]

These authors critique this heterosexist script, along with the notions that sex
must be spontaneous and flow smoothly and beautifully, arguing that "this
standard exists for us all, and harms us all."[4] Indeed, the sexual proscriptions
about how and how often to have sex are detrimental to disabled and nondisabled people who are trying to forge a positive sexual self-image.

Considering this social context, it is rather remarkable that only a few of
the focus group participants shared anxiety and sexual concerns. For example,
when asked to describe intimacy in her life, Rachel mentions that Jack likes to
be the one to transfer her from bed to chair, but she quickly goes into talking
about her conflicted feelings regarding disability and sexuality:

> So that is his little intimacy or he'll just pick me up and he'll transfer me, and
> they [the personal care assistants] are like, "Well, we can get her," [and he
> says] "No, I want to hold her right now." So, so, that's what, that's what we
> do. But I still feel, I'm still with the old values, got to please my man. I'm
> not doing that, I'm not a good wife, that kind of stuff. And he says, "I don't
> care about that. I just want to be with you. I don't care." I'm still trying to get
> that through my head, you know, it's hard when you have media and every-
> thing around you saying you got to have sex, you got to have sex.

Rachel feels very close to Jack, and she can think of numerous examples of
physical and emotional intimacy; however, she feels inadequate because she
cannot replicate what is represented in popular culture and sex education.

Sexual concerns frequently added to the disabled partner's anxiety about
the stability of their relationships. In Focus Group 1, Ellen admits to longing
for the sex life they had before her disability.

> ELLEN: But do you think sometimes too that the person with the dis-
>   ability . . . Everybody is in a different situation. Um, maybe the
>   person with disabilities finds it difficult to do things that they
>   could do maybe ten or five years or ten years ago and you feel
>   that maybe the relationship or the sex is one-sided; that the
>   "good" partner [*laughs at saying that*] is doing all the work.
>   And I don't know how to put this [*laughter*], but it's . . .
>   because it happens with us I have tightness in my inner thighs,

and the poor man, by the time we're done is like ugh! [*making painful face*]

TRACY: Oh, my gosh! [*laughter*]

ADAM: I'm not trying to be creepy, but do you mind? [*to Kevin*]

KEVIN: No, it's, it's part of the intimacy!

ADAM: Exactly! [*laughter*]

ELLEN: But, you know, from my end of it, it's like, I'm sorry, I apologize for my muscles not working. That's, that's, not looking at you, but that I was happy to see you. [*to Rachel*] I'm thinking cool, she is having the same problems I am!

RACHEL: Oh, absolutely.

ELLEN: But you know what, there, there is still that intimacy. I mean, the snuggling and everything else. It's just, you wish you could go back to when you first had your relationship where everything worked properly! And everything was relaxed.

Even though her partner, Kevin, is not concerned with Ellen's physical functioning, she wishes that she could get her nondisabled body back.

Decades after his injury, Dan continues to feel limited by his physical impairment. In his journal, he writes:

> As a male with a disability and not able to perform as an able body, it is mentally difficult to have sex. There are many things I wish I could do, but am limited in my mobility. I think this frustration has built up over the years and has led to a decrease in sexual activity. This is strictly on my part and I know it affects my wife. She feels I don't desire her anymore. I feel less than satisfied.

Kay has known Dan only in the wheelchair. She knows that his body performs sexually differently than nondisabled bodies but, in both the focus group and her journal, she notes her continued desire for Dan, her acceptance of his disabled body. Dan, on the other hand, is frustrated that his body will not perform as he wants it to, that he cannot do the activities a husband and father is supposed to be able to do.

Considering the social barriers that people with disabilities face, and society's beliefs about what counts as good and proper sex, it is totally understandable that Dan, Ellen, and Rachel struggle with viewing themselves as sexually desirable and satisfying partners. What is surprising from this research, however, is how infrequently disabled/nondisabled couples viewed their sex lives as impaired. The vast majority felt they had excellent sexual relationships and believed that they and their partners were sexy. Even Dan, Ellen, and Rachel had positive things to say. Thus, contrary to expectations, disabled/nondisabled couples had good sex lives—some even argued that they had *better* sex lives.

I believe that one of the reasons this information is so new is that most interlocutors are comparing nondisabled sex with disabled sex.[5] In other words, sex is predefined going into the research as penile/vaginal penetration. Other ways of expressing sexuality and sexual intimacy are either ignored completely or viewed through a heteronormative lens in which other forms of sex are perverse, unsatisfying, or pathetic. I set out on a different mission, intent on listening to, reading about, and watching disabled/nondisabled couples discuss sex, refusing to define for them (even when asked) what I meant by sex and intimacy. This tactic revealed rich and complex sexual modalities, most of which incorporated aspects of physical care into sexual intimacy. In what follows, I provide numerous examples of disabled/nondisabled sexuality. Although these couples' sexuality rarely looked normal, they were all actively engaged in rewriting sexual scripts to facilitate their bodies and needs. In the process, they were normalizing new forms of desire.

Normal Desire

In the focus groups, there was a notable desire to portray the couples' sex lives as "just the same" or "just like" the sex lives of nondisabled couples. Similarly, when asked about caregiving, participants first responded by generally mentioning that providing physical care was simply "second nature," "normal," just like "any couple" would do. Most said that care and sexuality were unrelated; care neither improved nor impinged on sex. For example, Bob says:

> Like I said [care is] just figuring out how to lead as normal a life as you can and if you don't . . . I don't think that we even think about it in terms of caretaking. We just think about it in terms of coping. How do we cope with whatever the next issue is or with whatever the particular roadblock to whatever it is we want to do is?

Connie qualifies Bob's statement of normalcy by saying, "He makes it a non-issue, for us. It's just, *we got another way of doing it*" (emphasis added). As participants talked more about what counted as care, sex, and intimacy, a more complicated and interesting picture emerged. In other words, as participants began to give concrete examples of how they do care and do sex and intimacy, there was increasing recognition that they do it (all of it!) differently.

The focus group atmosphere allowed participants to step outside of talking about their intimate lives within the dominant framework, allowing them to articulate the ways in which sex was different for them (not less than, just different), and the ways in which caregiving and sexual intimacy frequently intersected. In fact, most of the couples felt that physical caregiving activities often enhanced intimacy. For example, when asked how providing care interacts with sexuality or intimacy in the relationship, Richard and Emma respond:

> RICHARD: It enhances it, I think. [*laughter*]
>
> EMMA: [*inaudible*] When you're in the shower and he is bathing me it's . . . it's not sexual, but yet it is. I can't explain it the right way.
>
> RICHARD: It's a . . . um, high-level sexual, but I mean, it is certainly not, certainly not intercourse, but it's, it's, pleasurable, it's pleasurable.
>
> EMMA: It is very intimate . . . it is a very loving, sensual, state-of-being.

For Richard and Emma, the routine task of bathing has become part of their sexual intimacy. Another participant, Allison, who is blind, explains that holding hands with her partner, Jason, is a way for them to express intimacy and closeness even though, on a practical level, he is simply guiding her across a street. In both of these examples, the disabled/nondisabled couple is able to eroticize care activities to enhance intimacy. The routine activities of daily care become opportunities for sexuality and intimacy because, as Olivia puts it, "You can be perverted whenever you want."

Connie and Bob also felt that the dailiness of close, physical care aided sexual intimacy. Discussing personal care, they have this candid exchange:

> CONNIE: Taking care of [someone] is intimate. Yes, I don't need help with anything taking a bath or a shower but, if we're at anybody else's house or at a motel and they don't have a walk-in shower, I cannot climb over a bathtub. He knows that, whether we are staying at my mother's house or, and he would be in the bathroom with me at . . . and helping me get into the bathtub. He said, "I just got to make sure I put dry clothes on afterwards," or he's naked along with me while I'm getting into the bathtub and stuff. So, yeah, but . . .
>
> BOB: Which never bothers me so I don't look at it as care [*inaudible*]. [*laughter*]

Everyone laughs, but they are not laughing at Bob for getting sexual enjoyment out of helping bathe Connie. The laughter here, and in all of the intimate joking in the focus groups, is clearly expressing a sense of understanding, a way to show that we are all in on the same private joke.

The authors and filmmakers discussed in previous chapters were much more up-front with their sexual distinctiveness. Unlike the focus group participants, the authors and filmmakers had the privilege of ready access to feminist and queer circles that unabashedly celebrated non-normative sexualities and forms of intimacy. Thus, the self-representations that I analyzed in this study were rich with stories about disabled sex and the role of care. For most, acts of giving physical care facilitated sexual intimacy. By giving care, the nondisabled partner (and disabled partner) received physical, sexual closeness. In these cases, the giving and receiving were mutual and simultaneous. Writing about the physical care that George gives, Nancy Mairs writes that "we carry on a constant, often hardly conscious, corporeal conversation regardless of our other pursuits and preoccupations. Without my disability to throw us together thus habitually, our bodies might spend their days racing separately from one activity to another, coming across each other only in time to tumble into sleep."[6] She also says, "Our bodies conceptualize not only themselves but also each other, murmuring: Yes, you are there; yes, you are you; yes, you can love and be loved."[7] These passages exemplify the constant tension between self and other, the ways in which she is connected, as well as separate from, George's body. Mairs's subjectivity and personal identity are quite literally formed through the process of mirror talk or mutual recognition as she explains that George "loves me into being."[8] But significantly, it is a subjectivity that is wholly dependent on bodies and, thus, reminiscent of Weiss's notion of intercorporeality.[9] Mairs's reference to her body's relation to George's body (and the bodies of others) makes clear that corporeal recognition is imperative.[10]

From the caregiver perspective, Morton Kondracke and Marion Deutsche Cohen both also indicate that care tasks can be physically satisfying to them. Thus, when Cohen asks rhetorically "what happens when one of the lovers is, in twelve-year-old Bret's words, in charge of both bodies," part of that answer is the pleasurable oneness between lovers, between caregiver and cared-for.[11] I too experienced this physical gratification when caring for Max. The experience is beyond words, but it is similar to the physical connection that lovers feel when having really great sex, or the connection a couple may experience during couples' yoga. It is an in-tune-ness as bodies move together and communicate silently but knowingly that is rewarding and sustaining. Maurice Hamington's concept of "caring habits" in *Embodied Care: Jane Addams, Maurice Merleau-Ponty, and Feminist Ethics* comes close to explaining the physical satisfaction that can come with care. For Hamington, "care habits" are the "embodied practices of interaction."[12] He says "the body 'knows' many things, including how to care. . . . Caring habits are practices of the body's caring knowledge."[13] Drawing on Nel Noddings's understanding of "engrossment"—the caregiver's preoccupation with the cared-for—and Merleau-Ponty's phenomenology of the body, to outline care habits, Hamington suggests that care theory needs to attend to the embodied aspects of care. Noddings explains the state of engrossment as "I receive the other into myself, and I see and feel with the other. I become a duality."[14] As flesh connects in the act of caregiving, a "weaving relations between bodies" occurs as bodies familiar to each other "read" and "speak" through touch.[15] This sensing is subconscious (habit), but pleasurable nonetheless, and Hamington sees its recognition as key to understanding how care is sustainable and ontologically fundamental.

I also think that recognition of physical pleasure in care is key to recasting care. And each of the authors in this analysis is attentive to the physical pleasures of care. I read one of the photographs that accompany Cohen's text as illustrative. Jeff has his back toward the camera and he is sitting on the edge of the bed. Cohen is facing him (and readers) with her arms wrapped around Jeff's shoulders and neck. We know from the caption under the photograph that this is a break "between steps two and three of getting Jeff out of bed," but it is also a very intimate moment.[16] If it were not for the caption, readers would simply think it was a couple embracing. It is not intimate in the sexual sense, but in the "constant, often hardly conscious," intercorporeal sense that Mairs writes about.[17] Cohen writes that even now, with Jeff in the nursing home, their bodies remain pleasurably connected:

> Now I sit with Jeff lovingly, my hand around his, his around mine. (I have to put his around mine. Just a few days ago, I remarked, "I know that was just a spasm, but it still feels good, your gripping my hand," and he smiled.) I sit with him, sometimes lie with him, if he's been placed sufficiently to one side of the bed so there's room for me. Long quiet looks, maybe some kissing, even petting, as much as the feeding tube and catheter will allow.[18]

In this passage, physical intimacy also begins to blend into a more explicit sexual connectiveness. Other times, the care moments seem to actually facilitate sexual intimacy, as when Cohen notes that "toilet" (helping Jeff in the bathroom), "at least at the beginning, had intimate overtones."[19] Likewise, Kondracke describes bath time as another opportunity for more sexual play:

> I lift Milly from her wheelchair onto a shower-chair, give her a shampoo, and wash her back and face. She washes her chest. Then I ease her to a standing position and our joke is, "I'll wash the backside, you wash the front." After a rinse-off, I wrap Milly in towels, making her look like a robed Arab prince, and wheel her to brush her teeth and then put her clothes on. We have another standing joke when I help her get into her bra. I always say, as I move a breast into it, "Aha, this is the good part." And she always laughs.[20]

In all of these instances, intimacy or sexuality is not normative—it is not the way in which readers may expect sexual intimacy, but the authors write about it passionately and at length, indicating how important and pleasurable such blending of care and intimacy/sexuality can be for disabled/nondisabled couples. All of the authors in this analysis (except for Cohen) continue to have more traditional sexual relations with their partners (some more than others), but the messy moments in which care blends into intimacy that blends into sexuality get much more play.[21]

These renderings of sexuality, care, and the disabled body expose both the sexy and the "ugly," which, as Cheryl Marie Wade argues, is vital to correcting omissions in the disability rights movement.[22] Writing about sexually intimate moments can help correct the belief that disabled/nondisabled relationships are sexless, and it can also show outsiders how sexual intimacy may look different in these relationships. In addition, it is politically necessary that the need for personal care be represented; otherwise, the realities of the disabled body are glossed over. As Cohen writes, we've got to "spill the dirty details"; otherwise, support for disabled people and their partners will continue to dwindle.[23]

The films *Shameless: The ART of Disability*, *Sick: The Life and Death of Bob Flanagan Supermasochist*, and *Want* are careful to expose the dirty details while insisting that the need for care in no way hinders intimacy between sexual partners.[24] In fact, like the autobiographies and focus groups, the films suggest a blurring of care and sexuality, in which care contributes to the couples' overall intimacy. For example, for Bob Flanagan, regular floggings also had the therapeutic effect of clearing Flanagan's lungs of mucus, thus explicitly blending care and sexuality.[25] Care and sex and intimacy are also blended in *Shameless*, albeit less explicitly. After Frazee returns from the hospital, she and her partner are at their cottage in the woods, enjoying nature and time together. The audience even becomes privy to a romantic bubble bath that the two take. This sequence helps make clear that the care Frazee needs in no way hinders sex and intimacy. *Shameless* also includes an interesting sequence with Klein and her husband, Michael, in which they openly discuss why Michael stays with Klein after the stroke. In voice-over Michael says:

> The men of women who've had strokes leave their wives a shocking 80% of the time. Why didn't I leave? Oh, poverty of imagination, I suppose. [*laughter*] No, I didn't leave because our relationship basically didn't change. I mean that's the major issue, that Bonnie takes care of me. And she took care of me when she was in the ICU and quadriplegic, she was taking care of Seth and me and Naomi.

While Michael says this, he is helping Klein across a rocky beach and into a canoe that they then paddle together. As these films make clear, the excesses of the disabled body require a level of care between partners that increases intimacy.[26]

Want is less traditionally narrative than *Shameless* or *Sick*, relying instead on seemingly unrelated scenes, juxtaposed to call attention to community, belonging, desire, care, and intimacy. Thus, for example, it moves from Loree giving fellatio to her partner's dildo in the bathroom to Loree receiving help with toileting, associating care with sexuality and intimacy. The care sequence is particularly innovative because it is composed of clips of at least five different people helping Loree with toileting. Using a montage here emphasizes the breadth, camaraderie, and intimacy of her community, even around something readers will likely consider deeply private—using the bathroom. While *Want* does not tell a traditional story, it does relay the filmmaker's desires for recognition and inclusion as well as offering a snapshot of a life that blends community care, intimacy, and queer sexuality.

For all of the disabled/nondisabled couples, sex, intimacy, and care combined together to form the core of their loving relationships. Although, at first, the focus groups tried to paint a picture of heteronormativity, examples of nonnormative sex and intimacy quickly flowed. Care was exposed not as a burden to sexual intimacy, but a way to facilitate touching, closeness, trust, and, sometimes, a way to jump-start a more traditional sexual encounter. Thus, even though sex, intimacy, and care may look different for disabled/nondisabled couples, there was nothing lacking or missing from their relationships.

Better Sex and Intimacy

Perhaps because talking so openly about sex and care was new and exciting, several of the focus group participants became exuberant and empowered, and began to assert that their difference was *better*. In his journal entries, Kevin tracks some of the care activities he performs for Ellen, and his feelings about this "work."

> I get to spend time each morning stretching her legs/feet to loosen up tight muscles for better walking. I consider this intimate because she trusts me and allows me to stretch her and not cause her pain.

> I helped her into/out of bathroom stall. It could have been embarrassing and awkward for both of us, but (at least for me and I think for her) it wasn't. We worked together and experienced an intimate moment that brought us closer and more comfortable and trusting of each other.

> Looking over the past two weeks . . . I think we both show each other caring and enjoying intimacy—not like other couples—but maybe even better. We have developed a trust between us that has allowed us to experience a closeness that I don't think many "normal" couples would ever experience. We have our ups and downs like all couples . . . but I think we're doing alright.

As the participants wrote or talked about their experiences with caregiving, many, like Kevin, reached the conclusion that perhaps they were better off than "regular" couples. For example, Gene explains:

> I'm trying to think of the best way to put this. There are times when it kind of increases intimacy, and I'm talking both sexual intimacy and just the closeness. In fact, I think we get a lot more closeness out of those up-close and personal moments that we have together. . . . Looking at other relationships before her, I would say this is the closest, strongest relationship, and I'm sure that that [physical care] has a lot to do with it.

Here, Gene is arguing that the physical care not only enhances sexual and emotional intimacy, but makes them stronger and closer than nondisabled couples. This sentiment is echoed by other participants as well. For example, Sabrina, who has MS, says, "I think truly it makes you closer than it does other couples because you have to deal with things that you'd never have to deal with." In Sabrina's case, her partner, Adam, has had to catheterize her when she is unable to do it herself. Thus, she feels that their relationship exhibits more trust and intimacy than that of nondisabled couples.

For many, it was precisely this knowledge of "private matters"—of their partners' bladders, bowels, and other bodily functions—that provided the basis of this increased level of closeness and trust.

> KAY: I think we know each other in a way that a lot of couples will never know each other. [*laughter*]
>
> SARAH: Exactly.
>
> TED: That's quite true there. [*laughter*]
>
> KAY: You know more about each other's bodily, bodily . . . daily habits than maybe you'd—
>
> SARAH: That's a different way of looking at it, but—
>
> KAY: Than a lot of people do. [*laughter*]

Although Kay and other participants laughed at the "level of intimacy," all did agree, on a very serious level, that such bodily knowledge facilitated intimacy.

Comparing his level of intimacy with Ellen with that of his married friends, Kevin states: "I'm a lot more involved in things than any of my buddies or any other guys I work with other than with their patients that they're with, and so I think that is a wonderful thing because I know my wife a lot better than a lot of these guys ever will!" People with disabilities simply cannot have the same kind of privacy and body boundaries as nondisabled people have been socialized to maintain.

For the disabled partners in particular, body trust was integral to their own self-esteem and their confidence about their relationship with their nondisabled partners. Many talked about needing assurance from their nondisabled partner that exposure to supposedly shameful body parts and processes did not impair their ability to see their disabled partner as a full person, dignified and sexy. Verbal and physical confirmation that exposure to the dirty details did not kill the spark led to an acceptance that allowed care and sexuality to blend together, making it possible for intimate care to enhance sexual intimacy.

Kevin was particularly impacted by the suggestion that his sexual relationship was better in some ways than that of his nondisabled peers. In his journal, the night of the focus group, he writes: "We talked about many things on the way home last night. How we feel our intimacy has traveled way beyond sexuality. The openness we have about almost ANY and ALL subjects, including biological functions that may be too embarrassing for some couples." Getting past the embarrassment of bladder and bowel functions, the exposure of dressing, grooming, and bathing another body brought Kevin and Ellen (and other couples in the study) into a new, higher level of trust, facilitating deeper levels of emotional and sexual intimacy.

The focus group participants' assertion that their relationships were more intimate, perhaps even better, than the sexual relationships of nondisabled people is echoed in other studies and guides about sex and disability that do not assume a heteronormative focus. For example, Gary Karp has written extensively on sex and relationships after spinal cord injury. In his guide *Life on Wheels: The A to Z Guide to Living Fully with Mobility Issues*, he argues that it is imperative to move beyond restrictive notions of what counts as "good sex." People with disabilities that have rich, satisfying sexual lives with both casual and long-term partners are able to include kissing, cuddling, oral sex, touching, dirty talk, and other forms of sexual expression in "sex." This expansive definition opens up possibilities to explore what sex is ultimately about, "an experience of unity, of joining, of feeling as if there is no longer any boundary between you and your partner. . . . The remarkable sense of bliss, the shift in consciousness, and the quality of relief and clarity are all experiences possible in sexual intimacy."[27] Some people with disabilities report being able to remap their bodies so that they are able to orgasm from stroking on the head, nape of the neck, or nipples, or even just by thinking about it.[28] This ability to expand one's sexual repertoire has also led many to claim that disabled people make better lovers. Randi Chance writes:

> With the broadening of the repertoire comes greater experimentation and greater communication between partners about what is pleasurable (Neistadt & Freda, 1987; Westgren & Levi, 1999). An adjustment in sex role expectations often leads to more tenderness by the male partner and a more active participation by the female partner, resulting in a more satisfying relationship

for both (Chigier, 1980). Many disabled men have reported becoming better lovers, better able to concentrate on their partners' pleasure. Many, indeed, pride themselves on their proficiency, especially in performing oral sex (Kroll & Klein, 1992).[29]

It is precisely the move away from the focus on penetration and orgasm that facilitates deeper sensual experiences for disabled people and their partners. In addition, people with disabilities often develop communication skills and the ability to resist dominant notions of beauty and strength, all of which can add to better sexual intimacy. As Lesley Childs argues, "Disabled people make the best lovers because we're experienced at asking for what we want in a nice way. We have to become ingenious at finding ways around problems and barriers."[30] The self-representations in this study mirror Chance's findings and Karp's and Child's experiences; disability facilitated sexual relationship for the disabled/nondisabled couples by requiring the couple to step outside of heteronormative boundaries and explore new dimensions of trust, body awareness, and communication.[31]

Queer Pleasures

In the focus groups and autobiographical self-representations, couples acknowledged that the disabled body requires physical, personal care. However, instead of hindering sexual intimacy, couples felt that this care helps intimacy. In fact, their words seem to suggest a blurring of care and sexuality, in which care contributes to the couples' overall intimacy. Of course, bathing, dressing, toileting, and transferring are not normative forms of sexuality or intimacy. Because of this, I believe that disabled/nondisabled sexuality—even when heterosexual—is truly "queer" in the "queer theory" sense of the word. As this research makes clear, nonheteronormative ways of expressing love and sexual desire are common in disabled/nondisabled intimate relationships.

I do not believe, however, that most of the focus group members would necessarily self-identify as queer. As I mentioned in Chapter 1, there is still a desire for average persons to claim normality, to hide the ways in which their sex lives may be different. I think this is especially true because care and sexuality are considered incompatible, even perverse, in popular culture.[32] As noted earlier, needing physical care for activities like using the bathroom, bathing, and eating is linked to dependency and is considered infantilizing. This is the type of care that mothers give to babies, and, in society, it is taboo to associate sexuality with this activity. Mother-child care is idealized as maternal, not sexual. Suggesting that infants have sexuality, or that infants derive oral pleasure from breastfeeding (let alone the suggestion that mothers may feel sexual pleasure from care activities), is likely to cause anxiety and even condemnation from laypeople. Because it is so taboo to associate care of children with sexuality, I believe we have a deep-seated need to disassociate sex from disability, especially when the impairment requires a high level of assistance with intimate, personal care.

From the psychoanalytic perspective, however, the sexual pleasure of intimate care makes perfect sense. Sigmund Freud suggested that babies have an infantile sexuality, deriving oral pleasure from breastfeeding, and genital and anal pleasure from diaper changing and potty training.[33] He argued that for both sexes, mothers are the first love object. To emerge into adult sexuality and form love relationships with people other than the mother, humans repress this infantile sexuality; however, in the case of physical disability, it may be that intimate care can be so easily eroticized because of these early connections between care and sexual pleasure. By making this connection between mother/infant sexuality and disabled/nondisabled sexuality, I do not mean to imply that disabled/nondisabled couples are backward or perverse in any way. Quite the contrary, I believe they tap into an aspect of sexuality that is present in all of us, but shamed out of us by the false separation of private and public.

Disabled/nondisabled couples participate in what Tobin Siebers calls a "sexual culture" that actively foils the separation between the public and private, and refigures sexual desires, behaviors, and responses. Siebers argues that "the sexual experiences of disabled people expose with great clarity both the fragile separation between the private and public spheres, as well as the role played by this separation in the history of regulating sex."[34] Sex has historically been relegated to the private sphere, something to do behind closed doors, not spoken about in public, and supposedly free of public intervention. Feminists; lesbian, gay, bisexual, and transgendered people; and people of color have long problematized this divide as a facade that hides the ways the "personal is political." Siebers believes disabled people can further dismantle the harmful separation by exposing its unintelligibility and failures because, for disabled people, the zones of the body considered private are regularly handled and made public by necessity. Doctors, nurses, rehabilitation specialists, medical students, personal care assistants, and hospital janitors are a few of those who are not family members that examine, clean, clothe, and care for the private parts of disabled people. "Their professionalization hinges on being able to invade privacy while divorcing that invasion from its sexual associations."[35] But despite their constant attempts, private parts that pee and poop and need to be cleaned and cared for are also sexual parts.[36] Disabled people expose the reality of connection between public and private, and the way in which private is *really* a sphere for the nondisabled, the rich, the white, and the heterosexual.

Eschewing the shame imposed by the dominant culture that upholds this public/private divide is one way that the disabled/nondisabled couples in this study queer sexuality, potentially freeing up new forms of sexual expression for all people. Some of the couples experienced their sex lives as better than the intimate relations of nondisabled couples precisely because the myth of private had been dismantled. They tapped into the association of care and sex, which is inside all of us, to form new sexual expressions that fit their lives and their bodies. There is absolutely nothing shameful about such innovation. Disabled/nondisabled sexuality exposes shame as a socially constructed response to non-heteronormative pleasures. In doing so, the pleasures of care are opened up for all of us.

Notes

1. Some disabled people continue to be institutionalized, especially when family members are unable to provide or pay for community care. In addition, disabled people are still at risk for sterilization. If the court declares the disabled person as unable to give consent, his or her guardian can give consent for sterilization through a process called "substitute consent."

2. See, for example, Milligan and Neufeldt, "The Myth"; and Wolfe, "The Influence."

3. Kaufman, Silverberg, and Odette, *The Ultimate Guide*, pp. 3–4.

4. Ibid., p. 2.

5. There are a few books that do show that disabled people have good sex lives (for example, Gary Karp has written several positive pieces about disability and sexuality, such as *Life on Wheels* and *Disability and the Art of Kissing*). In addition, Mitchell Tepper has researched sex and disability for over a decade and found numerous examples of people with disabilities who enjoy sex and sexual partners, as related in his article "What Does Your Partner Find Sexy About Your Disability?" I say "new" because the public discourse on the topic, including popular culture and most of the academic research, offers only images of decline, shame, and dissatisfaction.

6. Mairs, *Waist-High*, p. 54.

7. Ibid., p. 50.

8. Ibid.

9. Weiss, *Body Images*.

10. Mairs talks about the relationship between her body and the bodies of others, including the reader's body, throughout *Waist-High*.

11. Cohen, *Dirty Details*, p. 86.

12. Hamington, *Embodied Care*, p. 12.

13. Ibid., p. 4.

14. Noddings, *Caring*, p. 30.

15. Hamington, *Embodied Care*, pp. 51–53.

16. Cohen, *Dirty Details*, p. 67.

17. Mairs, *Waist-High*, p. 54.

18. Ibid., p. 130.

19. Ibid.

20. Kondracke, *Saving Milly*, p. 123.

21. Mairs, *Waist-High*; Hockenberry, *Moving Violations*; Klein and Blackbridge, *Slow Dance*; Kondracke, *Saving Milly*.

22. Wade, "It Ain't."

23. Cohen, *Dirty Details*, p. 26.

24. *Shameless: The ART of Disability*, directed by Bonnie Sherr Klein, 2006 (Montreal, Quebec: National Film Board of Canada), DVD; *Sick*, directed by Kirby Dick, 1997 (Santa Monica, CA: Lion's Gate Home Entertainment), DVD; *Want*, directed by Loree Erickson, 2007 (Toronto, Ontario: Femmegimp Productions), DVD.

25. McRuer, *Crip Theory*, p. 182.

26. Notice the contrast to the more mainstream films discussed in Chapter 2. For example, *Murderball* (2005), a theatrically released documentary not made by or for people with disabilities, suggests care (specifically, dependence on partners for physical tasks) may hinder relationships. After Zupan and his girlfriend tell the cameras that they have a wonderful relationship, the film cuts to a montage of Zupan's girlfriend pumping gas, loading groceries, and so forth. The camera in each of these shots lingers on Zupan watching passively and helplessly, thereby undercutting the assertion that their relationship is good.

27. Karp, *Life on Wheels*, pp. 245–246.

28. Ibid., pp. 252–253; Kaufman, Silverberg, and Odette, *The Ultimate Guide*, p. 229; and McNeff, "Meet the Sexperts."

29. Chance, "To Love," p. 202.

30. Childs interviewed in Clark, "Sex and Disability."

31. Chance, "To Love and Be Loved"; Karp, *Life on Wheels*; Clark, "Sex and Disability."

32. I am indebted to Jeffrey Tobin for helping me think through the connection between infantile sexuality and care.

33. See Freud's *Three Essays on the Theory of Sexuality*.

34. Siebers, *Disability Theory*, p. 136.

35. Ibid., p. 145.

36. Siebers relates a story written by the late activist and journalist Mark O'Brien, who spent most of his life in an iron lung as the result of childhood polio, in which O'Brien accidentally ejaculates from an impersonal sponge bath given by a nurse. The nurse does not comment, and a janitor silently, stoically, cleans up the ejaculate from the hospital floor.

8

New Understandings of Care, Gender, and Sexuality

For the most part, the self-representations that I analyzed in this book offer readers and audiences alternative understandings of care and sexuality in disabled/nondisabled intimate relationships. Frequently, these representations are explicitly speaking back to, and critiquing, dominant representations that paint their relationships as burdensome, sexless, and tragic. These texts are not, however, entirely happy, overcoming narratives. They portray disabled/nondisabled relationships as complex, sometimes positive, sometimes negative, but ultimately valuable and sustaining. Such representations are not always easy to read. For example, I admit being uncomfortable with some of Marion Deutsche Cohen's rants about "nights, toilet, and lifting."[1] As a nondisabled partner, I wanted Cohen to paint the picture better. At several points, I became angry at Cohen for making the pains so visible. I know that Cohen also portrayed the joys, but the raw exposure of the tribulations made it difficult to ingest because I was so invested in showing a positive image of disabled/nondisabled intimate relationships.

One night I was struggling with this very ambivalence, reading and rereading Cohen's text. It was hot in the bedroom, so I took off my pajama bottoms and slipped back into the sheets. As I was enjoying how good the cool sheets felt on my legs, I realized that I had not experienced this feeling for over six years. When Max was alive, he frequently ate meals in bed, especially when the MS fatigue was bad. It was simply easier to just eat in bed than work on transferring, dressing, sitting at the table, and the undressing and transferring again. This meant, however, that there were *always* crumbs in our bed. Even though I changed the sheets often, and I nightly tried to wipe out the crumbs, I could never get them all, it seemed. At the beginning of our relationship I tried to sleep, as I had always done, in just a nightshirt, but inevitably I ended up just like the girl in *The Princess and the Pea*.[2] That one teeny, tiny

157

crumb felt like a brick and I was unable to sleep. Eventually I resigned myself to this reality and got used to sleeping in bottoms.

So, two years after Max's death, I took off my bottoms and felt no crumbs and I was happy. Then, I was sad and felt guilty for being happy. The bed crumbs also meant that Max was always around, in bed, and available to talk with me. My office was in our bedroom, so I wrote and graded and he ate and watched TV or read. But through it all, we were constantly together. There were crumbs, but I had a brilliant man that I could turn to at any moment and ask for another word for "complexity," or ask how Immanuel Kant viewed moral autonomy. Like Cohen, I hated some aspects of Max's disability, but loved other parts. It was . . . complex, but beautiful.

Unfortunately, as I demonstrated in the first part of this book, the applied fields and popular culture have largely failed to accurately portray the complexities of love and sex for disabled/nondisabled partners. Drawn from dominant understandings of autonomy and independence, the need for care is framed as an emotional and physical burden on the partner. The disabled partner is rendered helpless, as only care receiving. The nondisabled partner is portrayed as saddled with duty, tired, and overwhelmed from caregiving. Because of this care dynamic and the taboo around the disabled body and mixing of care and sex, these partnerships are rarely represented as sexual.

The disability rights movement's intervention into this discourse has attempted to reframe the disabled person's need for care by advocating for personal care assistants and distancing disability from care. Tom Shakespeare has suggested that "care" be replaced with "help"[3] in the disability rights discourse because, as Nick Watson et al. outline, care is

> associated with the confinement of disabled people, the modern equivalent to the custodial strategy that was the standard social response to disabled people by incarcerating them in "total institutions" (Goffman, 1961) and constituting them as objects of medical scrutiny. . . . [Care] locates power with the caregiver rather than the recipient.[4]

"Help" is a less politically loaded term for people with disabilities. Thus, personal care assistants give help and support to their employers; they do not care for them. Such a reframing does indeed shift the power away from the personal care assistant or caregiver; however, these tactics are ultimately limiting because they fail to undermine dominant understandings of autonomy and independence. Arguing that disabled people can be just like the nondisabled with the use of personal care assistants reifies the supposed distinction between disabled and nondisabled people and obscures those people whose impairments are disabling. Ramps and personal care assistants may help some people with disabilities live like the nondisabled, but there are many disabled people whose lives continue to be different despite access and inclusion. Pain, fatigue, and other body realities are not erased by the presence of personal care assistants or consumer-controlled payment schemes (i.e., England's direct payment program).

In addition, this solution fails to acknowledge the material and social reality of caregivers as well as the relationship between employee and employer. Women, people of color, and poor people are the typical care workers. These jobs are physically and emotionally exhausting, and they usually pay low wages with no benefits. Furthermore, Watson et al. note that there is "some evidence that disabled people and their assistants do not experience personal assistance in purely contractual, unemotional and instrumental terms."[5] Indeed, the nature of the work connotes a level of trust and intimacy that is not found in typical employer-employee relationships. In addition, this instrumental frame is difficult, if not impossible, to apply to the many disabled people who "employ" family members. In advocating for the disabled person's right to control his or her own care, the disability rights movement has failed to consider the rights of the caregiver and the interpersonal dynamics of the care relationship.

On the other side of the care debates are feminists who are concerned with the well-being of the caregiver. Grounded in a materialist framework, these feminist care researchers have "focused on the 'burden' of care, and documented various ill-effects that could result from caring . . . including stress, limitations and emotional impacts."[6] As I mentioned in Chapter 1, their work has spurred much activism around improving the lives of caregivers. In the past several decades, organizations to support informal caregivers, such as the National Family Caregivers Association and the National Alliance for Caregiving, have popped up. These organizations link informal caregivers with resources (e.g., respite care), provide social support, and keep members aware of policy that affects community care. Some of these organizations, along with the National Organization for Women's mothers and caregivers economic rights campaign, advocate for privatizing care by paying family caregivers and regulating their working conditions.

All of these efforts, however, focus exclusively on the caregiver. In this framework, the compensation is paid to the informal caregiver (not to the disabled person); the caregiver essentially becomes a state employee (not the disabled person's employee). It is easy to see how this simply transfers power to the caregiver, rendering the disabled person a passive recipient. Additionally, some feminist thinkers, such as Virginia Held, are weary of this "marketization" of care. Held argues that these tactics fail to consider the ways in which the market can pervert the emotional and ethical aspects of the care relationship. She agrees that "moving an activity that was previously unpaid to the side of being paid is often a gain, not just for the person doing the work but others also and for the quality of the work."[7] However, "subordinating caring labor to the norms of the market" can also be dangerous.[8] Markets have not, to date, been able to "express and promote many of the values important to [care] practices, such as mutually shared caring concern."[9] Indeed, in both remuneration schemes outlined above, the care relationship is eclipsed.

Other feminists, those I have called feminist care philosophers, have attempted to rescue care through nonmarket means. As Michael Fine and Caroline Glendinning explain, "rather than emphasizing the negative ('burdensome') features of care," these theorists have developed "a discourse on the 'ethic of care' [emphasizing] its socially positive and desirable features."[10] Feminist care ethics is concerned with the social value of care, the ways in which care promotes collective responsibility and empathy. Some of these philosophers, such as Joan Tronto, argue that care ethics is a precursor to justice and that "the right to receive and to give care needs to be thought of as an issue of social justice."[11] In this framework, care is an esteemed activity and caregivers are valorized.

The problem with all of these tactics, however, is that they are concerned with either the caregiver or the care receiver. Bill Hughes et al. provide the following succinct characterization of the political split:

> Generally, for feminist scholars, the emphasis is on the giver of care (usually female), whilst in disability studies the recipient of care (male or female) is the locus of interest. Given the political agenda and standpoint of these two social movements, the contrast in focus is understandable. However, whilst these groups have a different agenda, both regard the parties involved in the caring relationship as constituted and colonized by its dynamic.[12]

Like feminist disability scholars before me, I do not believe this divide is inevitable. In fact, both movements can inform each other and strengthen their individual agendas. However, this divide will not heal until feminist and disability activists/scholars work toward a coalitional politics concerned about both givers and receivers of care. Following Jenny Morris, Jan Walmsley, Margaret Lloyd, and other disabled feminist scholars, I argue that a first step is to undermine the notion that people in care relationships are only either caregivers or care receivers.[13] In other words, we must highlight the reciprocity and mutuality of care relationships. As the self-representations that I analyzed in Part 2 demonstrate, disabled/nondisabled intimate relationships are characterized by mutual support. Couples pay special attention to help maximize the ways in which the disabled partner can give care in an effort to create a sense of equality in the relationship. Thus, a coalitional politics between feminist and disability activists/scholars must be based on care relationships.

From this coalitional politics grounded in relationships, new perspectives on old problems can develop. Three potentially fruitful areas for future coalitional scholarship and activism include the privatization of care, queer theory, and creating new images. First, I believe feminist and disability activists/

scholars alike must retain a healthy skepticism of market-based solutions to care. The efforts of both direct payment systems and feminists to monetize housework have problematic side effects. I do not advocate, however, abandoning market strategies altogether, because previous research and the findings of this study suggest that families that deal with disability face economic hardship.[14] Furthermore, S. McCann and D. S. Evans found that finances were one of the main concerns for people receiving care—they were concerned "about the level of financial support for themselves and their carers" as well as the health and well-being of the caregivers.[15] Care receivers recognized that caregivers may sacrifice other financial or social opportunities in order to provide care. Disabled care receivers also felt that they should not have to rely solely on the caregiver for financial and physical support. Clearly, disabled/nondisabled couples need a variety of support, including respite care, money, and flexible services. It may be that some level of market-based assistance is inevitable and useful. The key will be working together to develop sophisticated assessments of the costs and benefits of privatizing care, and proposing policy solutions that work for both disabled and nondisabled alike.

Because queer theory foils the public/private distinction, I believe queer frames may be a particularly useful way to think about intimate care for the disabled body, including the ways in which this care is sexualized both inside and outside of disabled/nondisabled intimate relationships. I believe that care and sexuality in disabled/nondisabled relationships are taboo subjects because of heteronormative ways to think about bodies, erogenous zones, and proper sexuality. However, as I highlighted in Chapter 7, care activities often become part of the couple's sexual intimacy in disabled/nondisabled relationships. Future work should consider the implications of queering disabled/nondisabled intimate relationships as well as queering care more generally.

Finally, feminist and disability activists/scholars must work on providing new images and new narratives of disabled/nondisabled relationships. These images can help dislodge the negative, demeaning representations enforced in dominant discourses and illuminate new ways of relating that can inform all social relationships. Drawing on Luce Irigaray's notion of otherness and the later work of Michel Foucault, Hughes et al. "propose that the feminization of care in a phallocentric culture makes participants in the caring relationship—regardless of gender identity—necessarily subordinate."[16] Relegated to the realm of the other, disabled/nondisabled couples that give and receive care are misrepresented or not represented at all. Their existence is unspeakable in the language of the dominant culture. Thus, Hughes et al. suggest that "those involved in caring relationships" need to represent "its delight and drudgery and to fashion a dignified 'aesthetics of existence.'"[17] For Foucault, "life as a work of art is characterized by creativity, and attained through work on the self [which] involves the intensification of relations to oneself."[18] Dedicated to the care of the self in social and political contexts, "an aesthetics of existence is thus an ongoing project that requires ethical work."[19] This book adds to the literature by offering glimpses of beautiful lives.

More research on disabled/nondisabled relationships—especially those imbued with other forms of social difference such as sexual orientation and race—is needed. Much of the research to date, including this project, has examined white, heterosexual couples. In addition, future research should consider how other domains, such as the influence of children, public policy, and support organizations, influence the experience of care and sexuality in disabled/nondisabled relationships. Most of all, we need new images and new narratives about care and intimacy in disabled/nondisabled relationships. In this effort, I will conclude with one more story about Max and me.

Max could not stand without a walker, and even then he was mostly using the strength of his arms to keep him upright. To maintain bone density and flexibility, he was supposed to stand using the walker several times a day. We did it once or twice a month. I actually enjoyed helping him with this task because it was one of the few times we stood face-to-face. It was always quite shocking to me and I would become giddy from the novelty, and we would gaze into each other's eyes and kiss. Sometimes, if he was feeling energetic, Max would also wiggle his rear end and do a little jig to make us both laugh. Despite the fun we had with the exercises, he avoided them like the plague because it was so exhausting. Two or three sit-stands wiped Max out. I also think it was scary for him. The MS sometimes interfered with his sense of balance; he would become dizzy or disoriented suddenly when he was just sitting in his chair. Loud noises or fast movements startled him badly and could cause instant vertigo. So, he was very worried about falling during these exercises and checked and double-checked with me to ensure that I was braced and ready for him. I was always ready, but he never did fall.

In the water, however, Max could stand—even walk—without the exertion. And wrapped in a life jacket, he was not as worried about falling. He would stand, chest deep in the water, and walk along the edge of the pool holding on to the wall for balance. Of course it was a lot of work getting to the YMCA, dressing in swim trunks, being lowered into the pool with a mechanical lift, and then being lifted out, dried, and dressed again. So, unfortunately, we did not do this type of exercise often either, but we did do it often enough that Max eventually felt safe enough in the water with me to go without the life jacket. I stood behind him and wrapped my arms around his chest and started walking backward, slowly and steadily, but at a good enough speed to let him lift his feet and legs and "float." In this position, Max could stretch and slowly kick his legs, moving muscles that he never could on land. It was excellent exercise and it was one of the ways that I cared for Max, but it was also a very intimate, erotic experience. I will always remember what it was like to feel Max's whole body move with mine in the water. Although we lay next to each other every night, it was only in the water that our whole bodies could move freely together. So, among the children just learning to swim and the old ladies doing water aerobics, we glided through the water, heads together, deeply in love.

Notes

1. Cohen, *Dirty Details.*
2. Andersen, *The Princess and the Pea.*
3. Shakespeare, *Help.*
4. Watson et al., "(Inter)dependence," p. 335.
5. Ibid., p. 338.
6. Fine and Glendinning, "Dependence, Independence," p. 603.
7. Held, "Care and the Extension," p. 23.
8. Ibid.
9. Ibid., p. 32.
10. Fine and Glendinning, "Dependence, Independence," p. 604.
11. Ibid., p. 605.
12. Hughes et al., "Loves Labours," p. 260.
13. Morris, "'Us' and 'Them'?"; Walmsley, "Contradictions in Caring"; Lloyd, "Does She Boil Eggs?" and "The Politics of Disability and Feminism."
14. Clarke and McKay, *Exploring Disability.*
15. McCann and Evans, "Informal Care," p. 228.
16. Hughes et al., "Loves Labours," p. 260.
17. Foucault's "aesthetics of existence" has been criticized by many feminists for celebrating autonomous male individuals; however, following Margaret McLaren, I read Foucault's work on the "beautiful life" as open to all people and as inherently involving social relationships. See McLaren, *Feminism, Foucault*, pp. 68–74, for a good review of the feminist discourse on the "aesthetics of existence." Hughes et al., "Loves Labours," p. 271.
18. McLaren, *Feminism, Foucault*, p. 70.
19. Ibid.

Appendix A:
Methods

Focus Group Methodology

After exploring several methodological options (e.g., individual interviews, couple interviews, and questionnaires), I selected the focus group or "feminist group interview."[1] Used for decades in market research, focus groups are becoming increasingly popular in the social sciences.[2] They are generally defined as a group interview, composed of six to twelve people, "that places particular importance on interaction between participants."[3] Focus groups are particularly "appropriate for the generation of new ideas formed within a social context."[4]

I felt that focus groups best fit my research questions and goals for three reasons. First, focus groups allow participants to control the discussion and, potentially, can reveal information a researcher previously has not considered because participants build on and add to each other's opinions.[5] Focus groups construct collective knowledge among the participants. Sharlene Nagy Hesse-Biber and Patricia Lina Leavy suggest that focus groups create a "happening."[6] Leavy explains that a "happening" is "a conversation that, while pre-arranged and 'focused' by the researcher, remains a dynamic narrative process. Within the context, group members communicate their thoughts, feelings, and experiences on their own terms."[7] The happening is the result of the unique interaction between participants. As Tim Freeman puts it, "focus groups aim to promote self-disclosure among participants, by explicitly capitalizing on group dynamics in discussions. Participants are encouraged to question each other's responses, elicit clarification and explore caveats to their statements."[8] Thus, the happening draws out new understandings for the researcher and the participants, creating a rich data set. Joan Callahan, quoted by Shulamit Reinharz, explains that she chose the focus group methodology based on her "belief that the women's participation and the flow of ideas and information would be enhanced by being able to listen to each other's experience and to interact with each other . . . a group interview format facilitates women building on each other's ideas and augments the identification of patterns through their shared experience."[9] In this sense, the focus group mirrors feminist consciousness-raising groups. Marginalized individuals begin to notice common experiences and supposedly private, individual problems become uncovered as collective battles. The focus group can expose shared social experiences to the researcher and participants alike.

My second motivation for selecting focus groups is the long history of research *on* people with disabilities.[10] In particular, the sex lives of individuals with disabilities have been overresearched in the applied fields (see Chapter 3); thus, performing more individual interviews risks reproducing this dynamic. Focus groups offer participants the space to talk about the issues of care and sexual intimacy without focusing on the particularities of their own lives, unless they so desire. In other words, information about care and intimacy can be gained without putting individual couples under the microscope. Jenny Kitzinger argues that focus groups are particularly good for reaching what she calls "difficult" populations—groups that are socially marginalized, oppressed, or hard to reach—because the design provides "safety in numbers" and an environment of mutual support among people with similar life experiences.[11] Thus, especially for people who feel that they have little to contribute to research, the process of group dialogue can "help people explore and clarify their views and attitudes efficiently."[12] In other research modes, the researcher is more obviously in control—asking the questions, setting the terms of the discussion, probing only when he or she believes the participants' comments are significant. In focus groups, the locus of power is more squarely in the group; "priority is given to the respondents' hierarchy of importance, their language and concepts, their frameworks for understanding the world."[13] As Esther Madriz notes, "focus groups allow access to research participants who may find one-on-one, face-to-face interactions 'scary' or 'intimidating.'"[14]

Third, many couples who deal with disability report social isolation.[15] Focus groups potentially can facilitate community building among couples who are experiencing similar forms of disability discrimination and isolation.[16] As a feminist researcher concerned with the transformative potential of research, I wanted to select a method that encouraged community building and the production of new group knowledge.[17] Ideally, disabled/nondisabled couples could be a source of support for each other even beyond the onetime interaction of the focus group.

Focus groups are not, however, entirely ideal. Although all of the participants share the experience of being in a disabled/nondisabled intimate relationship, they differ from each other in many ways. The couples in the focus groups varied in terms of age, class, education, religion, and race and ethnicity. Thus, power dynamics can inevitably operate within the group, potentially silencing less privileged individuals. In addition, some individuals may not feel comfortable sharing personal information in a group setting, or may not be able to think of pertinent information at the time of the focus group.[18] To help mediate these potentially negative variables, I used a journaling or diary method as an additional, optional follow-up study to the focus groups.[19] In the journals, participants could write about their personal experiences, thoughts, and issues around care, sexuality, and disability during the two-week period following the focus group. The journals provided a space for participants to speak freely about topics they may have been unwilling or uncomfortable to discuss in the focus group. The journals could also capture thoughts generated by the focus group discussion, yielding much richer data than the initial group meeting.

Finally, in order to help account for the power dynamics among participants and between myself and the group, I used feminist standpoint theory (as elaborated in the "Data Analysis" section below) to guide interpretation. Standpoint theory ensured that the ways in which the participants and I were situated in the social-political landscape, and how these locations may have influenced our knowledge production, were not eclipsed in the findings. In line with standpoint theory, I disclosed my investment in the project at the beginning of each focus group. I explained that my partner had MS and that I helped with most of his personal care needs. Thus, it was clear to all of the participants that the idea for the project was personal and that I was one of them. I also added my own stories next to theirs during the focus group conversations. I believe that these techniques made the participants feel more comfortable with me. I was the researcher, but I was also a group member; therefore, the potential alienating power dynamic between researcher and subjects was, to a point, mitigated. Furthermore, following Kitzinger's work on focus groups, I do not necessarily assume that the power dynamics in the group will compromise the data. She argues that "instead of generalizing about the effect of the 'groups' we need to pay close attention to the composition of the groups and how the characteristics of any particular group may influence what is said. We can then explore what this tells us about social pressures and the construction and the communication of knowledge."[20] After all, knowledge is always and inevitably formed in relation to others. Focus groups mirror this reality.

Methods

I did not focus on a particular physical disability in this part of the project. Instead, I limited the scope to physical disabilities that limit activities of daily living (bathing, dressing, toileting, and eating). I excluded emotional and cognitive disabilities because the issues that these disabilities raise are very different from physical disabilities, especially around decisionmaking and political and personal autonomy. For example, family reaction to a couple in which one partner has a severe cognitive impairment and the other partner is nondisabled will likely be rooted in concerns about sexual consent in the relationship, not about the level of physical care that the nondisabled partner provides. In addition, I excluded physical disabilities that do not limit activities of daily living because the focus of this research was on the caregiving relationship in which assistance is needed with instrumental and practical activities of daily life. Examining the relationship experience across physical disability is also a choice that reflects the demands of the disability rights movement. Limiting research to a specific disability, such as spinal cord injury or multiple sclerosis, may suggest that the impairment itself impacts the relationship in unique ways. A pandisability approach focuses, instead, on the ways in which society creates particular conditions, such as inaccessible buildings or bias toward people with disabilities, that impact the disability experience.[21] Such an approach encourages people with disabilities to form coalitions across various types of impairment, focusing on the ways in which they are similarly disabled, and to see themselves as a political, social, and cultural identity group.

For this part of the research project, I recruited twelve couples into four focus groups in four different areas of Ohio.[22] Focus Group 1 was located in a large city (City A) and consisted of four couples; Focus Group 2 was located in a medium-sized city (City B) and consisted of two couples; Focus Group 3 was located in a medium-sized city (City C) and consisted of three couples; Focus Group 4 was located in a large city (City D) and consisted of three couples. In each area of Ohio, I contacted regional disability-specific organizations (e.g., MS Society and Adapted Recreational Sports) and Centers for Independent Living. I explained the research and asked for the organization's support in recruitment. For some locations, this meant sending a recruitment announcement through an electronic listserv. At other locations, flyers were posted in their offices or mailed out to constituents. Regardless of the distribution method, recruitment announcements read:

> Couples are needed for a research study on caregiving between intimate partners, in which one is physically disabled and the other is able-bodied. Eligible couples will participate in a focus group with other couples to discuss their experiences with caregiving and intimacy, and the representation of care and intimacy in popular culture.
>
> Eligible couples include same-sex and opposite-sex couples that have lived together (with the physical disability) for at least one year. Participants will be compensated $30 per person for their time.
>
> For more information & to determine eligibility please contact Sarah Smith at smith.2447@osu.edu or 614-202-1791. This project is being conducted by Dr. Christine Keating and Sarah Smith from The Ohio State University and has been approved by the Institutional Review Board (Protocol number 2007B0092).

When a potential participant contacted me, I provided more information about the study, including the expected time commitment (two hours for the focus group), and answered any questions. If the person was still interested in participating, I asked a series of eligibility screening questions. In order to be eligible, the person had to answer yes to all of the following questions: Are you currently in an intimate relationship? Does one partner have a physical disability and is the other partner able-bodied? Does the physical disability limit an activity of daily living? Have you lived together for at least one year (as disabled)? Do you currently live in Ohio? Are both partners aged eighteen to sixty-five? Finally, I asked if either partner had an emotional or cognitive (developmental/mental) disability. If they answered yes, I probed to determine if the emotional or cognitive impairment was severe enough to warrant exclusion from the study. Cognitive impairments like dyslexia and mild Attention Deficit Hyperactivity Disorder (ADHD), as well as emotional impairments like mild anxiety or seasonal depression, did not render participants ineligible for this study. Major impairments like schizophrenia, autism, and other disorders that may impact decision-making warranted exclusion from the study so that the focus could remain on physical care.

If the couple was eligible and willing to participate, I took down their contact information and explained that, once enough couples had been gathered in their area, I would contact them again to schedule the focus group. Recruitment continued until I had enough couples in a given area (minimum of two couples, maximum of four couples, per focus group). If I had recruited more than four couples in a particular area, I called them back in order (e.g., the first couple to contact me in City A was the first couple I called to schedule the focus group). This process of quota sampling continued until all four focus groups were scheduled.

Focus groups were held at locations that would be most convenient for participants in that particular area and were conducted during September and October 2007. Since many of the participants in City A had been recruited through a disability-related organization in that area, this focus group was held in a boardroom of that organization's offices after normal business hours. In City B, the focus group was held in one couple's home because the two couples lived very close to each other and knew one another. An independent living and disability rights organization was the location for the City C focus group because it had been instrumental in recruiting participants for the group (all participants had ties to the organization). In City D, the focus group met in the community space of a local Panera restaurant to minimize driving distance for participants. Regardless of location, participants were reimbursed for metered parking fees (or bus or cab fare if needed) and for child care. This was important so that economic barriers would not prevent lower-income couples from participating.

Upon arrival to the group, I reviewed the consent-to-participate form with each couple, explaining that the focus group would be audiotaped, but that their names and other identifying information would be removed from the transcript to protect their confidentiality. I also told participants (verbally and in writing) that they could refuse to answer any questions and that they could leave the study at any time without negative consequences. They would be compensated $30 each ($60 per couple) for their time even if they left the study. Because focus group participants might decide to share private information with the group, I reminded each participant that what was shared by other participants should be kept confidential. I provided each participant with a copy of the consent form and a resource list that included disability rights organizations and information about couples and individual counseling. Since some of the focus group discussions could dredge up negative emotions or spark disagreements for the couple, it was important that I provide resources that would help participants work through difficulties. However, no participants reported adverse effects or sought help after the focus group. Before beginning the discussion, each participant completed a short demographic questionnaire.

As Chapters 2 and 3 demonstrate, disabled/nondisabled couples' lives are dominated by hegemonic understandings of love and sexuality that reflect ableist manifestations of dependence/independence. For example, providing personal care, especially with tasks such as toileting, is represented as interfering with the couples' sexual lives. Physical care is understood only as a burden, and the disabled partner is viewed as wholly dependent. During the focus groups, I asked participants to speak to these dominant representations and, as a group, construct self-representations that might understand care and intimacy differently. Importantly, the script was intentionally semistructured and open-ended so that participants could take the conversation where they felt it needed to go. All participants understood that the goal of the research was to better understand how they experienced care and intimacy in their relationship, and they were encouraged to deviate from these sections of the script as needed to reach the shared goal of the group.

The script was divided into three sections: (1) how outsiders treat the couple; (2) media representations; and (3) personal definitions of care and intimacy. After briefly introducing themselves to the other group members, I asked participants to begin discussing how outsiders (friends, family, physicians, even strangers) view their relationship. I probed as needed for stories about how such outsiders have treated the couples. Next, I brought up media representations (if they had not already been mentioned), asking participants whether they felt popular culture influenced how they are treated by outsiders. To spark further conversation, I showed each group a short television public service announcement created by Mothers Against Drunk Driving.[23] I selected this public service announcement because it quickly relates many of the ableist attitudes commonly found in popular culture. In the public service announce- ment, a young man is reading on a park bench and the screen reads "your best friend." An attractive woman walks up and kisses him as the screen reads "your girlfriend." The camera moves to the inside of an institutional-looking room with a man in a wheelchair gazing on the pair and the text reads "you." The screen fades to black and says, "You have a lot to lose."

Finally, I encouraged the participants to offer their own understandings of how care, dependence/independence, and intimacy and sexuality operate in their own lives. Typically, participants had already offered anecdotal accounts that countered dominant hegemonic representations of their relationships. As facilitator, I brought the conversation back to these accounts to probe for sim- ilar and different perspectives and experiences.

At the end of each focus group, I explained the optional follow-up study in which each participant would journal about his or her thoughts about and experiences with care, intimacy, and disability for the following two-week period. If a participant chose to complete this part of the study, he or she was given a blank journal and preaddressed, stamped envelope to return the jour- nal. Participants also had the option of completing the journal on the computer and e-mailing the entries. This option was especially important for those par- ticipants who could not write, but used voice recognition software to "type." Either way, participants were paid $30 for this portion of the study. Like the focus groups, they could write as much or as little as they wanted.

Although I have kept in touch informally with some of the participants, and plan to send each participant a copy of the book, I did not perform mem- ber checks (in which they would review the transcript and edit as needed), nor did I ask them to participate in data analysis. Ideally, I would have at least given each participant a transcript and asked for feedback; at best, I would have asked them to interpret the findings with me. This is certainly what fem- inist researchers recommend.[24] However, I chose not to collaborate with par- ticipants on data interpretation for several reasons. Primarily, it was a decision driven by time and financial limitations. Collaborative analysis and member checking can become messy.[25] I was concerned that working with participants on interpretation would delay the completion of the project, especially since the focus groups were only one aspect of a much larger research project. Addi- tionally, I felt that it was only fair to offer financial compensation to partici- pants who worked with me on collaboration or took the time to review the data; however, I could not offer a monetary payment. On a theoretical level, I am not convinced that interpretative collaboration or member checks necessar- ily lead to better analysis. From the perspective of feminist standpoint theory, it is inaccurate to assume that a participant's edits to the transcript will lead to more "valid" data.[26] As subjects situated by race, class, sexual orientation, and so forth, they do not have unmediated access to their truth. However, in retrospect, I wish that I had been able to do collaborative interpretation with participants because I believe it would have improved the emancipatory goals of this project. In addition, the process of collaboration may have led to additional insights, adding another level to the data.

Data Analysis

I transcribed the focus group audio recordings into a Microsoft Word document. I changed the names of the participants and removed any identifying information (e.g., employer, children's names) from the text to ensure participant confidentiality. I transcribed the recordings largely verbatim; however, I did not always note stutters, pauses, and other noises as some qualitative analysts suggest to do.[27] That is because these sounds are simply part of many of the participants' normal speech patterns and do not necessarily indicate hesitation or nervousness. I did note in the transcript text laughter, nonspeech sounds (e.g., moans), nonverbal behaviors such as eye rolling, and significant pauses that I was sure were not disability related.

After transcribing the text, I began coding the data into identity themes. The semistructured interview schedule detailed above was designed to address some of the themes found in the applied fields literature (Chapter 3) and in the published self-representations. I used these same themes to begin data analysis.[28] However, I modified and substantially enhanced these initial themes by drawing from the traditions of grounded theory and schema analysis.[29] Grounded theory uses close, line-by-line reading of the data to allow new themes and relationships to emerge.[30] As I did the first round of coding, I noted topics that did not fit into the themes on the initial coding sheet. These new topics became new themes if they appeared frequently or if I felt they could be particularly significant. With this method, theoretical understandings emerge from the data.

Grounded theory methods cannot, however, detect the effects of power operating within the group or capture the impact of social location on knowledge formation. As Kathy Charmaz notes, "most grounded theorists write as if their data have an objective status. Strauss and Corbin (1998) write of 'the reality of the data' and tell us, 'The data do not lie' (p. 85). Data are narrative constructions. . . . They are re-constructions of experience; they are not the original experience itself."[31] The themes that emerge from the data are shaped by the interaction of the participants in the focus group, the time and day of the interview, the location of the interview, and the standpoint of the participant. These and other factors mediate what is said and not said. The standpoint of the participant is particularly important to feminist data analysis because it recognizes the impact of social difference on experience. Donna Haraway, quoted in Virginia Olesen, explains that "standpoints are cognitive-emotional-political achievements, crafted out of located social-historical-bodily experience—itself always constituted through fraught, noninnocent, discursive, material, collective practices."[32]

Considering the impact of standpoint and other factors, I did not approach the data as fully transparent. During coding, I made sure to pay attention to participants' race, class, disability status, and gender, noting where a participant's experience of and beliefs about social difference become apparent. For example, "sexism" became a theme in the final coding. In addition, I drew from the tradition of schema analysis, which is "based on the idea that people must use cognitive simplifications to help make sense of the complex information to which they are constantly exposed."[33] Using schema analysis, I noted specific words that appeared frequently, metaphors, and absences—places in which explanation is not given because a participant assumes other group members understand or share belief or perspective. Drawing from grounded theory, standpoint theory, and schema analysis, I added new themes to the coding sheet after the two rounds of coding. Using the final coding sheet, I entered texts and codes into NVivo Version 7, a qualitative data analysis software program. NVivo is an excellent data management tool—all pieces of text coded at a certain theme can be generated quickly for analysis.

Demographics

The demographics of all participants are displayed in Table 1.1 (Chapter 1). Although all recruitment announcements indicated that I was interested in talking with both same-sex and opposite-sex couples, only opposite-sex couples contacted me. In addition, only one participant was African American. All other participants, including his wife, identified as white or Caucasian. The sample was more diverse in terms of age. The mean age was thirty-nine years old, ranging from age twenty-three to sixty-four. Based on representations in popular culture and research from the applied fields that indicate it is more likely for disabled women to be divorced or abandoned by male partners than disabled men to be by female partners,[34] I expected the sample to be heavy with disabled men. However, the woman was the disabled partner in ten of the twelve couples in this sample. As expected, only two of the couples experienced the onset of the disability after the start of their relationship: for the vast majority of the sample, the disability was present when the pair met.

This group of selected couples is obviously not a representative sample, nor was it intended to be. The intention was simply to talk with disabled/nondisabled couples outside of a clinical, therapeutic setting in order to better understand how average people experience disability, intimacy, and care in their relationships. It is also important to note that the sample I recruited was more likely to be happy with their relationship because they were willing to talk in a group about their experiences. Couples experiencing distress would most likely be reluctant to share such problems in a group (unless, of course, that group is explicitly a therapy or support group). The demographics are important, however, in guiding the data analysis because social location impacts disability experiences and beliefs.

Content Analysis Methods

It actually was quite difficult to find articles that discussed love and care in disabled/nondisabled intimate relationships. I experimented with various keywords that would yield articles about care, sexuality, or both in disabled/nondisabled intimate relationships, including "sex," "disability," "care," "carer," "partner," and "spouse." Ultimately, conducting two separate searches proved to be most productive.[35] In the first search, I used the keywords "caregiving" and "spouse" and retrieved ninety-eight potential articles.[36] In the second search, I used the keywords "sexuality" and "disability," which yielded 179 potential articles. Then, I read each abstract from the search results to determine the article's relevance and inclusion in the analysis. I excluded articles that focused on end-of-life or bereavement issues, intellectual or emotional disabilities, or relations other than intimate relationships. After this exclusion process, twenty-three articles from the "sexuality and disability" search and forty-one articles from the "caregiving and spouse" search remained (see Appendix B). One article appeared in both searches. Finally, I analyzed the sixty-three articles using a form created for this study to ensure the same information was collected on each article (see Figure A.1). On each

---

Figure A.1   Information Gathered for Content Analysis

Article Name:
- Was this article found from the "Sexuality and Disability" search, the "Caregiving and Spouse" search, or both?
- Demographics of study participants (if relevant).
- Is the article primarily concerned with the disabled partner, the nondisabled partner, or both? Is there a rationale for this choice? Does the choice support the research question?
- How does the article represent the relationship?
- Does the article address intimacy or sex? If so, is it related to the discussion of care?
- Do the methods support the dominant image of care, or do they attempt to uncover other aspects of the care relationship?
- Describe any intertextuality.

form, I recorded how the article framed caregiving, sexuality and intimacy in the relationship, and whether the authors were focused on the well-being of both or only one of the partners. I entered these results for each article into the software program NVivo 8 so that various qualitative analyses could be conducted as need.

Notes

1. Shulamit Reinarz, *Feminist Methods*, uses the term "feminist group interview" to distinguish the method from focus groups used for market research or sociology. For Reinarz, the feminist group interview is distinct from the focus group because it is dedicated to women's knowledge and explicitly seeks to add value to the lives of women (instead of to a product or company). I primarily use the term "focus group" because it is, at this point, the more widely used term among qualitative researchers (including those outside of the business world). It should be clear, however, that like the feminist group interview, the focus groups in this study were also dedicated to improving the lives of people with disabilities and their partners.

2. See, for example, Breen, "A Practical Guide"; Kitzinger, "The Methodology of Focus Groups"; and van Staveren, "Focus Groups."

3. Freeman, "'Best Practice,'" p. 492.

4. Breen, "A Practical Guide," p. 466.

5. Freeman, "'Best Practice,'" p. 492; Madriz, "Focus Groups," p. 838; Reinharz, *Feminist Methods*, p. 223.

6. Hesse-Biber and Leavy, *The Practice of Qualitative Research*, p. 19.

7. Leavy, "The Practice of Feminist Oral History," p. 173.

8. Freeman, "'Best Practice,'" p. 492.

9. Quoted in Reinharz, *Feminist Methods*, p. 223.

10. Two excellent examples of how people with disabilities are sometimes treated as objects and/or pin cushions by researchers are Anne Finger, *Elegy for a Disease*; and Kenny Fries, *Body, Remember*. Barnes, Mercer, and Shakespeare, *Exploring Disability*, pp. 213–220; Swain, French, and Cameron, *Controversial Issues*, pp. 131–136.

11. Kitzinger, "The Methodology of Focus Groups," p. 112.

12. Freeman, "'Best Practice,'" p. 493.

13. Kitzinger, "The Methodology of Focus Groups," p. 108.

14. Madriz, "Focus Groups," p. 835.

15. Parker, *With This Body*, pp. 114–115.

16. Madriz, "Focus Groups," p. 842.

17. Olesen, "Early Millennial Feminist," p. 252.

18. Freeman, "'Best Practice,'" p. 493; Kitzinger, "The Methodology of Focus Groups," p. 110.

19. There is little in the feminist literature about the use of journaling as a data collection method; however, it is similar to other feminist research methods such as content analysis of preexisting diaries (Reinharz, *Feminist Methods*, p. 147) and asking participants to write their oral history or narrative (p. 143). Journaling or diaries are, however, prominent in health research that seeks to measure daily health-related behaviors (e.g., safer sex practices and eating habits). For a rather innovative examination of the use of journals in social science research, see Välimäki et al. In their study, they tested the usefulness of diaries for family caregivers of people with Alzheimer's disease. They found

that diaries provided good research data and seemed to help participants: "The writing experience had been pleasant, even therapeutic, in some families, helping: 'me to think more clearly about this'" (p. 73).

20. Kitzinger, "The Methodology of Focus Groups," pp. 112–113.

21. See, for example, Shapiro, *No Pity*; and Stroman, *The Disability Rights Movement*.

22. In her review of the focus group methodology literature from sociology and anthropology, van Staveren says that "three to four groups on one subject are generally enough and a duration of one to two hours per group is advised" ("Focus Groups," p. 132).

23. Kitzinger recommends using a "group exercise" in the focus group to maximize participation and minimize facilitator involvement ("The Methodology of Focus Groups," p. 107). Drawing attention to the exercise—such as having the group sort cards into various categories—requires participants to work together, to reach consensus, or to clarify disagreements. Using the public service announcement ("Girlfriend," Mothers Against Drunk Driving Canada, 2005) required participants to discuss their reactions to the image and help warm up the group for a good discussion of popular culture.

24. For example, Kirsch, *Ethical Dilemmas*.

25. See, for example, Borland, "'That's Not What I Said.'"

26. Acker, Barry, and Esseveld, "Objectivity and Truth"; Naples, *Feminism and Method*.

27. For example, Peräkylä, "Analyzing Talk and Text"; Yow, *Recording Oral History*, pp. 227–233.

28. Miles and Huberman, *Qualitative Data Analysis*; Ryan and Bernard, "Data Management," p. 781; Willms et al., "A Systematic Approach."

29. Agar and Hobbs, "How to Grow Schemata."

30. Charmaz, "Grounded Theory."

31. Ibid., p. 514.

32. Quoted in Olesen, "Early Millennial Feminist," p. 243.

33. Ryan and Bernard, "Data Management," p. 783.

34. Singh and Sharma, "Sexuality and Women," p. 29.

35. Searches that included both sexuality and care (or some version of care, such as caregiving, caregiver, etc.) yielded few articles. Therefore, I ultimately divided the searches into two so that I could mine the literature on sexual relationships of people with disabilities and partner/spousal care of people with disabilities.

36. Using the term "spouse" also highlights the heterosexual bias to the literature. Using "caregiving" and "partner" as the search terms produces only forty-two results, most of which are not relevant to the intimate relationship. Those articles that are about intimate partners show up on the "caregiving" and "spouse" search, which also produces more results in general. Therefore, I ultimately used the "caregiving" and "spouse" search for Chapter 3. Thus, using "partner" instead of "spouse" did not reveal additional research about same-sex relationships.

Appendix B:
Self-Representations
and Articles Analyzed

Autobiographies and
Documentary Self-Representations

Cohen, Marion Deutsche. *Dirty Details: The Days and Nights of a Well Spouse*. 1996.
Cohen details her experiences of providing physical care to her husband, Jeffrey, who has multiple sclerosis. Cohen is a writer and mathematics professor.

Hockenberry, John. *Moving Violations: War Zones, Wheelchairs, and Declarations of Independence*. 1996.
Hockenberry became paraplegic in a car accident in 1976. This book is a collection of autobiographical essays. Although Hockenberry is now married to Alison, the essays in the book are about relationships with women before Alison.

Klein, Bonnie Sherr, and Persimmon Blackbridge. *Slow Dance: A Story of Stroke, Love, and Disability*. 1997.
Klein, a feminist filmmaker, details the stroke that left her permanently impaired, and her relationship with her husband, Michael.

Kondracke, Morton. *Saving Milly: Love, Politics, and Parkinson's Disease*. 2001.
Kondracke, a journalist, tells the story of his relationship with his wife, Milly, and their battle with Parkinson's disease.

Mairs, Nancy. *Waist-High in the World: A Life Among the Nondisabled*. 1996.
Mairs's autobiographical essay collection explores her experience of having multiple sclerosis, her life as a writer, and her relationship with her husband, George.

Murphy, Robert. *The Body Silent*. 1987.
As a trained anthropologist, Murphy provides text that is part autobiography, part ethnography of the physically disabled. Quadriplegic from a spinal tumor, Murphy describes his physical dependency and his relationship with his anthropologist wife, Yolanda.

Shameless: The ART of Disability. Directed by Bonnie Sherr Klein, 2006.
The film follows five disabled activists/artists in Canada—Bonnie Sherr Klein, Geoffrey McMurchy, David Roche, Catherine Frazee, and Persimmon Blackbridge—as they create self-representations for KickstART!, a disability arts festival. Along the way, the five friends discuss disability discrimination, media stereotypes, love and relationships, the limits of the body, and other disability issues. *Shameless* is Klein's first film since her stroke in 1987. She is best known for her documentary film *Not a Love Story* (1981), about pornography and its negative effect on women.

Sick: The Life and Death of Bob Flanagan Supermasochist. Directed by Kirby Dick, 1997.
The film follows another disabled artist/activist, Bob Flanagan, self-described "supermasochist." At the time of his death in 1996 at age forty-three, Flanagan was the oldest living survivor of cystic fibrosis, a hereditary disease that causes the body to produce excess phlegm in the lungs, resulting in difficult breathing, constant cough, pancreatic and bowel problems, and increased infections. The film chronicles Flanagan's last two years of his life (including, eerily, his death), focusing especially on Flanagan's relationship with his life partner Sheree Rose, their mistress/slave relationship, and Flanagan's bondage, discipline, dominance, submission, sadism, and masochism (BDSM) performance art. Video excerpts from Flanagan's earlier performances are edited into the film.

Want. Directed by Loree Erickson, 2007.
Want is a short autobiographical film by Loree Erickson about her desire to be seen as more than a person with a disability and to make visible queer crip sexuality and community. Viewers see scenes of Loree having sex with a female partner, scenes of Loree being cared for by friends, and footage that Loree has taken on the streets.

Articles Analyzed from the Sexuality and Disability Search (*n* = 23)

Barnoff, Lisa, Christina Sinding, and Pamela Grassau. "Listening to the Voices of Lesbians Diagnosed with Cancer: Recommendations for Change in Cancer Support Services." *Journal of Gay and Lesbian Social Services* 18, no. 1 (2005): 17–35.
Christopherson, Jeannine Marguerite, et al. "A Comparison of Written Materials vs. Materials and Counselling for Women with Sexual Dysfunction and Multiple Sclerosis." *Journal of Clinical Nursing* 15, no. 6 (2006): 742–750.
Gagliardi, Barbara A. "The Experience of Sexuality for Individuals Living with Multiple Sclerosis." *Journal of Clinical Nursing* 12, no. 4 (2003): 571–578.
Galvin, Rose D. "Researching the Disabled Identity: Contextualising the Identity Transformations Which Accompany the Onset of Impairment." *Sociology of Health and Illness* 27, no. 3 (2005): 393–413.
Hassouneh-Phillips, Dena, and Elizabeth McNeff. "'I Thought I Was Less Worthy': Low Sexual and Body Esteem and Increased Vulnerability to Intimate Partner Abuse in Women with Physical Disabilities." *Sexuality and Disability* 23, no. 4 (2005): 227–240.

Karimzadeh, Mansoureh, et al. "The Psychological Impact of Infertility in the Male Able Bodied and Spinal Cord Injured Population." *Sexuality and Disability* 24, no. 4 (2006): 185–193.

Kedde, Harald, and Willy van Berlo. "Sexual Satisfaction and Sexual Self Images of People with Physical Disabilities in the Netherlands." *Sexuality and Disability* 24, no. 1 (2006): 53–68.

Laursen, Birgitte Schantz, et al. "Ongoing Pain, Sexual Desire, and Frequency of Sexual Intercourse in Females with Different Chronic Pain Syndromes." *Sexuality and Disability* 24, no. 1 (2006): 27–37.

Li, Candy Mung-nga, and Matthew Kwai-sang Yau. "Sexual Issues and Concerns: Tales of Chinese Women with Spinal Cord Impairments." *Sexuality and Disability* 24, no. 1 (2006): 1–26.

McCabe, Marita P., and George Taleporos. "Sexual Esteem, Sexual Satisfaction, and Sexual Behavior Among People with Physical Disability." *Archives of Sexual Behavior* 32, no. 4 (2003): 359–369.

Melby, Todd. "Facilitated Sex." *Contemporary Sexuality* 37, no. 11 (2003): 1–6.

Mona, Linda R. "Sexual Options for People with Disabilities: Using Personal Assistance Services for Sexual Expression." *Women and Therapy* 26, nos. 3–4 (2003): 211–221.

Murray, C. D., and B. Harrison. "The Meaning and Experience of Being a Stroke Survivor: An Interpretative Phenomenological Analysis." *Disability and Rehabilitation* 26, no. 13 (2004): 808–816.

Rodarte, Irene Torices, and Martha Patricia Bonilla Muñoz. "Inventory of Sexual Experiences and Response in Disability (IEReSDi): Construction and Validation of the Scale of the Sexual Response in People with Disabilities." *Sexuality and Disability* 22, no. 3 (2004): 181–195.

Sakellariou, Dikaios. "If Not Disability, Then What? Barriers to Reclaiming Sexuality Following Spinal Cord Injury." *Sexuality and Disability* 24, no. 2 (2006): 101–111.

Schmidt, E. Z., et al. "Sexuality in Multiple Sclerosis." *Journal of Neural Transmission* 112, no. 9 (2005): 1201–1211.

Singh, Roop, and Sansar C. Sharma. "Sexuality and Women with Spinal Cord Injury." *Sexuality and Disability* 23, no. 1 (2005): 21–33.

Svetlik, Doris, et al. "Declines in Satisfaction with Physical Intimacy Predict Caregiver Perceptions of Overall Relationship Loss: A Study of Elderly Caregiving Spousal Dyads." *Sexuality and Disability* 23, no. 2 (2005): 65–79.

Taleporos, George, and Marita P. McCabe. "Relationships, Sexuality and Adjustment Among People with Physical Disability." *Sexual and Relationship Therapy* 18, no. 1 (2003): 25–43.

Valtonen, Kirsi, et al. "Satisfaction with Sexual Life Among Persons with Traumatic Spinal Cord Injury and Meningomyelocele." *Disability and Rehabilitation* 28, no. 16 (2006): 965–976.

Vansteenwegen, Alfons, I. Jans, and Arlynn T. Revell. "Sexual Experience of Women with a Physical Disability: A Comparative Study." *Sexuality and Disability* 21, no. 4 (2003): 283–290.

Wiegerink, Diana, et al. "Social and Sexual Relationships of Adolescents and Young Adults with Cerebral Palsy: A Review." *Clinical Rehabilitation* 20, no. 12 (2006): 1023–1031.

Zitzelsberger, Hilde. "(In)visibility: Accounts of Embodiment of Women with Physical Disabilities and Differences." *Disability and Society* 20, no. 4 (2005): 389–403.

Articles Analyzed from the Caregiving and Spouse Search (*n* = 41)

Beach, Scott R., et al. "Risk Factors for Potentially Harmful Informal Caregiver Behavior." *Journal of the American Geriatrics Society* 53, no. 2 (2005): 255–261.

Blake, Holly, Nadina B. Lincoln, and David D. Clarke. "Caregiver Strain in Spouses of Stroke Patients." *Clinical Rehabilitation* 17, no. 3 (2003): 312–317.

Boeije, Hennie R., Mia S. H. Duijnstee, and Maria H. F. Grypdonck. "Continuation of Caregiving Among Partners Who Give Total Care to Spouses with Multiple Sclerosis." *Health and Social Science in the Community* 11, no. 3 (2003): 242–252.

Boeije, Hennie R., and Anneke Van Doorne-Huiskes. "Fulfilling a Sense of Duty: How Men and Women Giving Care to Spouses with Multiple Sclerosis Interpret This Role." *Community, Work and Family* 6, no. 3 (2003): 223–244.

Bookwala, Jamila, et al. "Concurrent and Long-Term Predictors of Older Adults' Use of Community-Based Long-Term Care Services: The Caregiver Health Effects Study." *Journal of Aging and Health* 16, no. 1 (2004): 88–115.

Burton, Lynda C., et al. "Transitions in Spousal Caregiving." *The Gerontologist* 43, no. 2 (2003): 230–241.

Campbell, Thomas L. "The Effectiveness of Family Interventions for Physical Disorders." *Journal of Marital and Family Therapy* 29, no. 2 (2003): 263–281.

Cannuscio, Carolyn C., et al. "Employment Status, Social Ties, and Caregivers' Mental Health." *Social Science and Medicine* 58, no. 7 (2004): 1247–1256.

Chappell, Neena L. "Correcting Cross-Cultural Stereotypes: Aging in Shanghai and Canada." *Journal of Cross-Cultural Gerontology* 18, no. 2 (2003): 127–147.

Choi, Heejeong, and Nadine F. Marks. "Transition to Caregiving, Marital Disagreement, and Psychological Well-Being: A Prospective U.S. National Study." *Journal of Family Issues* 27, no. 12 (2006): 1701–1722.

Cremeans-Smith, Julie K., et al. "Spouses' and Physicians' Perceptions of Pain Severity in Older Women with Osteoarthritis: Dyadic Agreement and Patients' Well-Being." *Pain* 106, nos. 1–2 (2003): 27–34.

Druley, Jennifer A., et al. "Emotional Congruence in Older Couples Coping with Wives' Osteoarthritis: Exacerbating Effects of Pain Behavior." *Psychology and Aging* 18, no. 3 (2003): 406–414.

Ducharme, Francine, et al. "Older Husbands as Caregivers of Their Wives: A Descriptive Study of the Context and Relational Aspects of Care." *International Journal of Nursing Studies* 43, no. 5 (2006): 567–579.

Ellenbogen, Phyllis S., et al. "The Impact of Spinal Cord Injury on the Employment of Family Caregivers." *Journal of Vocational Rehabilitation* 25, no. 1 (2006): 35–44.

Feld, Sheila, Ruth E. Dunkle, and Tracy Schroepfer. "When Do Couples Expand Their ADL Caregiver Network Beyond the Marital Dyad?" *Marriage and Family Review* 37, nos. 1–2 (2005): 27–44.

Feld, S., et al. "Expansion of Elderly Couples' IADL Caregiver Networks Beyond the Marital Dyad." *International Journal of Aging and Human Development* 63, no. 2 (2006): 95–113.

Fultz, Nancy H., et al. "The Impact of Own and Spouse's Urinary Incontinence of Depressive Symptoms." *Social Science and Medicine* 60, no. 11 (2005): 2537–2548.

Giarelli, Ellen, Ruth McCorkle, and Cheryl Monturo. "Caring for a Spouse After Prostrate Surgery: The Preparedness Needs of Wives." *Journal of Family Nursing* 9, no. 4 (2003): 453–485.

Gordon, Phyllis A., and Kristin M. Perrone. "When Spouses Become Caregivers: Counseling Implications for Younger Couples." *Journal of Rehabilitation* 70, no. 2 (2004): 27–32.

Hash, Kristina. "Caregiving and Post-Caregiving Experiences of Midlife and Older Gay Men and Lesbians." *Journal of Gerontological Social Work* 47, nos. 3–4 (2006): 121–138.

Hendrix, Christina, and Charlene Ray. "Informal Caregiver Training on Home Care and Cancer Symptom Management Prior to Hospital Discharge: A Feasibility Study." *Oncology Nursing Forum* 33, no. 4 (2006): 793–798.

Hirst, Michael. "Carer Distress: A Prospective, Population-Based Study." *Social Science and Medicine* 61, no. 3 (2005): 697–708.

Ingersoll-Dayton, Berit, and Michael Raschick. "The Relationship Between Care-Recipient Behaviors and Spousal Caregiving Stress." *The Gerontologist* 44, no. 3 (2004): 318–327.

Joseph, Elizabeth Betcy, and Ranbir S. Bhatti. "Psychosocial Problems and Coping Patterns of HIV Seropositive Wives of Men with HIV/AIDS." *Social Work in Health Care* 39, nos. 1–2 (2004): 29–47.

Kang, Suk-Young. "Predictors of Emotional Strain Among Spouse and Adult Child Caregivers." *Journal of Gerontological Social Work* 47, nos. 1–2 (2006): 107–131.

Kim, Catherine, et al. "Quality of Preventive Clinical Services Among Caregivers in the Health and Retirement Study." *Journal of General Internal Medicine* 19, no. 8 (2004): 875–878.

Kim, Youngmee, et al. "Gender Differences in Caregiving Stress Among Caregivers of Cancer Survivors." *Psycho-Oncology* 15, no. 12 (2006): 1086–1092.

Lee, Sunmin, et al. "Caregiving and Risk of Coronary Heart Disease in U.S. Women: A Prospective Study." *American Journal of Preventative Medicine* 24, no. 2 (2003): 113–119.

Lin, Pi-Chu, and Change-Ming Lu. "Hip Fracture: Family Caregivers' Burden and Related Factors for Older People in Taiwan." *Journal of Clinical Nursing* 14, no. 6 (2005): 719–726.

Luttik, Marie Louise, et al. "For Better and for Worse: Quality of Life Impaired in HF Patients as Well as in Their Partners." *European Journal of Cardiovascular Nursing* 4, no. 1 (2005): 11–14.

Martire et al. "Older Spouses' Perceptions of Partners' Chronic Arthritis Pain: Implications for Spousal Responses, Support Provision, and Caregiving Experiences." *Psychology and Aging* 21, no. 2 (2006): 222–230.

Mbanaso, Michael Udo, Jeffrey Shavelson, and John Ukawuilulu. "Elderly African Americans as Intragenerational Caregivers." *Journal of Gerontological Social Work* 47, nos. 1–2 (2006): 3–15.

Pinquart, Martin, and Silvia Sörensen. "Associations of Stressors and Uplifts of Caregiving with Caregiver Burden and Depressive Mood: A Meta-Analysis." *Journal of Gerontology: Psychological Sciences* 58B, no. 2 (2003): P112–P128.

———. "Ethnic Differences in Stressors, Resources, and Psychological Outcomes of Family Caregiving: A Meta-Analysis." *The Gerontologist* 45, no. 1 (2005): 90–106.

Raschick, Michael, and Berit Ingersoll-Dayton. "The Costs and Rewards of Caregiving Among Aging Spouses and Adult Children." *Family Relations* 53, no. 3 (2004): 317–325.

Ruiz, John M., et al. "Does Who You Marry Matter for Your Health? Influence of Patients' and Spouses' Personality on Their Partners' Psychological Well-Being

Following Coronary Artery Bypass Surgery." *Journal of Personality and Social Psychology* 91, no. 2 (2006): 255–267.

Smith, Tamara L., and Ronald W. Toseland. "The Effectiveness of a Telephone Support Program for Caregivers of Frail Older Adults." *The Gerontologist* 46, no. 5 (2006): 620–629.

Soskolne, Varda, et al. "Caregiving Stressors and Psychological Distress Among Veteran Resident and Immigrant Family Caregivers in Israel." *Social Work in Health Care* 43, nos. 2–3 (2006): 73–93.

Svetlik, Doris, et al. "Declines in Satisfaction with Physical Intimacy Predict Caregiver Perceptions of Overall Relationship Loss: A Study of Elderly Caregiving Spousal Dyads." *Sexuality and Disability* 23, no. 2 (2005): 65–79.

Toseland, Ronald W., et al. "Supporting Caregivers of Frail Older Adults in an HMO Setting." *American Journal of Orthopsychiatry* 74, no. 3 (2004): 349–364.

Wolff, Jennifer L., and Judith D. Kasper. "Caregivers of Frail Elders: Updating a National Profile." *The Gerontologist* 46, no. 3 (2006): 344–356.

Bibliography

Acker, Joan, Kate Barry, and Johanna Esseveld. "Objectivity and Truth: Problems in Doing Feminist Research." In *Beyond Methodology: Feminist Scholarship as Lived Research*, edited by Mary Margaret Fonow and Judith A. Cook, 133–153. Bloomington: Indiana University Press, 1991.

Agar, M., and J. Hobbs. "How to Grow Schemata Out of Interviews." In *Directions in Cognitive Anthropology*, edited by Janet W. D. Dougherty, 413–431. Urbana: University of Illinois Press, 1985.

Aguilera, Raymond. "Disability and Delight: Staring Back at the Devotee Community." *Sexuality and Disability* 18, no. 4 (2000): 255–261.

Albrecht, Gary L. "Disability Humor: What's in a Joke?" *Body and Society* 5, no. 4 (1999): 67–74.

Altman, Mara. "Something in the Way He Moves." *The Village Voice*, February 6, 2007. http://www.villagevoice.com (February 13, 2007).

An Affair to Remember. DVD. Directed by Leo McCarey. 1957; Beverly Hills, CA: Twentieth Century Fox Home Entertainment, 2002.

Andersen, Hans Christian. *The Princess and the Pea*. Trans. Athea Bell. Natick, MA: Picture Book Studio, 1987.

Asch, Adrienne, and Michelle Fine. "Nurturance, Sexuality and Women with Disabilities: The Example of Women and Literature." In *The Disability Studies Reader*, edited by Lennard Davis, 241–259. New York: Routledge, 1997.

As Good As It Gets. DVD. Directed by James L. Brooks. 1997. Culver City, CA: Columbia TriStar Home Video, 1998.

Avatar. DVD. Directed by James Cameron. 2009. Beverly Hills, CA: Twentieth Century Fox, 2010.

Barnes, Colin, Geof Mercer, and Tom Shakespeare. *Exploring Disability: A Sociological Introduction*. Cambridge, England: Polity Press, 1999.

Barnoff, Lisa, Christina Sinding, and Pamela Grassau. "Listening to the Voices of Lesbians Diagnosed with Cancer: Recommendations for Change in Cancer Support Services." *Journal of Gay and Lesbian Social Services* 18, no. 1 (2005): 17–35.

Beach, Scott R., et al. "Risk Factors for Potentially Harmful Informal Caregiver Behavior." *Journal of the American Geriatrics Society* 53 (2005): 255–261.

Beauty and the Beast. VHS. Directed by Gary Trousdale and Kirk Wise. 1991. Burbank, CA: Walt Disney Home Video, 1992.

183

Benjamin, Jessica. *The Bonds of Love: Psychoanalysis, Feminism, and the Problem of Domination.* New York: Pantheon Books, 1988.

———. *Like Subjects, Love Objects: Essays on Recognition and Sexual Difference.* New Haven: Yale University Press, 1995.

Blake, Holly, Nadina B. Lincoln, and David D. Clarke. "Caregiver Strain in Spouses of Stroke Patients." *Clinical Rehabilitation* 17, no. 3 (2003): 312–317.

Blink. DVD. Directed by Michael Apted. 1994. New Line Home Video, 2003.

Block, Pamela. "Sexuality, Fertility, and Danger: Twentieth-Century Images of Women with Cognitive Disabilities." *Sexuality and Disability* 18, no. 4 (2000): 239–254.

Boeije, Hennie R., Mia S. H. Duijnstee, and Maria H. F. Grypdonck. "Continuation of Caregiving Among Partners Who Give Total Care to Spouses with Multiple Sclerosis." *Health and Social Science in the Community* 11, no. 3 (2003): 242–252.

Boeije, Hennie R., and Anneke Van Doorne-Huiskes. "Fulfilling a Sense of Duty: How Men and Women Giving Care to Spouses with Multiple Sclerosis Interpret This Role." *Community, Work and Family* 6, no. 3 (2003): 223–244.

The Bone Collector. Directed by Phillip Noyce. Performed by Denzel Washington and Angelina Jolie. 1999.

Bookwala, Jamila, et al. "Concurrent and Long-Term Predictors of Older Adults' Use of Community-Based Long-Term Care Services: The Caregiver Health Effects Study." *Journal of Aging and Health* 16, no. 1 (2004): 88–115.

Borland, Katherine. "'That's Not What I Said': Interpretive Conflict in Oral Narrative Research." In *The Oral History Reader,* edited by Robert Perks and Alistair Thomson, 320–332. London: Routledge, 1998.

Born on the Fourth of July. DVD. Directed by Oliver Stone. 1989. Universal City, CA: Universal Studios, 2000.

Breen, Rosanna L. "A Practical Guide to Focus-Group Research." *Journal of Geography in Higher Education* 30, no. 2 (2006): 463–475.

Bubeck, Diemut Grace. "Justice and the Labor of Care." In *The Subject of Care: Feminist Perspectives on Dependency,* edited by Eva Feder Kittay and Ellen K. Feder, 160–185. Lanham, MD: Rowman & Littlefield, 2002.

Burton, Lynda C., et al. "Transitions in Spousal Caregiving." *The Gerontologist* 43, no. 2 (2003): 230–241.

Butler, Judith. *Gender Trouble: Feminism and the Subversion of Identity.* New York: Routledge, 1999.

Cahill, Madeleine A., and Martin F. Norden. "Hollywood's Portrayals of Disabled Women." In *Women, Disability, and Identity,* edited by Asha Hans and Annie Patri. New Delhi: Sage, 2003.

Campbell, Thomas L. "The Effectiveness of Family Interventions for Physical Disorders." *Journal of Marital and Family Therapy* 29, no. 2 (2003): 263–281.

Cannuscio, Carolyn, et al. "Employment Status, Social Ties, and Caregivers' Mental Health." *Social Science and Medicine* 58, no. 7 (2004): 1247–1256.

Chance, Randi. "To Love and Be Loved: Sexuality and People with Physical Disabilities." *Journal of Psychology and Theology* 30, no. 3 (2002): 195–208.

Chappell, Neena L. "Correcting Cross-Cultural Stereotypes: Aging in Shanghai and Canada." *Journal of Cross-Cultural Gerontology* 18, no. 2 (2003): 127–147.

Charmaz, Kathy. "Grounded Theory: Objectivist and Constructivist Methods." In *Handbook of Qualitative Research,* 2nd ed., edited by Norman K. Denzin and Yvonna S. Lincoln. Thousand Oaks, CA: Sage, 2000.

Children of a Lesser God. DVD. Directed by Randa Haines. 1986. Hollywood, CA: Paramount Pictures, 2000.

Choi, Heejeong, and Nadine F. Marks. "Transition to Caregiving, Marital Disagreement, and Psychological Well-Being: A Prospective U.S. National Study." *Journal of Family Issues* 27, no. 12 (2006): 1701–1722.

Christopherson, Jeannine Marguerite, et al. "A Comparison of Written Materials vs. Materials and Counselling for Women with Sexual Dysfunction and Multiple Sclerosis." *Journal of Clinical Nursing* 15, no. 6 (2006): 742–750.

City Lights. DVD. Directed by Charlie Chaplin. 1931. Pyrmont, NSW: MK2/Warner Bros., 2004.

Clark, Jill. "Sex and Disability: What Can We Learn?" TimesOnline, February 15, 2009. http://women.timesonline.co.uk/tol/life_and_style/women/relationships/article5716226.ece.

Cohen, Marion Deutsche. *Dirty Details: The Days and Nights of a Well Spouse*. Philadelphia: Temple University Press, 1996.

Coming Home. Directed by Hal Ashby. Performed by Jane Fonda and Jon Voight. 1978. Santa Monica, CA: Metro-Goldwyn-Mayer.

Connell, R. W. *Masculinities*. Berkeley: University of California Press, 1995.

Couser, G. Thomas. *Recovering Bodies: Illness, Disability, and Life Writing*. Madison: University of Wisconsin Press, 1997.

Crawford, Danette, and Joan M. Ostrove. "Representations of Disability and the Interpersonal Relationships of Women with Disabilities." *Women and Therapy* 26, nos. 3–4 (2003): 179–194.

Cremeans-Smith, Julie K., et al. "Spouses' and Physicians' Perceptions of Pain Severity in Older Women with Osteoarthritis: Dyadic Agreement and Patients' Well-Being." *Pain* 106, nos. 1–2 (2003): 27–34.

Davidson, Michael. "Introduction." *Journal of Literary Disability* 1, no. 2 (2007): i–vi. http://www.journalofliterarydisability.com/issues/vol01no02/Introduction.pdf.

Druley, Jennifer A., et al. "Emotional Congruence in Older Couples Coping with Wives' Osteoarthritis: Exacerbating Effects of Pain Behavior." *Psychology and Aging* 18, no. 3 (2003): 406–414.

Ducharme, Francine, et al. "Older Husbands as Caregivers of Their Wives: A Descriptive Study of the Context and Relational Aspects of Care." *International Journal of Nursing Studies* 43, no. 5 (2006): 567–579.

Eakin, Paul John. *How Our Lives Become Stories: Making Selves*. Ithaca: Cornell University Press, 1999.

Egan, Susanna. *Mirror Talk: Genres of Crisis in Contemporary Autobiography*. Chapel Hill: University of North Carolina Press, 1999.

Ellenbogen, Phyllis S., et al. "The Impact of Spinal Cord Injury on the Employment of Family Caregivers." *Journal of Vocational Rehabilitation* 25, no. 1 (2006): 35–44.

Eustice, Carol, and Richard Eustice. "In Sickness and in Health: Chronic Illness Interjects Complications into Marriage." About.com: Arthritis, November 4, 2008. http://arthritis.about.com/cs/sex/a/sicknesshealth.htm?p=1 (November 29, 2010).

Feder, Ellen K., and Eva Feder Kittay. "Introduction." In *The Subject of Care: Feminist Perspectives on Dependency*, edited by Eva Feder Kittay and Ellen K. Feder, 1–13. Lanham, MD: Rowman & Littlefield, 2002.

Feld, Sheila, Ruth E. Dunkle, and Tracy Schroepfer. "When Do Couples Expand Their ADL Caregiver Network Beyond the Marital Dyad?" *Marriage and Family Review* 37, nos. 1–2 (2005): 27–44.

Feld, S., et al. "Expansion of Elderly Couples' IADL Caregiver Networks Beyond the Marital Dyad." *International Journal of Aging and Human Development* 63, no. 2 (2006): 95–113.

Fine, Michael, and Caroline Glendinning. "Dependence, Independence or Inter-dependence? Revisiting the Concepts of 'Care' and 'Dependency.'" *Ageing and Society* 25, no. 4 (2005): 601–621.

Finger, Anne. *Elegy for a Disease: A Personal and Cultural History of Polio*. New York: St. Martin's Press, 2006.

Finkelstein, Vic. "The Social Model of Disability Repossessed." The Disability Studies Archive UK, December 1, 2001. http://www.leeds.ac.uk/disability-studies/archiveuk/finkelstein/soc%20mod%20repossessed.pdf (May 15, 2009).

Folbre, Nancy. "Reforming Care." *Politics and Society* 36, no. 3 (2008): 373–387.

Frank, Arthur W. *The Wounded Storyteller: Body, Illness, and Ethics*. Chicago: University of Chicago Press, 1995.

Freeman, Tim. "'Best Practice' in Focus Group Research: Making Sense of Different Views." *Methodological Issues in Nursing Research* 56, no. 5 (2006): 491–497.

Freud, Sigmund. *Three Essays on the Theory of Sexuality*. Ed. James Strachey. New York: Basic Books, 1975 (originally published 1905).

Frida. DVD. Directed by Julie Taymor. 2002. Burbank, CA: Buena Vista Home Video, 2003.

Fries, Kenny. *Body, Remember: A Memoir*. New York: Dutton, 1997.

Fultz, Nancy H., et al. "The Impact of Own and Spouse's Urinary Incontinence of Depressive Symptoms." *Social Science and Medicine* 60, no. 11 (2005): 2537–2548.

Gagliardi, Barbara A. "The Experience of Sexuality for Individuals Living with Multiple Sclerosis." *Journal of Clinical Nursing* 12, no. 4 (2003): 571–578.

Galvin, Rose D. "Researching the Disabled Identity: Contextualising the Identity Transformations Which Accompany the Onset of Impairment." *Sociology of Health and Illness* 27, no. 3 (2005): 393–413.

Garland-Thomson, Rosemarie. *Extraordinary Bodies: Figuring Physical Disability in American Culture and Literature*. New York: Columbia University Press, 1997.

Giarelli, Ellen, Ruth McCorkle, and Cheryl Monturo. "Caring for a Spouse After Prostate Surgery: The Preparedness Needs of Wives." *Journal of Family Nursing* 9, no. 4 (2003): 453–485.

Gibbs, Nancy. "Pillow Angel Ethics." *Time,* January 7, 2007. http://www.time.com/time/nation/article/0,8599,1574851,00.html (accessed November 30, 2010).

"Girlfriend." Mothers Against Drunk Driving Canada. 2005. http://www.madd.ca/english/news/pr/madd_best_friend_1.mov.

Gordon, Phyllis A., and Kristin M. Perrone. "When Spouses Become Caregivers: Counseling Implications for Younger Couples." *Journal of Rehabilitation* 70, no. 2 (2004): 27–32.

Greengross, Wendy. *Entitled to Love: The Sexual and Emotional Needs of the Handi-capped*. London: Malaby Press, 1976.

Hamington, Maurice. *Embodied Care: Jane Addams, Maurice Merleau-Ponty, and Feminist Ethics*. Urbana: University of Illinois Press, 2004.

Hanna, William John, and Betsy Rogovsky. "Women with Disabilities: Two Handicaps Plus." *Disability, Handicap and Society* 6, no. 1 (1991): 49–63.

Hash, Kristina. "Caregiving and Post-Caregiving Experiences of Midlife and Older Gay Men and Lesbians." *Journal of Gerontological Social Work* 47, nos. 3–4 (2006): 121–138.

Hassouneh-Phillips, Dena, and Elizabeth McNeff. "'I Thought I Was Less Worthy': Low Sexual and Body Esteem and Increased Vulnerability to Intimate Partner Abuse in Women with Physical Disabilities." *Sexuality and Disability* 23, no. 4 (2005): 227–240.

Held, Virginia. "Care and the Extension of Markets." *Hypatia* 17, no. 2 (2002): 19–33.

Hendrix, Christina, and Charlene Ray. "Informal Caregiver Training on Home Care and Cancer Symptom Management Prior to Hospital Discharge: A Feasibility Study." *Oncology Nursing Forum* 33, no. 4 (2006): 793–798.

Hesse-Biber, Sharlene Nagy, and Patricia Lina Leavy. *The Practice of Qualitative Research.* Thousand Oaks, CA: Sage, 2006.

Hirst, Michael. "Carer Distress: A Prospective, Population-Based Study." *Social Science and Medicine* 61, no. 3 (2005): 697–708.

Hockenberry, John. *Moving Violations: War Zones, Wheelchairs, and Declarations of Independence.* New York: Hyperion, 1996.

hooks, bell. *All About Love: New Visions.* New York: HarperCollins, 2000.

Hughes, Bill. "Disability and the Body." In *Disabling Barriers—Enabling Environments,* edited by J. Swain, V. Finkelstein, S. French, and M. Oliver, 63–69. London: Sage, 2004.

Hughes, Bill, et al. "Loves Labours Lost? Feminism, the Disabled People's Movement and an Ethic of Care." *Sociology* 39, no. 2 (2005): 259–275.

Hump the Stump. DVD. 2009. Robert Hill Entertainment.

The Hunchback of Notre Dame. VHS. Directed by Gary Trousdale and Kirk Wise. 1996. Burbank, CA: Walt Disney Home Video, 1997.

Ice Castles. VHS. Directed by Donald Wyre. 1978. New York: Columbia Pictures Home Entertainment.

Ingersoll-Dayton, Berit, and Michael Raschick. "The Relationship Between Care-Recipient Behaviors and Spousal Caregiving Stress." *The Gerontologist* 44, no. 3 (2004): 318–327.

Irvine, Janice. "Regulated Passions: The Invention of Inhibited Sexual Desire and Sexual Addiction." In *Deviant Bodies,* edited by J. Terry and J. Urla, 314–337. Bloomington: Indiana University Press, 1995.

Jackson, Stevi. "Love and Romance as Objects of Feminist Knowledge." In *Making Connections: Women's Studies, Women's Movements, Women's Lives,* edited by M. Kennedy, C. Lubelska, and V. Walsh, 39–50. London: Taylor & Francis, 1993.

Jennifer 8. DVD. Directed by Bruce Robinson. 1992. Hollywood, CA: Paramount Pictures, 2000.

Johnny Belinda. DVD. Directed by Jean Negulesco. 1948. Warner Home Video, 2006.

Joseph, Elizabeth Betcy, and Ranbir S. Bhatti. "Psychosocial Problems and Coping Patterns of HIV Seropositive Wives of Men with HIV/AIDS." *Social Work in Health Care* 39, nos. 1–2 (2004): 29–47.

Kafer, Alison. "Insperarable: Gender and Disability in the Amputee-Devotee Community." In *Gendering Disability,* edited by Bonnie G. Smith and Beth Hutchison, 107–118. New Brunswick, NJ: Rutgers University Press, 2004.

Kang, Suk-Young. "Predictors of Emotional Strain Among Spouse and Adult Child Caregivers." *Journal of Gerontological Social Work* 47, nos. 1–2 (2006): 107–131.

Karimzadeh, Mansoureh, et al. "The Psychological Impact of Infertility in the Male Able Bodied and Spinal Cord Injured Population." *Sexuality and Disability* 24, no. 4 (2006): 185–193.

Karp, Gary. *Disability and the Art of Kissing.* San Rafael, CA: Life on Wheels Press, 2008.

———. *Life on Wheels: The A to Z Guide to Living Fully with Mobility Issues,* 2nd ed. New York: Demos Medical, 2009.

Kaufman, Miriam, Cory Silverberg, and Fran Odette. *The Ultimate Guide to Sex and Disability.* San Francisco: Cleis Press, 2003.

Kedde, Harald, and Willy van Berlo. "Sexual Satisfaction and Sexual Self Images of People with Physical Disabilities in the Netherlands." *Sexuality and Disability* 24, no. 1 (2006): 53–68.

Kilborn, Peter T. "Divorce Rate Is Higher Among Disabled, Experts Say." *New York Times*, May 31, 1999.

Kim, Catherine, et al. "Quality of Preventive Clinical Services Among Caregivers in the Health and Retirement Study." *Journal of General Internal Medicine* 19, no. 8 (2004): 875–878.

Kim, Youngmee, et al. "Gender Differences in Caregiving Stress Among Caregivers of Cancer Survivors." *Psycho-Oncology* 15, no. 12 (2006): 1086–1092.

Kirsch, Gesa E. *Ethical Dilemmas in Feminist Research: The Politics of Location, Interpretation, and Publication.* Albany: SUNY Press, 1999.

Kittay, Eva Feder. *Love's Labor: Essays on Women, Equality, and Dependency.* New York: Routledge, 1999.

Kitzinger, Jenny. "The Methodology of Focus Groups: The Importance of Interaction Between Research Participants." *Sociology of Health and Illness* 16, no. 1 (1994): 103–121.

Klein, Bonnie Sherr, and Persimmon Blackbridge. *Slow Dance: A Story of Stroke, Love, and Disability.* Toronto: Knopf Canada, 1997.

Kondracke, Morton. *Saving Milly: Love, Politics, and Parkinson's Disease.* New York: Ballantine Books, 2001.

La Caze, Marguerite. "Love, That Indispensable Supplement: Irigaray and Kant on Love and Respect." *Hypatia* 20, no. 3 (2005): 92–114.

Laursen, Birgitte Schantz, et al. "Ongoing Pain, Sexual Desire, and Frequency of Sexual Intercourse in Females with Different Chronic Pain Syndromes." *Sexuality and Disability* 24, no. 1 (2006): 27–37.

Leavy, Patricia Lina. "The Practice of Feminist Oral History and Focus Group Interviews." In *Feminist Research Practice*, edited by Sharlene Nagy Hesse-Biber and Patricia Lina Leavy, 149–186. Thousand Oaks, CA: Sage, 2007.

Lee, Sunmin, et al. "Caregiving and Risk of Coronary Heart Disease in U.S. Women: A Prospective Study." *American Journal of Preventative Medicine* 24, no. 2 (2003): 113–119.

Lesbian Handicap Sex. DVD. 2009. Heatwave Entertainment.

Li, Candy Mung-nga, and Matthew Kwai-sang Yau. "Sexual Issues and Concerns: Tales of Chinese Women with Spinal Cord Impairments." *Sexuality and Disability* 24, no. 1 (2006): 1–26.

Lin, Pi-Chu, and Change-Ming Lu. "Hip Fracture: Family Caregivers' Burden and Related Factors for Older People in Taiwan." *Journal of Clinical Nursing* 14, no. 6 (2005): 719–726.

Linton, Simi. *Claiming Disability: Knowledge and Identity.* New York: New York University Press, 1998.

The Little Mermaid. VHS. Directed by John Musker and Ron Clements. 1989. Burbank, CA: Walt Disney Home Video, 1990.

Lloyd, Margaret. "Does She Boil Eggs? Towards a Feminist Model of Disability." *Disability, Handicap and Society* 7, no. 3 (1992): 207–221.

———. "The Politics of Disability and Feminism: Discord or Synthesis?" *Sociology* 25, no. 3 (2001): 715–728.

Luttik, Marie Louise, et al. "For Better and for Worse: Quality of Life Impaired in HF Patients as Well as in Their Partners." *European Journal of Cardiovascular Nursing* 4, no. 1 (2005): 1–14.

Madriz, Esther. "Focus Groups in Feminist Research." In *Handbook of Qualitative Research*, 2nd ed., edited by Norman K. Denzin and Yvonna S. Lincoln, 835–850. Thousand Oaks, CA: Sage, 2000.

Magnificent Obsession. DVD. Directed by Douglas Sirk. 1954. Irvington, NY: Criterion Collection, 2008.

Maguire, Gregory. *Wicked: The Life and Times of the Wicked Witch of the West*. New York: Harper Paperbacks, 1996.

Mairs, Nancy. *Waist-High in the World: A Life Among the Nondisabled*. Boston: Beacon Press, 1996.

"Manipulated." *Law & Order: Special Victims Unit*. Season 7, Episode 15. Directed by Matt Earl Beesley, February 7, 2006.

Martire et al. "Older Spouses' Perceptions of Partners' Chronic Arthritis Pain: Implications for Spousal Responses, Support Provision, and Caregiving Experiences." *Psychology and Aging* 21, no. 2 (2006): 222–230.

Mbanaso, Michael Udo, Jeffrey Shavelson, and John Ukawuilulu. "Elderly African Americans as Intragenerational Caregivers." *Journal of Gerontological Social Work* 47, nos. 1–2 (2006): 3–15.

McCabe, Marita P., and George Taleporos. "Sexual Esteem, Sexual Satisfaction, and Sexual Behavior Among People with Physical Disability." *Archives of Sexual Behavior* 32, no. 4 (2003): 359–369.

McLaren, Margaret. *Feminism, Foucault, and Embodied Subjectivity*. Albany: SUNY Press, 2002.

McNeff, Elizabeth A. "Issues for the Partner of the Person with a Disability." In *Sexual Function in People with Disability and Chronic Illness: A Health Professional's Guide*, edited by Marsha L. Sipski and Craig J. Alexander, 595–616. Gaithersburg, MD: Aspen, 1997.

McNeff, Lizzi. "Meet the Sexperts." *New Mobility*, February 2005. http://www .newmobility.com/articleViewIE.cfm?id=968 (January 20, 2010).

McRuer, Robert. *Crip Theory: Cultural Signs of Queerness and Disability*. New York: New York University Press, 2006.

Melby, Todd. "Facilitated Sex." *Contemporary Sexuality* 37, no. 11 (2003): 1–6.

The Men. Directed by Fred Zinnemann. Performed by Marlon Brando and Teresa Wright. 1950. Santa Monica, CA: Republic Pictures.

Meyer, Madonna Harrington, ed. *Care Work: Gender, Class, and the Welfare State*. New York: Routledge, 2000.

Miles, M. B., and A. M. Huberman. *Qualitative Data Analysis: An Expanded Sourcebook*, 2nd ed. Thousand Oaks, CA: Sage, 1994.

Milligan, Maureen S., and Aldred H. Neufeldt. "The Myth of Asexuality: A Survey of Social and Empirical Evidence." *Sexuality and Disability* 19, no. 2 (2001): 91–109.

Million Dollar Baby. Directed by Clint Eastwood. Performed by Clint Eastwood, Hilary Swank, and Morgan Freeman. 2004. Burbank, CA: Warner Home Video, 2005.

Mintz, Susanna B. "Transforming the Tale: The Auto/body/ographies of Nancy Mairs." *Auto/Biography Studies* 14, no. 2 (1999): 254–272.

Mitchell, David. "Body Solitaire: The Singular Subject of Disability Autobiography." *American Quarterly* 52, no. 2 (2002): 311–315.

Mitchell, David, and Sharon Snyder. "Narrative Prosthesis and the Materiality of Metaphor." In *The Disability Studies Reader*, 2nd ed., edited by Lennard Davis, 205–216. New York: Routledge, 2006.

Mona, Linda R. "Sexual Options for People with Disabilities: Using Personal Assistance Services for Sexual Expression." *Women and Therapy* 26, nos. 3–4 (2003): 211–221.

Morris, Jenny. "'Us' and 'Them'? Feminist Research, Community Care and Disability." *Critical Social Policy* 11 (1991): 22–39.

Murderball. Directed by Henry Alex Rubin and Dana Adam Shapiro. 2005. New York: Lion's Gate Home Entertainment.

Murphy, Robert Francis. *The Body Silent*. New York: W. W. Norton, 1990 (originally published 1987).

Murray, C. D., and B. Harrison. "The Meaning and Experience of Being a Stroke Survivor: An Interpretative Phenomenological Analysis." *Disability and Rehabilitation* 26, no. 13 (2004): 808–816.

My Left Foot. Directed by Jim Sheridan. Performed by Daniel Day-Lewis. 1989. New York: HBO Video.

Naples, Nancy A. *Feminism and Method: Ethnography, Discourse Analysis, and Activist Research*. New York: Routledge, 2003.

National Organization for Women. "A Feminist Future: Policy and Program Goals for Mothers and Caregivers Economic Rights." http://www.now.org/issues/mothers/goals.html (May 14, 2009).

———. Mothers and Caregivers Economic Rights. http://www.now.org/issues/mothers/index.html (November 28, 2010).

———. "NOW and Disability Rights." http://www.now.org/issues/disability/index.html (November 28, 2010).

Noddings, Nel. *Caring: A Feminine Approach to Ethics and Moral Education*. Berkeley: University of California Press, 1984.

Notting Hill. DVD. Directed by Roger Michell. 1999. Universal City, CA: Universal Studios.

Olesen, Virginia. "Early Millennial Feminist Qualitative Research: Challenges and Contours." In *The Sage Handbook of Qualitative Research*, 3rd ed., edited by Norman K. Denzin and Yvonna S. Lincoln, 235–278. Thousand Oaks, CA: Sage, 2005.

Oliver, Kelly. "Subjectivity as Responsivity: The Ethical Implications of Dependency." *The Subject of Care: Feminist Perspectives on Dependency*, edited by Eva Feder Kittay and Ellen K. Feder, 322–333. Lanham, MD: Rowman & Littlefield, 2002.

Oliver, M. *Understanding Disability: From Theory to Practice*. London: Macmillan, 1996.

Olkin, Rhonda. "Women with Physical Disabilities Who Want to Leave Their Partners: A Feminist and Disability-Affirmative Perspective." *Women and Therapy* 26, nos. 3–4 (2003): 237–246.

O'Reilly, Kevin B. "Confronting Eugenics: Does the Now Discredited Practice Have Relevance to Today's Technology?" *AMNews*, July 2, 2007. http://www.ama-assn.org/amednews/2007/07/09/prsa0709.htm (July 9, 2007).

Orphans of the Storm. DVD. Directed by D. W. Griffith. 1921. Los Angeles, CA: Delta Entertainment, 2004.

Parens, Erik, and Adrienne Asch. "The Disability Rights Critique of Prenatal Genetic Testing: Reflections and Recommendations." *Hastings Center Report* (September–October 1999).

Parker, Gillian. *With This Body: Caring and Disability in Marriage*. Buckingham, England: Open University Press, 1993.

Parritt, Simon, and Jean O'Callaghan. "Splitting the Difference: An Exploratory Study of Therapists' Work with Sexuality, Relationships and Disability." *Sexual and Relationship Therapy* 15, no. 2 (2000): 151–169.

Parsons, Talcott. *The Social System*. New York: Free Press, 1964.

Passion Fish. DVD. Directed by John Sayles. 1992. Culver City, CA: Columbia TriStar Home Video, 1998.

Peräkylä, Anssi. "Analyzing Talk and Text." In *The Sage Handbook of Qualitative Research*, 3rd ed., edited by Norman K. Denzin and Yvonna S. Lincoln, 869–886. Thousand Oaks, CA: Sage, 2005.

Pinquart, Martin, and Silvia Sörensen. "Associations of Stressors and Uplifts of Caregiving with Caregiver Burden and Depressive Mood: A Meta-Analysis." *Journal of Gerontology: Psychological Sciences* 58B, no. 2 (2003): P112–P128.

———. "Ethnic Differences in Stressors, Resources, and Psychological Outcomes of Family Caregiving: A Meta-Analysis." *The Gerontologist* 45, no. 1 (2005): 90–106.

Price, Janet, and Margrit Shildrick. "Bodies Together: Touch, Ethics and Disability." In *Disability/Postmodernity: Embodying Disability Theory*, edited by Mairian Corker and Tom Shakespeare, 62–75. London: Continuum, 2002.

Raschick, Michael, and Berit Ingersoll-Dayton. "The Costs and Rewards of Caregiving Among Aging Spouses and Adult Children." *Family Relations* 53, no. 3 (2004): 317–325.

"Real Women, Real Courage." *Glamour*, June 2007.

Reinharz, Shulamit. *Feminist Methods in Social Research*. New York: Oxford University Press, 1992.

Reynolds, Dawn. "Disability and BDSM: Bob Flanagan and the Case for Sexual Rights." *Sexuality Research and Social Policy* 4, no. 1 (2007): 40–52.

Richardson, Diane. "Heterosexuality and Social Theory." *Theorizing Heterosexuality: Telling It Straight*, edited by Diane Richardson, 1–20. Buckingham, England: Open University Press, 1996.

Robinson, Betsy C. "Validation of a Caregiver Strain Index." *Journal of Gerontology* 38, no. 3 (1983): 344–348.

Rodarte, Irene Torices, and Martha Patricia Bonilla Muñoz. "Inventory of Sexual Experiences and Response in Disability (IEReSDi): Construction and Validation of the Scale of the Sexual Response in People with Disabilities." *Sexuality and Disability* 22, no. 3 (2004): 181–195.

Ruiz, John M., et al. "Does Who You Marry Matter for Your Health? Influence of Patients' and Spouses' Personality on Their Partners' Psychological Well-Being Following Coronary Artery Bypass Surgery." *Journal of Personality and Social Psychology* 91, no. 2 (2006): 255–267.

Ryan, Gery W., and H. Russell Bernard. "Data Management and Analysis Methods." In *Handbook of Qualitative Research*, 2nd ed., edited by Norman K. Denzin and Yvonna S. Lincoln, 769–802. Thousand Oaks, CA: Sage, 2000.

Sakellariou, Dikaios. "If Not Disability, Then What? Barriers to Reclaiming Sexuality Following Spinal Cord Injury." *Sexuality and Disability* 24, no. 2 (2006): 101–111.

Samuels, Robert C. "The Hockenberrys: A Family Portrait." *New Mobility*, August 2002. http://www.newmobility.com/articleViewIE.cfm?id=578 (January 2, 2010).

Schmidt, E. Z., et al. "Sexuality in Multiple Sclerosis." *Journal of Neural Transmission* 112, no. 9 (2005): 1201–1211.

Schulz, Celia H. "Collaboration in the Marriage Relationship Among Persons with Disabilities." *Disability Studies Quarterly* 28, no. 1 (2008).

Schutte, Ofelia. "Dependency Work, Women, and the Global Economy." In *The Subject of Care: Feminist Perspectives on Dependency*, edited by Eva Feder Kittay and Ellen K. Feder, 138–158. Lanham, MD: Rowman & Littlefield, 2002.

Shakespeare, Tom. *Disability Rights and Wrongs*. London: Routledge, 2006.

———. *Help*. Birmingham, England: British Association of Social Workers, 2000.

———. "Joking a Part." *Body and Society* 5, no. 4 (1999): 47–52.

Shakespeare, Tom, Kath Gillespie-Sells, and Dominic Davies. *The Sexual Politics of Disability: Untold Desires*. London: Cassell, 1996.

Shameless: The ART of Disability. Directed by Bonnie Sherr Klein. National Film Board of Canada, 2006. Montreal, Quebec.

Shapiro, Joseph P. *No Pity: People with Disabilities Forging a New Civil Rights Movement*. New York: Three Rivers Press, 1994.

Shildrick, Margrit. "Contested Pleasures: The Sociopolitical Economy of Disability and Sexuality." *Sexuality Research and Social Policy* 4, no. 1 (2007): 53–66.

———. "Unreformed Bodies: Normative Anxiety and the Denial of Pleasure." *Women's Studies* 34, nos. 3–4 (2005): 327–344.

Shrek. DVD. Directed by Andrew Adamson and Vicky Jenson. 2001. Universal City, CA: DreamWorks Home Entertainment.

Shuttleworth, Russell P. "The Search for Sexual Intimacy for Men with Cerebral Palsy." *Sexuality and Disability* 18, no. 4 (2000): 263–282.

Sick: The Life and Death of Bob Flanagan Supermasochist. Directed by Kirby Dick. 1997. Santa Monica, CA: Lion's Gate Home Entertainment.

Siebers, Tobin. "Disability in Theory: From Social Constructionism to the New Realism of the Body." *American Literary History* 13, no. 1 (2001): 737–754.

———. *Disability Theory*. Ann Arbor: University of Michigan Press, 2008.

Simpson et al. "Improving the Rehabilitative Management of Client Sexual Health Concerns After Neurological Disability: Evaluation of a Staff Sexuality Training Programme in New Zealand." *Clinical Rehabilitation* 20 (2009): 847–859.

Singh, Roop, and Sansar C. Sharma. "Sexuality and Women with Spinal Cord Injury." *Sexuality and Disability* 23, no. 1 (2005): 21–33.

Skloot, Floyd. "A Measure of Acceptance." *In the Shadow of Memory*. Lincoln: University of Nebraska Press, 2004.

Smith, Tamara L., and Ronald W. Toseland. "The Effectiveness of a Telephone Support Program for Caregivers of Frail Older Adults." *The Gerontologist* 46, no. 5 (2006): 620–629.

Sontag, Susan. *AIDS and Its Metaphors*. New York: Picador, 1989.

———. *Illness as Metaphor*. New York: Picador, 1978.

Soskolne, Varda, et al. "Caregiving Stressors and Psychological Distress Among Veteran Resident and Immigrant Family Caregivers in Israel." *Social Work in Health Care* 43, nos. 2–3 (2006): 73–93.

Speziale, Bette A. "Couples, Sexual Intimacy, and Multiple Sclerosis." *Journal of Family Psychotherapy* 8, no. 1 (1997): 13–32.

The Spiral Staircase. DVD. Directed by Robert Siodmak. 1946. Culver City, CA: Metro-Goldwyn-Mayer Home Entertainment.

Stein, Joel. "Porn Goes Mainstream." *Time*, June 24, 2001. http://www.time.com/time/magazine/article/0,9171,989038,00.html (September 3, 2010).

Stroman, Duane F. *The Disability Rights Movement: From Deinstitutionalization to Self-Determination*. Lanham, MD: University Press of America, 2003.

Stronach, Ian, and Julie Allan. "Joking with Disability: What's the Difference Between the Comic and the Tragic in Disability Discourses?" *Body and Society* 5, no. 4 (1999): 31–45.

Stubblefield, Anna. "'Beyond the Pale': Tainted Whiteness, Cognitive Disability, and Eugenic Sterilization." *Hypatia* 22, no. 2 (2007): 162–181.

Support and Housing Assistance for People with Disabilities. http://www.shad.org.uk (March 12, 2007).

Suthers, Kristen. "Women Still Shouldering the Burden: Caregiving in the 21st Century." *The Women's Health Activist* 31, no. 4 (2006): 4–5.

Svetlik, Doris, et al. "Declines in Satisfaction with Physical Intimacy Predict Caregiver Perceptions of Overall Relationship Loss: A Study of Elderly Caregiving Spousal Dyads." *Sexuality and Disability* 23, no. 2 (2005): 65–79.

Swidler, Ann. *Talk of Love: How Culture Matters*. Chicago: University of Chicago Press, 2001.

Taleporos, George, and Marita P. McCabe. "Development and Validation of the Physical Disability Sexual and Body Esteem Scale." *Sexuality and Disability* 20, no. 3 (2002): 159–176.

———. "Relationships, Sexuality and Adjustment Among People with Physical Disability." *Sexual and Relationship Therapy* 18, no. 1 (2003): 25–43.

Tepper, Mitchell. "Providing Comprehensive Sexual Health Care in Spinal Cord Injury Rehabilitation: Implementation and Evaluation of a New Curriculum for Health Care Professionals." *Sexuality and Disability* 15, no. 3 (1997): 131–165.

———. "What Does Your Partner Find Sexy About Your Disability?" May 24, 2002. www.yourable.com (March 18, 2008).

The Theory of Flight. VHS. Directed by Paul Greengrass. 1998. Fine Line Features, 1999.

Thomas, Carol. *Sociologies of Disability and Illness: Contested Ideas in Disability Studies and Medical Sociology*. New York: Palgrave Macmillan, 2007.

Toseland, Ronald W., et al. "Supporting Caregivers of Frail Older Adults in an HMO Setting." *American Journal of Orthopsychiatry* 74, no. 3 (2004): 349–364.

Twigg, Julia. "The Body in Social Policy: Mapping a Territory." *Journal of Social Policy* 31, no. 3 (2002): 421–439.

Välimäki, Tarja, Katri Vehvil inen-Julkunen, and Anna Maija Pietil. "Diaries as Research Data in a Study of Family Caregivers of People with Alzheimer's Disease: Methodological Issues." *Journal of Advanced Nursing* 59, no. 1 (2007): 68–76.

Valtonen, Kirsi, et al. "Satisfaction with Sexual Life Among Persons with Traumatic Spinal Cord Injury and Meningomyelocele." *Disability and Rehabilitation* 28, no. 16 (2006): 965–976.

Vance, Daniel J. "Disability and Divorce." *Atlantic Highlands Herald*, December 8, 2005. http://www.ahherald.com/disabilities/2005/dw051208_divorce.htm (November 10, 2007).

van Staveren, Irene. "Focus Groups: Contributing to a Gender-Aware Methodology." *Feminist Economics* 3, no. 2 (1997): 131–135.

Vansteenwegen, Alfons, I. Jans, and Arlynn T. Revell. "Sexual Experience of Women with a Physical Disability: A Comparative Study." *Sexuality and Disability* 21, no. 4 (2003): 283–290.

Wade, Cheryl Marie. "It Ain't Exactly Sexy." *The Ragged Edge*, November–December 1991.

Wait Until Dark. DVD. Directed by Terence Young. 1967. Burbank, CA: Warner Home Video, 2003.

Walmsley, Jan. "Contradictions in Caring: Reciprocity and Interdependence." *Disability, Handicap and Society* 8, no. 2 (1993): 129–141.

Want. Directed by Loree Erickson. 2007. Toronto, Ontario: Femmegimp Productions.

Waterdance. DVD. Directed by Neal Jimenez and Michael Steinberg. 1992. Culver City, CA: Columbia TriStar Home Video, 2001.

Watson, Nick, et al. "(Inter)Dependence, Needs and Care: The Potential for Disability and Feminist Theories to Develop an Emancipatory Model." *Sociology* 38, no. 2 (2004): 331–350.

Waxman, Barbara Faye. "It's Time to Politicize Our Sexual Oppression." *The Ragged Edge*, March–April 1991.

Weiss, Gail. *Body Images: Embodiment as Intercorporeality*. New York: Routledge, 1999.

Wendell, Susan. *The Rejected Body: Feminist Philosophical Reflections on Disability*. New York: Routledge, 1996.

Westlund, Andrea C. "The Reunion of Marriage." *The Monist* 91, nos. 3–4 (2008): 558–577.

What Ever Happened to Baby Jane? Directed by Robert Aldrich. Performed by Joan Crawford and Bette Davis. 1962. Burbank, CA: Warner Home Video, 2006.

Wicked: A New Musical. Adapted by Stephen Schwartz and Winnie Holzman. Directed by Joe Mantello. Chicago: Oriental Theater, July 27, 2005.

Wiegerink, Diana, et al. "Social and Sexual Relationships of Adolescents and Young Adults with Cerebral Palsy: A Review." *Clinical Rehabilitation* 20 (2006): 1023–1031.

Wilkerson, Abby. "Disability, Sex Radicalism, and Political Agency." *NWSA Journal* 14, no. 3 (2002): 33–57.

Willms et al. "A Systematic Approach for Using Qualitative Methods in Primary Prevention Research." *Medical Anthropology Quarterly* 4, no. 4 (1990): 391–409.

Wolfe, Pamela S. "The Influence of Personal Values on Issues of Sexuality and Disability." *Sexuality and Disability* 15, no. 2 (1997): 69–90.

Wolff, Jennifer L., and Judith D. Kasper. "Caregivers of Frail Elders: Updating a National Profile." *The Gerontologist* 46, no. 3 (2006): 344–356.

Young, Jason. *Media Education Foundation Study Guide: The Price of Pleasure*. Media Education Foundation, 2008.

Yow, Valerie Raleigh. *Recording Oral History: A Practical Guide for Social Scientists*. Thousand Oaks, CA: Sage, 1994.

Zitzelsberger, Hilde. "(In)visibility: Accounts of Embodiment of Women with Physical Disabilities and Differences." *Disability and Society* 20, no. 4 (2005): 389–403.

Zupan, Mark, and Tim Swanson. *Gimp*. New York: HarperCollins, 2006.

Index

About the Book

In this exploration of intimate relationships between people with physical disabilities and those without, Sarah Smith Rainey shatters the myth of sexless, burdensome partnerships. And in its place, she reveals a rich and rewarding continuum of emotional and physical intimacies.

Rainey draws on interviews, autobiographies, and films to show how disabled/nondisabled couples not only build mutually satisfying relationships by giving and receiving in equal measure, but also move beyond traditional gender roles to create new forms of sexual intimacy. She also takes note of the challenges that these couples face. With sensitivity and clarity, she offers an unparalleled portrait of the lived experience of disability and sexuality.

Sarah Smith Rainey teaches women's studies at Bowling Green State University.